Sex Crime
Sex offending and society

Terry Thomas

WILLAN
PUBLISHING

Published by:

Willan Publishing
Culmcott House
Mill Street, Uffculme
Cullompton, Devon
EX15 3AT, UK
Tel: +44(0)1884 840337
Fax: +44(0)1884 840251
e-mail: willan.publishing@virgin.net

Published simultaneously in the USA and Canada by:

Willan Publishing
c/o ISBS, 5804 N.E. Hassalo St,
Portland, Oregon 97213-3644, USA
Tel: +001(0)503 287 3093
Fax: +001(0)503 280 8832

First published 2000

ISBN 1-903240-00-x (cased)
ISBN 1-903240-01-8 (paper)

British Library Cataloguing-in-Publication Data
A catalogue record for this book is available from the British Library.

Typeset by Doyle & Co, Colchester
Printed and Bound by T.J. International Ltd, Padstow, Cornwall

Sex

Sex o

The College of West Anglia

Ramnoth Road • Wisbech •• PE13 2JE • Tel: (01945 582561)

Learning
Resource
Centre

Crime and Society Series
Series Editor: Hazel Croall

Preface

The aim of this volume is to introduce the reader to the subject of sexual offending and sex offenders, to set this form of offending in context and to examine the measures taken in terms of law, penal policy and social policy to bring these offenders to justice and increase everyone's protection from sex offenders.

As a field of study, sexual offending – and the policies to combat it – has been a rapidly moving terrain over the last five years. Attitudes towards sexual offending and to victims of that offending have been changing in response to the greater attention now being paid to the phenomenon and our growing awareness of its extent and the damage it causes.

This book looks also at the policy and legal framework which has been developed both to bring offenders to justice and to increase protection from abusers. It looks at the formulation of that legal framework and its implementation by police officers, probation officers, the judiciary, lawyers, teachers and others. Sometimes the implementation does not work out as the formulation had intended. Always there is the 'discovery' of the unforeseen that 'we need to do something about'.

The primary focus of the book is that of law, policy and practice in England and Wales. The variations in approaches to sexual offending in Scotland and Northern Ireland are brought in where appropriate; a variation that reminds us of the relativity of sexual offending and how different communities reserve the right to define it differently and respond to it differently.

The approach to sexual offending that has been taken is, of necessity, an interdisciplinary approach, reflecting the nature of the activity itself and the various responses to it. Hopefully, this approach will allow those practitioners already referred to – police officers, probation officers, social workers, the judiciary and others – who have to work with these offenders every day to place that work in its wider context: in the terminology of the times, to see where that work 'joins up' with the work of others and fits into the overall strategies that exist. The same hope is offered to the general reader, who could be forgiven for wondering 'what's going on?' in this field when he or she has only the frenetic reporting of today's newspapers to go on.

Thanks are due to staff at the Leeds Metropolitan University library, the Brotherton Library, University of Leeds and the British Library at Wetherby, as well as to a number of colleagues along the way who have directly or indirectly given pointers to how this volume should proceed, and have put various items of interest in my direction. These include Keith Soothill for comments on early drafts, Bill Hebenton, Sue Griffiths, Ilan Katz, Olwen Lyner, Corinne Wattam, Jenny Cieslik, Joanne Smith, Alan Deacon, Ken Pease, Pat Fairfoot, Liz Jeffery, Sheila Banks, Alison Bennett, Joe Cocker, Makhan Shergill, and Frans Mulschlegal; the author remains responsible for the final product. Thanks to Pete Nutman, who appreciated the need for time to write at Leeds Metropolitan University; thanks also to Pam Reynolds, Sharon Eaton and Lorraine Drake for invaluable word processing skills.

Contents

List of tables

Tables of statutes, statutory instruments and cases cited

Statutory instruments cited

Cases cited

Sources cited

The Times 2, 69, 87, 93, 101, 109, 112, 152
Today 88
Yorkshire Evening Post (Leeds) 20, 23
Yorkshire Post 18, 19, 20, 70

House of Commons debates and written answers
4 August 1869   Col. 1261 42
5 March 1903   Col. 1683 47
26 June 1908   Col. 284 47
26 June 1908   Col. 288 47
27 March 1985   Cols. 244–245 WA 139
15 October 1990   Cols. 721–722 65
16 January 1992   Cols. 1207–1216 131
23 January 1992   Cols. 477–478 129
28 March 1994   Cols. 747–756 93
12 June 1996   Cols. 328–341 73
12 June 1996   Col. 363 75
25 October 1996   WA 965 107
28 October 1996   WA 779 140
27 January 1997   Cols. 30–31 .... 110, 111
27 January 1997   Col. 42 112
27 January 1997   Col. 60 110
4 February 1997   Col. 7 Standing Committee D 111
4 February 1997   Col. 9 Standing Committee D 111
4 February 1997   Cols. 16–17 Standing Committee D 113
4 February 1997   Cols. 17–18 Standing Committee D 113
4 February 1997   Col. 56 Standing Committee D 112
4 February 1997   Col. 58 Standing Committee D 112
20 February 1997   Col. 1029 70
25 February 1997   Col. 132 WA 64
7 July 1997   Col. 748–749 101-102
17 July 1998   Cols. 348–349 WA 144
28 January 1999   Col. 353 WA 101
15 February 1999   Cols. 601–602 103
22 February 1999   Col. 112 WA 7
25 February 1999   WA 72369 101
9 March 1999   WA 75034 Col. 127 3
12 May 1999   Col. 159 WA 117
28 June 1999   Col. 85 WA 117
5 July 1999   Cols. 432–435 WA 143
23 July 1999   Col. 732 WA 8, 145
25 October 1999   Col. 691 WA 153

House of Lords debates
7 June 1864   Col. 1339 41
7 June 1864   Col. 1342 42
7 June 1864   Col. 1345 42

1
Introduction

Sexual offending is often considered as somehow inherently 'different' from other forms of offending. Sexual offenders occupy a special place in contemporary society's secular demonology. Sexual crime is a mainstay of the tabloid and broadsheet newspapers, where offenders become 'monsters', 'beasts' and 'sex fiends'. Within prison walls, 'ordinary' offenders see it as normal to harass and bully the sex offender and professionals find them equally difficult to work with. According to one observer:

> ... concern about sexual crimes has become a panic. Women increasingly see themselves at risk of sexual assault, and rape now heads the list of crimes which the public characterises as serious. Those who perpetrate such crimes are hated and despised more than almost any other offender. Built up into modern folk-devils by the popular press, their treatment at the hands of many people working in the criminal justice system reflects their sub-normal status in the popular mind.
>
> (Sampson, 1994, p. x)

A particular hostility has been directed at the sex offender who offends against children. Although experts may debate the true meaning of the word 'paedophile', there is little doubt that the paedophile has become the 'hate figure' of our time in the popular imagination.

Despite the demonology and the hatred, the sex offender is also noted for his (and less often her) 'invisibility'. We may hold to the stereotype of the 'man in the grubby raincoat' hanging around street corners, but in truth the sex offender appears in all walks of life and in all guises.

The sex offending itself takes many forms: from the man who indecently exposes himself, to the anonymous stranger who abducts, assaults and kills, to the man who possesses illegal pornography; from the man who offends only against his own children, to the men who find employment in children's homes or schools just to give them access to children and opportunities to offend.

In Bolton, a 23-year-old man is convicted for creating child pornography by superimposing photographs of children onto obscene photographs of adult men ('Pervert with an album of child filth' *Manchester Evening News*, 7 November 1998). A teenager is convicted of six indecent assaults in West Yorkshire ('Boy aged thirteen is placed on register of sex offenders' *Guardian*, 19 November 1997) and a serial rapist of women, who has twice been acquitted because victims were too frightened to give evidence, is imprisoned for 21 years ('You lack a factor that distinguishes man from beast, namely humanity' *Scotsman*, 17 January 1998).

An ageing rock star in his 50s takes his personal computer in for repairs and finds himself convicted of possessing indecent images of children found stored there ('Glitter jailed for child porn charges' *Guardian*, 13 November 1999). A gang of boys aged between 14 and 17 are given lengthy custodial sentences for gang-raping an Austrian tourist in London before throwing her into a canal ('Faces of Evil' *Daily Mail*, 19 April 1997). Police make simultaneous arrests in 12 different countries in Operation Cathedral, to seize over a million indecent internet pictures of some 400 children ('Police to show images of net porn children' *The Sunday Times*, 11 November 1998), and a tribunal of inquiry takes almost four years to produce a 900-page report on the 'widespread sexual abuse of boys . . . in children's residential establishments in Clwyd between 1974 and 1990' (Waterhouse Report, 2000, para. 55.10)

Sex offenders are thick on the ground and make good copy for the newspapers. A serving prisoner is given day release to run in a charity marathon but has his invitation withdrawn when his conviction is revealed ('Rapist is withdrawn from charity marathon run' *Daily Telegraph*, 3 March 1994) and in Sri Lanka a British science-fiction writer is accused of offences against children just before Prince Charles was to confer a knighthood on him ('Sex claim author joins Prince at banquet' *PA News*, 5 February 1998). A police officer in Avon and Somerset receives a £20,000 grant from the Home Office to research the safety of children on international holiday exchanges ('Exchange trip pupils in danger of abuse' *The Times*, 21 April 1998) and, from overseas, a stream of stories comes back from the armed conflict in the Balkans, that rape is being systematically used by soldiers as a form of violence against civilian women.

At one extreme, the 'sex offender' label is attached to Fred and Rose West, as a country is transfixed by the horrific revelations of what happened at 25 Cromwell Street in Gloucester ('Burn in hell' *Sun*, 23 November 1995). At the other extreme, questions are asked of Boots the Chemist when they call the police in to look at negatives they have been asked to develop by an ITN news reader; they turn out to be innocent photographs of her own children.

The law may tell us in detail what is a sexual offence but an abstract definition remains nebulous. Here we might suggest only that it is the inducement or coercion of adults and children into sexual activities to which they have not consented. This might include the exploitative use of people in prostitution or other unlawful sexual practices, including the production of pornographic material. The absence of a true consent to sexual activities is the overarching feature of sexual offending.

Alongside this growing awareness is the associated question of what we do about the sex offender. How do we identify him in the first place and bring him to justice? Should that justice involve treatment, containment or straight punishment? How do we identify the known offender after his treatment or punishment in order to protect ourselves and children from him?

Forms of sex offending

What constitutes a sex offence also varies over time and place. An existing offence may be de-criminalised at the stroke of a statute (e.g. homosexual activities in England and Wales in 1967), and existing behaviour may be recognised as needing to be criminalised (e.g. male rape in 1994). What is a sex offence in one country may not be in another.

The exact number of sex offences committed each year is difficult to determine because of the varying forms, the nature of police recording and the unwillingness of some victims to report crimes in the first place. The Home Office recorded 36,690 sexual offences for the year ending September 1998 and 37,492 for the year ending September 1999 (Home Office, 2000a); this figure divides into approximately 6,000 rapes and the remainder indecent assaults. Reports suggest, however, that this is a massive under-reporting (see e.g. 'Hidden toll of rape victims' *Guardian*, 18 February 2000).

More detailed figures from the Home Office show the number of convictions and cautions for specific sexual offences against children to have fallen between 1985 and 1995. Indecent assaults on girls under 16 fell from 2,416 to 2,116 (a drop of 12 per cent) and on boys from 674 to 476 (a drop of 29 per cent). Unlawful sexual intercourse with girls under 16 fell 61 per cent and on girls under 13 by 27 per cent. Convictions and cautions for gross indecency with girls under 14 fell from 206 to 129 and on boys under 14 from 122 to 84 (Grubin, 1998, p. 4). As with the adult figures, cautions and convictions may not reflect the true incidence of these crimes.

The number of males convicted for the offence of indecency between males has also shown a steady decrease between 1987 and 1997. In 1987, 951 males of all ages were convicted for this crime, rising to a peak of 1,503 in 1989; by 1996, however, the figure had dropped to 219 and rose slightly to 237 in 1997 (HC Debs, 9 March 1999, WA 75034, col. 127).

The common theme to nearly all sexual offending is the lack of a real consent, whether by age, by coercion or from consent being given to a 'prohibited relationship'. Adults may be coerced into sexual activities against their will by threats or violence, and that will include coercion caused by poverty and economic imperatives that turn women (and men) to prostitution. Offences may be committed against women with mental impairments who are unable to give a true consent, and offences are committed when adults enter 'prohibited' (incestuous) relationships. Violent attacks on women where there is no sexual element can still be seen as sexual assaults simply because they are targeted as women.

Some offences may be committed even when there is consent between the adult parties concerned and most notably when activities are committed in a public rather than a private place, when they are deemed to offend our concepts of public decency.

Children and young people below the 'age of consent' may be engaged in unlawful sexual intercourse, either with or without their consent. Such offending can take place within a family ('intra-familial') or outside of the family ('extra-familial'); within a family it will probably be incestuous. Sexual offending outside of the family is sometimes referred to as the 'stranger-danger' that children should be wary of.

Allegations have been made that children have been subjected to 'ritual' or 'satanic' abuse, whereby the abuse is subsumed into ceremonies that serve to frighten the children into saying nothing afterwards. The truth of these allegations has been hotly disputed.

Children and young people also attend various institutions outside the family, such as nurseries, schools, youth clubs and sporting clubs; sometimes they require substitute care – when for various reasons their parents are unable to care – which might include a children's home or foster care. The extent of sex offending against children in all of these settings has been 'discovered' in the last 10 or 20 years and various safeguards put in place to reduce the risk to children in these 'out-of-home' settings. Some of this workplace sex offending can constitute organised abuse, sometimes referred to as 'rings' or 'networks' of offenders working together in various ways.

Children and young people may be coerced into prostitution against their will, and in other parts of the world this has been referred to as 'trafficking' when it involves moving victims (including adults) from one country to another. 'Sex tourists' is the term used to describe men who travel from North America, Europe, Japan and other developed countries to avail themselves of adult and child prostitutes in developing countries.

Sexual exploitation of children and adults can take place when they are involuntarily involved in the production of pornography which is then disseminated in either paper or electronic format; the latter could include distribution over the Internet.

The idea of outlining the 'forms' of sexual offending in this section is not to suggest a hierarchy of seriousness; all would be experienced as equally serious by the victims, unless, of course, they do not believe it to have been an offence at all. The idea has been to offer a sample of the variety of offending that we consider to be sexual offending; the reader will be able to add their own 'forms' to those not covered here.

The law

Although we can talk generally about sexual offending, in practice it will require a criminal court to decide whether or not a particular level of behaviour constitutes an offence. The courts will be interpreting the different common and statutory law for Scotland, Northern Ireland or England and Wales.

In 1985 the Howard League could report that:

> . . . the law makes no formal distinction between 'sexual' offences and other offences. How one differentiates is therefore largely a matter of individual choice, and the criteria for classification are open to debate.
>
> (Howard League, 1985, para. 2.3)

Today that position no longer holds.

Within the law various formal 'lists' of sexual offences have been drawn up for various purposes. For sentencing purposes, a 'list' exists in the Criminal Justice Act 1991 for England and Wales (see Table 1.1) and another in the Criminal Procedure (Scotland) Act 1995 for Scotland (see Table 1.2); they act as guides to the court that has to sentence a serious sexual offender.

The Sex Offenders Act 1997, which introduced the sex offender 'register', has 'lists' of which offenders might find themselves having to register. This 'list' is to be found in Schedule 1 to the Act and is actually subdivided into three 'lists' for England and Wales, Scotland and Northern Ireland.

The Schedule 1 'list' in the Sex Offenders Act is not to be confused with the more long-standing Schedule 1 'lists' that have given us the label 'Schedule 1 offender'. This Schedule 1 lists all the offences it is possible to commit against a child, including non-sexual offences such as neglect and physical abuse, and is to be found in the Children and Young Persons Act 1933 (as amended) (for England and Wales), the Children (Scotland) Act 1995 (for Scotland) and the Children and Young Persons Act (NI) 1968 (for Northern Ireland) (see Tables 6.1, 6.2 and 6.3 in Chapter 6).

Other 'lists' exist, such as the one that lists offences which can disqualify as a childminder (the Disqualification for Caring for Children Regulations 1991, S.I. No. 2094, Schedule); the list of offences which make a person 'automatically debarred' from teaching (the Education (Teachers) Regulations 1993, S.I. No. 543, as amended); and, if we move outside of legislation, yet another 'list' of sexual offences was drawn up by the Home Office in a 1996 consultation exercise that we will return to later (Home Office, 1996a, Annex A).

A *'sexual offence' (England and Wales)*
'Sexual offence' means any of the following –
(a) an offence under the Sexual Offences Act 1956, other than an offence under section 30, 31 or 33 to 36 of that Act;
(b) an offence under section 128 of the Mental Health Act 1959;
(c) an offence under the Indecency with Children Act 1960;
(d) an offence under section 9 of the Theft Act 1968 of burglary with intent to commit rape;
(e) an offence under section 54 of the Criminal Law Act 1977;
(f) an offence under the Protection of Children Act 1978;
(g) an offence under section 1 of the Criminal Law Act 1977 of conspiracy to commit any of the offences in paragraphs (a) to (f) above;
(h) an offence under section 1 of the Criminal Attempts Act 1981 of attempting to commit any of those offences;
(i) an offence of inciting another to commit any of those offences.
(Criminal Justice Act 1991, s. 31(1),
as amended by Criminal Justice and
Public Order Act 1994, Sch. 9, para. 45)

Table 1.1

A *'sexual offence' (Scotland)*
'Sexual offence' means –
(a) rape;
(b) clandestine injury to women;
(c) abduction of a woman or girl with intent to rape or ravish;
(d) assault with intent to rape or ravish;
(e) indecent assault
(f) lewd, indecent or libidinous behaviour or practices;
(g) shameless indecency;
(h) sodomy;
(i) an offence under section 170 of the Customs and Excise Management Act 1979;
(j) an offence under section 52 of the Civic Government (Scotland) Act 1982;
(k) an offence under section 52A of the Civic Government (Scotland) Act 1982;
(l) an offence under sections 1 to 3, 5, 6, 8, 10 and 13 of the Criminal Law (Consolidation) (Scotland) Act 1995.
(for full details see Criminal Procedure (Scotland) Act 1995, s. 120A,
as amended by the Crime and Disorder Act 1998, s. 86)

Table 1.2

None of these 'lists' has exactly the same content, which must be a signifier to some of the difficulties of defining a sexual offence. It may also explain why attempts are being made to review the law in England

and Wales. Paul Boateng, Minister of State at the Home Office, has said the review is needed because:

> . . . the law on sexual offences is confused and confusing. It is comprehensive but incoherent and has many anomalies that need resolving. Many of the offences were created long ago and reflect the social and legal system of their time . . . The law must be brought up to date, both to take on board human rights issues and to reflect the better understanding we now have of the patterns of sexual abuse. The courts must have the powers they need to deal with offenders and protect children and vulnerable people.
>
> (Home Office, 1999a)

One thing the review was not going to alter was the age of consent. The review was expected to be completed during the year 2000 (for details see HC Debs, 22 February 1999, col. 112 WA).

Whatever happens as a result of this review will not alter the current difficulties experienced by those who have to implement the law in terms of crime prevention, detection and arrest, prosecution and sentencing. Arguments over the punishment, containment or treatment of offenders will continue, as will the search for protection from the sex offender.

Consent

The concept of consent is central to defining sexual offending. Sexual activities are expected to be consensual, and we speak of 'consenting adults'. When one party to a sexual act has not consented, we are moving into the realms of sexual offending. The sexual offence of rape clearly takes place when penetrative sexual activity takes place without consent from the female (or male) victim, and that victim has been overcome by physical force or immediate threats of violence.

A consent is invalidated if it is given under duress; lawyers talk of the consent being 'negatived' by the presence of 'force, fear or fraud'. It is possible to compare consent here to the consent we give for medical treatment, where patients are said to give 'informed consent' (i.e. knowing the full implications) or 'real consent' (i.e. where no duress or coercion has been applied).

Consent has also been depicted as a continuum, with a positive consent at one end through to a reluctant agreement or submission at the other end; the latter can also be given without consent at all, which would mean a sex offence has been committed. A growing number of rapes are being reported that have been committed by people known to the victim and are referred to as 'acquaintance' or 'intimate' rapes as opposed to 'stranger' rapes (see Harris and Grace, 1999, pp. 5–7).

Consent to sexual activities is largely gender specific and socially constructed. The law may now recognise the crime of male rape but when it comes to consent we are mostly talking about women saying 'yes' or 'no' to heterosexual activity. Men have been culturally subsumed into being the partners that somehow 'always' want sex and indeed are sometimes said to have a 'sex drive' that is 'uncontrollable'. Such cultural thinking is not immutable and different cultures in different times and places have seen things differently. In Greek mythology the blind seer Teiresias, who had had the advantage of experiencing sex as both a man and a woman, was clear that women enjoyed it more than men on a ratio of about nine to one.

Children and young people are held to be unable to give a full autonomous consent because they lack the 'competence' to make the decision until they have reached a certain age – the age of consent. The age of consent for heterosexual activities in England, Scotland and Wales was fixed at 10 in 1285, raised to 13 in 1875 and to 16 in 1885, where it still stands (Sexual Offences Act 1956, s. 6). The age is examined from time to time to see if it should be altered (see e.g. Policy Advisory Committee on Sexual Offences, 1981), but it has remained at 16 for some time now, and there are no current plans to change it (see also Law Commission, 1995).

The age of consent for homosexual activities was fixed at 21 for England and Wales by the Sexual Offences Act 1967, section 1, with the same age being brought into Scottish Law in 1980 and Northern Ireland in 1982. Amending legislation lowered it to 18 in 1994 for all parts of the United Kingdom (Criminal Justice and Public Order Act 1994, s. 145).

Campaigners have continued to argue that the ages of consent for homosexual and heterosexual activities should be equalised. A case was put together by two men – Euan Sutherland and Chris Morris – with the backing of Stonewall, the homosexual rights group, to challenge the UK law in Europe. In July 1997, the European Commission on Human Rights accepted their arguments and found the present UK law contravened the European Convention on Human Rights. The next step would have been the UK appearing in the full European Court of Human Rights in Strasbourg, but the Government managed to broker an agreement to avoid the court hearing by promising to change the law at the earliest opportunity.

That opportunity came with the 1998 Crime and Disorder Bill, but unfortunately the requisite clause on equalisation was thrown out by the House of Lords, despite being overwhelmingly supported in the Commons. A second attempt was made through the Sexual Offences (Amendment) Bill published in December 1998, but the same thing happened. Any Bill rejected twice by the Lords can be presented for Royal Assent automatically in the next session of Parliament, and that was the intention at the time of writing (HC Debs, 23 July 1999, col. 732 WA).

Sexual activities, of whatever orientation, with young people below the age of consent is defined as 'unlawful sexual intercourse' even if a form of consent has been given and, in the case of a very young person, may be defined as rape.

Whilst most people would regard such under-age sexual activities as exploitation or criminal, arguments have been made that there should be no age of consent. Apologists for sex with children have even turned the concept on its head to argue it as a case of children's rights:

> ... children should have some say in what they do with their own bodies. They should be free to decide, as a matter of right, whether or not they want a sexual relationship.
>
> (O'Carroll, 1980, p. 127; see also Brongersma, 1988)

British law does accept that older children have a developing competence to make autonomous decisions and that autonomy and competence does not just appear on a given date in the calendar (*Gillick v. West Norfolk and Wisbech Area Health Authority and the DHSS* [1986] 1 AC 112). Discretion in the implementation of the law may be used when young people are only just below the age of consent and the defendant just above. A man under 24 years of age can also offer the defence that he had 'reasonable cause' to believe a girl was over 16 (Sexual Offences Act 1956, s. 6(3)).

Consent is declared invalid if the parties are entering a 'prohibited relationship'. A 'prohibited relationship' is defined in law and generally applies to relationships between parents and children or relatives that would be incestuous (Sexual Offences Act 1956, ss. 10–11). The incest taboo, the fear of in-breeding and the simple revulsion of the idea that those charged with caring for children should seek to have sex with those children are all reasons cited for prohibiting certain relationships.

The opposite side of the coin to 'prohibited relationships' is the idea that some recognised relationships give 'automatic' consent to sexual relations. For many years this was the case for married couples where the man had the relationship itself as a defence against a charge of rape; it was the orthodoxy that a man could not rape his own wife. The Law Lords have now overturned this common law idea that marriage means a man has a 'continual' consent from his wife for sexual activity at any time (*R v. R (Rape: marital exemption)* [1992] 1 AC 599).

Although there may well be agreement on what constitutes 'prohibited relationships' such as incest, there are still a number of 'prohibited relationships' where there is less agreement and indeed heated debate. The behaviour of two consenting adult males may, for example, be construed as a criminal act of indecency in certain circumstances. The participants may feel they have harmed no-one, but if their behaviour was in a public place they may have run up against the common law offence that declares their behaviour as obscene or disgusting enough to 'outrage public decency'. Here the prohibition is more about whether the act should be in private or public, rather than a reflection on the act itself. The purpose of the law is then to ensure that 'reasonable people may venture out in public without the risk of outrage to certain minimum accepted standards of decency' (Lord Simon of Glaisdale in *R v. Knuller (Publishing, Printing and Promotions) Ltd* [1973] 2 AC 435). The gay rights campaign group OutRage has taken its name from these common law provisions.

For many years sexual offending was synonymous with prostitution, which in turn was described as the 'crime without a victim'. The argument was that consent for this financial transaction was forthcoming on all sides, yet it was still circumscribed by laws forbidding soliciting, procuring or allowing premises to be used as a brothel – the public as opposed to the private aspects of prostitution. As we have seen earlier, more recent feminist approaches have argued that the women's consent is often not 'real' because she has been driven to her actions by poverty and lack of income; from this perspective prostitution becomes a form of abuse against women and even against those under 16, who are legally incapable of giving a 'real' consent.

Consent has had its limitations as a defence exposed elsewhere. In what became known as the 'Spanner Case' (named after the police operation), in 1990 a group of men were successfully prosecuted on charges of causing actual bodily harm and wounding under the Offences Against the Person Act 1861, section 47. The men's defence, that they all had an interest in sado-masochistic activities and that they had all consented to the acts, was not accepted; the prosecution was based on a home-made video of them that had come into the hands of the police.

On appeal the convictions were held to stand, but the custodial sentences imposed were reduced in length; the law appeared no clearer (*R v. Brown* [1993] 2 WLR 556 HL). With the support of Liberty, the civil rights organisation, the men went to the European Court of Human Rights in Strasbourg, but that court too upheld the right of the Government to prosecute in its role of protecting public health and morals; consent was not relevant (*Laskey, Jaggard and Brown v. UK* (1997) Times, 20 February).

Consent as a defence against allegations of sexual offending does, therefore, have its limitations. This legal ambivalence was displayed further when, in line with the *Brown* decision, a man in Wakefield was convicted for 'branding' his wife's buttocks. On appeal the case was thrown out as serving no useful purpose (*R v. Wilson* (1996) Times, 5 March). For most court hearings, however, the presence or absence of a 'real consent' is the turning point for deciding whether or not a sexual offence has taken place.

The private and the public

It has become the conventional wisdom that we live our lives in 'private' and 'public'. We move between these two spheres on a daily basis. Where exactly we draw the demarcation line is a matter of some debate and will vary from person to person, at different times of the day and between men and women. We value our privacy and we think we know when it has been 'invaded', even if we cannot accurately define what privacy is.

In general terms, the private sphere is characterised by being the unknown or unobserved area of life and an area in which 'free' behaviour is permitted without interference. It is the areas where individual and small group activities are permitted, including consensual sexual activities. As we have seen, the same activities in public space may well constitute crimes.

When the UK Government has looked at the law on sexual offending, it has always paid deference to matters of 'privacy'. The 1984 Criminal Law Revision Committee made out the case quoting verbatim from the 1957 Wolfenden Report:

> . . . the criminal law should not intervene in the private lives of citizens or seek to enforce any particular pattern of sexual behaviour further than is necessary 'to preserve public order and decency to protect the citizen from what is offensive or injurious and to provide sufficient safeguards against exploitation and corruption of others.'
>
> (Criminal Law Revision Committee 1984, para. 1.5; see also Wolfenden Report 1957, para. 13)

What actually constitutes the 'private zones' of life has been increasingly questioned. The privacy of the family or the household has been accepted to varying degrees since it was decreed 'an Englishman's [*sic*] home is his castle'. Women victims of criminal violence and sexual assault within the home would ask what value there is in delimiting such private zones wherein crimes against them are committed. The term 'domestic violence' has been questioned for its 'cosy' connotations that suggest this is perhaps a 'different' from of violence to public violence.

The most blatant example, until recently, has been the lack of recognition of rape in marriage (see above). Exactly the same behaviour carried out by a stranger in public would result in a lengthy prison sentence, but in the privacy of the household and circumscribed by 'marriage' it was not a crime at all. Some feminists have started to argue that privacy should only be applied to individuals totally alone in a house.

There is no definitive legal definition of privacy in the UK and consequently no right to privacy. From time to time the courts have been called on to attempt a definition (see e.g. *McConnell v. Chief Constable of Greater Manchester Police* [1990] 1 All ER 423 (CA)), and in turn they have lamented the lack of a statutory definition (*Kaye v. Robertson* [1991] FSR 62 (CA)).

United Kingdom law does go so far as to stipulate that certain sexual activities should only be undertaken in 'private'. The law decriminalising homosexual activities at the same time said those activities must be 'in private' (Sexual Offences Act 1967, s. 1). The law made no attempt to define what 'in private' meant, although later legislation has tried to throw some light on the subject (Criminal Justice and Public Order Act 1994, s. 143(3)). In 1997, seven men in Bolton were still prosecuted for homosexual activities that took place in a private household, but in the presence of others, which meant that it was considered not 'in private' ('Fight grows for gays in video case' *Guardian*, 23 January 1998).

International Conventions and Declarations have stated rights to privacy, including the UN Declaration of Human Rights (UN, 1948, art. 12) and the European Convention on Human Rights (Council of Europe, 1950, art. 8). The European Convention has now been assimilated into the UK's own Human Rights Act 1998 and it remains to be seen if this will clarify the domestic legal definition of privacy.

Sexual offending does take place in 'public space' but it is more likely to take place in 'private space', where there are rarely witnesses. For the criminal justice system, lawyers and victims, this has presented a major headache in bringing what went on, and determining whether or not there was consent, into the public arena of the court.

Dangerousness and risk

The idea that certain behaviour by individuals can be 'dangerous' has a long history. The Victorians thought that whole classes of people – the poor and dispossessed – could be called the 'dangerous classes'. For the most part of the twentieth century, the term was restricted in use to describe the behaviour of some mentally disordered people.

In 1977, in a seminal article, Bottoms described what he called the 'renaissance' of dangerousness as the label was increasingly used to describe criminal behaviour. Not only that, but practitioners in the criminal justice system including the police, probation officers and the judiciary were being called on, ever more, to divide criminal behaviour into what we might call 'dangerous' and that which was 'non-dangerous'. Penal disposals could then be decided upon in terms of the dangerousness posed (Bottoms, 1977).

The 'renaissance' of dangerousness in this fashion put practitioners into the business of trying to tell who exactly the dangerous person was. The word 'dangerous' having been, up until now, an adjective used to describe certain behaviour, now turned into a noun as we looked for the 'dangerous person'. Psychologists, social workers and psychiatrists were just some of the professionals who now engaged in the search for those attributes within a person that would justify them being assessed as 'dangerous people'. Once identified we could go on to assess the degree of risk they posed to other people.

Risk assessment takes a more detailed look at the same phenomena, but realises that an individual had to be seen, not in isolation, but in the context of their immediate social environment, be that family, household or community. Risk assessment is the process whereby information on the individual and his environment is collated – from various different agencies if necessary – to provide as complete a 'picture' as possible. Once assembled, the information has to be verified, sifted and weighted in significance; any deficiencies in the information has to be identified and that information duly gathered in.

In making a risk assessment, practitioners are making a prediction about a person's likely future behaviour. Everyone's future behaviour is, to some extent, uncertain and inherently unpredictable. Risk assessment accepts that we have enough information – including 'personal information' – about an individual to make an informed decision on that individual's future behaviour, albeit within a range of probabilities.

Sexual offenders are subjected to risk assessment when brought to court for bail or sentence decisions. They are assessed again at the start of their community or custodial sentence or on release from a period of detention. The assessment of risk is an ongoing process for practitioners working with sex offenders and an ongoing experience for those offenders.

Risk management follows on from assessment and involves the implementation of whatever measures are required to reduce the risk a sexual offender may pose. These measures may be community-based through supervision and conditions attached to that supervision, or may involve custodial containment.

Risk assessment and risk management will be a constant theme throughout this book; put together they can be considered under the umbrella term of 'risk analysis'.

Present approaches

This book attempts to introduce the reader to an overview of sexual offending as we have come to understand it today. Chapter 2 explores the explanations and responses made and put forward by the public, the press, politicians and the 'experts'. These different voices are often in competition with each other to try to define and 'claim' the phenomenon of sexual offending, and to say what should be done.

An illustrative history of sex offending is offered in Chapter 3, insofar as it can be distilled from historical sources. Particular attention is paid to themes and responses that have been made in the past which continue to have a resonance today. Such themes include the fear of the 'dangerous' person at large in the community and the need for the 'authorities' to identify him so that protective measures can be taken, and the need for 'experts' to understand what sexual offending is all about.

Chapter 4 outlines the current role of the police as the initial agency brought in to investigate sexual offending and detect those responsible. Chapter 5 carries the story on to the prosecution process and various difficulties encountered in the 'search for justice' where sexual offending is concerned. This 'search' ends with an examination of appropriate sentences for the convicted offender and (Chapter 6) how the agencies charged with carrying out those sentences go about their work.

Chapter 7 focuses on the particular mechanism of the UK's sex offender 'register'. In doing so, it emphasises the critical role that 'personal information' databases are seen to hold in the 'regulation' of the sex offender and the need to know where these offenders are at any given time; the 'register' is seen as one way of making 'visible' those who might otherwise be 'invisible'.

While Chapters 5 and 6 outline the 'search for justice', so Chapter 8 outlines the 'search for protection'. These are the protective measures taken within civil society to make communities safer from the threat of sexual offenders. This move toward protection – including child protection – can be seen as a parallel to the earlier 'search for justice', with the 'register' (Chapter 7) being the bridge between the two.

The book concludes with some speculation on future directions and developments, and an assessment of the role of 'personal information' and 'data' as the key to future regulation of the sex offender; that regulation also includes the use of such data for purposes of risk assessment and risk management. Throughout, the book seeks to act as a 'sourcebook' guiding the reader to other references for more detailed study.

2

The sex offender 'problem' – and responses

A number of different constituencies are competing with each other to claim and explain the phenomenon of the sex offender and to say what we should be doing with that offender. Criminologists refer to this as the struggle for 'dominion'. In its broadest terms, there are: community groups representing grass-roots; public opinion; the press and other media outlets; politicians seeking to be representative and responsible at the same time; and the 'experts' and practitioners in the form of doctors, penologists, therapists, police officers and others. The interaction between them all is complex – this is not a simple stand-off where the loudest voice gets to define what is happening.

The emotive nature of sex offending has often caused the formation of angry crowds to protest against the crimes and the criminals; the communal anger increases when the victim has been a child. Crowd reactions of this kind can be noted throughout history, with the precipitating event being the arrest of a sex offender, the trial, or the simple knowledge that the sex offender is living in a given locality.

The traditional role of the press has been to report such crowd disturbances. In the UK in recent years, however, we have seen the press as instigators of crowd reactions when they have published the identity and whereabouts of known sex offenders. The role of the police has normally been to ensure public order in the face of crowd violence, but they too have reportedly 'leaked' information on an offender's whereabouts to trigger that crowd into action in the first place. Probation officers and police officers, on the other hand, have complained that the press reporting of sex offenders has prevented them carrying out their duties.

In this chapter, we try to disentangle some of the messy threads of thought that overlap and pull these different constituencies in different directions: the local neighbourhood with genuine fears to express about the safety of their children; the politicians and press trying to voice those fears and at the same time take a lead in what we should be doing; and the practitioners such as probation officers, police officers, doctors and therapists trying to contain and regulate the activities of the sex offender. The aim is to reflect these different constituencies and their varying explanations and responses, rather than to lay claim to any single explanation and response that carries the imprint of a definitive 'truth'.

Popular explanations and responses

At the Conservative Party annual conference in October 1991, the MP for Littleborough and Saddleworth, Geoffrey Dickens, famously advised the Government how to combat sex offending:

> If you want to stop child abuse and rape of women, pass legislation and, on the second offence – not the first in case there is a mistake – put it before Parliament that you can castrate the buggers.
>
> (quoted in Sampson, 1994, p. 45)

Dickens's speech was well received and reported. It was a popular viewpoint to be hard and decisive on sex offenders, and it appealed to the crowd and the press alike. It is a viewpoint repeated often, and a viewpoint that challenges the 'expert' view that sex offenders can be helped and treated; it is a viewpoint that wants sex offenders 'locked up and the key thrown away' or simply wants them 'away from here and out of our neighbourhood'. When plans were announced in June 1999 to build accommodation for sex offenders in the grounds of Nottingham prison, a demonstration against the plans ensued; one demonstrator held a placard naming one of the offenders who might live there, saying he was wanted 'dead or alive', but with a cross deleting the last two words (see photograph on p. 2 *Guardian*, G2, 21 June 1999).

Communities have a genuine fear for their children and demonstrating is one way to voice it. The press and politicians will represent those fears and add their own motivations for taking up the cause. An intricate three-way relationship builds between these constituencies, which belies any direct power the media has to influence people. In turn, the audience reception of media reports and their own 'reading' of those reports to align them with existing knowledge and attitudes all plays a part (see Eldridge *et al.* 1997, esp. pp. 168–79).

The reporting of sex crime by the media and the double-edged relationship the media has with such offending has been well documented (see e.g. Soothill and Walby, 1991) and there is not the space here to go into the subject in great depth. On the one hand is the self-righteous indignation that such horrific crimes take place, and on the other, the knowledge that readers are compulsively fascinated with these stories and circulation figures may well depend on a regular supply of them; witness, for example, the *Sun*'s headline reporting of the conviction of Rose West for the crimes committed at 25 Cromwell Street ('Burn in Hell' *Sun*, 25 November 1995) accompanied by a 24-page special insert on 'the crime of the century'. From the Balkan conflict came apocryphal stories of reporters moving through the crowds of refugees asking if there were any women who had been raped and spoke English.

The same ambiguity can be seen in the wearing of children's clothes by adult women as the 'latest fashion' (see e.g. 'School's Out' *Independent on Sunday*, 17 August 1997) or by women pop stars deliberately cultivating a schoolgirl 'look':

> Most schoolgirls are aware of the undesirable effect that they have on a certain category of the population . . . powerlessness, naivete, and the general vulnerability of adolescence still exert an undeniable sexual pull.
>
> ('Little Girl Power' *Guardian*, 5 April 1999)

In the last ten years, the overall shift down-market of newspapers and broadcast news bulletins has also been noted, as journalists and news reporting have been forced to recognise market forces and competition. Franklin has documented this 'dumbing down' of the media's presentation of news, which he calls 'newszak':

> Newszak understands news as a product designed and 'processed' for a particular market and delivered in increasingly homogenous 'snippets' which make only modest demands on the audience. Newszak is news converted into entertainment.
>
> (Franklin, 1997, pp. 4–5)

Tabloid newspapers lead the way, followed by the 'broadsheets' and radio and television news, current affairs and documentaries. Ultimately, the 'fly on the wall' or 'docu-soap' replaces the traditional investigative documentary because they are cheaper to produce and the old-style documentaries that do appear have allegations of 'fabrication' thrown at them. For Franklin, this shift from news reporting as a public service to newszak, driven by market forces and competition, is raising serious questions about the role of the news and current affairs features and their contribution to mature democracies. It is in this world that crime and sex offending is being reported.

Some research found a decline in the quantity of media reports on rape between 1978 and 1992, accompanied by a tendency 'to concentrate on the more sensational cases which provide the most opportunity to titillate or to feed public outrage' (Grover and Soothill, 1995). One reason put forward for this fall-off has been 'boredom' and 'reader-fatigue' (Skidmore, 1995). Other trends have been noted:

> The continued reporting of such notorious cases as the Yorkshire Ripper and the Moors Murderers is akin to a 'sex offender soap'. Certainly, tabloid reporting of trivia helps to maintain a public interest in certain well-known cases.
>
> (Grover and Soothill, 1995)

And in the investigation of new sex crimes:

> [Journalists] have widened the reporting of sex crimes and have found new areas whereby they can titillate readers. This is particularly so in the search for the 'sex beast' in cases where no culprit has been identified and where the media is able to produce speculation in their construction of the sex fiend.
>
> (Grover and Soothill, 1995)

The other trend in the latter half of the 1990s has been the media's 'discovery' of the 'paedophile'. An analysis of articles about paedophiles in six leading British newspapers found nothing less than 'an explosion of interest in the topic [of paedophiles] among all these newspapers since 1996' (Soothill *et al.*, 1998). Paedophiles were big news; they were 'evil', 'monsters', 'beasts' and 'fiends' – the latter a word surely only ever used by journalists:

- 'They set a sex monster on my children' *Daily Mirror*, 15 August 1994
- 'Bestiality beyond imagination' *Daily Mail*, 17 May 1996
- 'Born a misfit, he became a monster' *Daily Mail*, 19 July 1996
- 'Monster bailed three times to attack again' *Yorkshire Post*, 23 November 1996
- 'I'll name the sex beasts' *Daily Mirror*, 9 June 1997
- 'Cops to unmask fiends' *News of the World*, 10 August 1997
- '6 more child sex fiends to go free' *Sun*, 13 March 1998
- 'Cage him before he kills again' *Daily Mirror*, 14 March 1998

Having constructed the paedophile in their own terms, the press were not going to engage in any deconstruction of him. It was pointed out, for example, that the press rarely reported successful appeals by sex offenders which, presumably, enabled them to throw off their 'monster' or 'beast' persona and return to being ordinary men again. The only time they were likely to report such appeals was if they could take another angle on it, as in the case of Stefan Kisko, where the police could be criticised for obtaining a confession from a man proved innocent by scientific techniques (Grover and Soothill, 1995).

The other effect of this 'name calling' of the individual who committed sex offences was to put them beyond the pale and out of reach of ordinary treatments and civil liberties. It also helped push the country into something of a 'moral panic' about sex offending, especially when that offending was against children.

The social theory of the moral panic as originally put forward by Cohen (1972) is the interaction between events on the ground, and their interpretation by 'primary signifiers' like courts, MPs, and inquiry reports and the media as 'secondary signifiers' in an escalating spiral of concern and outrage accompanied by demands that 'something must be done'. The triggering events invariably involve an element of violence, and that violence is on a scale that has crossed a threshold of acceptability and legality. The transgression of childhood innocence by adult aggressors was one such threshold.

In 1996 and 1997, the UK saw a series of popular 'uprisings' directed against sex offenders. A key element in these crowd reactions was the part played by the press and media reporting of sex crime and in particular the new role the press appeared to have taken upon themselves, actually to identify and publicise the whereabouts of sex offenders in the community. This 'outing' of sex offenders by the press was made against the backdrop of the political debate which had started on whether or not the police and other professionals should tell the public where 'known' sex offenders lived; the practice called 'community notification' or Megan's Law (see Chapter 7). It was as though the national and local press felt it was their duty to protect the community if the professionals were going to prevaricate.

The *Sunday Express* was amongst the first of the national newspapers to enter the fray with its campaign 'Will your child be next?'. The paper published five photographs and details of men with a record of sex offending whose addresses were unknown; readers were invited to identify their whereabouts:

> They could be living next to you, targeting your children right now. But you will not know their background – nor will your local police.
>
> ('Could these evil men be living next to you?'
> *Sunday Express*, 19 May 1996)

These men were all free citizens who had been punished by the criminal justice system and could be said to have 'done their time and paid their dues to society'. The implication was that these men were 'different', were likely to offend again and were not entitled to the restoration of normal civil rights and duties that anyone else might expect. Not only that, but there was an accusatory tone about the reporting that further implied the professionals had somehow 'got it wrong' and 'we', the public, were going to be suffering as a result.

The *Daily Mail* found a man in Lincolnshire who was on probation when they clearly thought he should have been in custody ('How could this man go free?' *Daily Mail*, 14 November 1996) and the *Yorkshire Post* reported on a man who had committed sex offences whilst on bail because of alleged incompetence by the Crown Prosecution Service ('Why was monster set free?' *Yorkshire Post*, 23 November 1996). The message was that 'the authorities' were getting it wrong a little too often.

The local press joined in. The *Bournemouth Echo* produced its own register of sex offenders from a trawl of its back editions; the register was available to professionals rather than the public. The *Yorkshire Post* photographed a known sex offender in the streets of Leeds ('Rapist just a face in the crowd' *Yorkshire Post*, 9 October 1996); the *Oxford Mail* found them visiting Chessington World of Adventure ('Mum's anger at pervert outings' *Oxford Mail*, 6 September 1996); and another Yorkshire paper found them at Flamingo Land and Lightwater Valley in North Yorkshire ('Theme parks off limits to sex offenders' *Yorkshire Evening Post*, 24 October 1996).

These press activities were soon being mirrored by local communal activities involving demonstrations, protests and vigilante action against sex offenders. In Manchester, a group of parents stormed the house of a known sex offender and marched on the local authority housing department to ask how many more there were ('Parents storm sex fiend's flat' *Manchester Evening News*, 7 November 1996). In Leeds, a gang burnt down the house of suspected child abuser ('"Child abuser" flees as vigilantes burn his home' *Guardian*, 8 July 1997) and protests were reported in Birmingham and Essex ('Nowhere to hide' *Daily Telegraph*, 22 March 1997).

Some of these activities were large and got beyond control. On the Logie estate in Aberdeen, a crowd of one hundred, described as mostly teenagers and young women, destroyed a house where they thought an offender was living. They described their estate as a 'dumping ground':

> At first it was disciplined – loud but disciplined. 'Perverts out!' was the most popular chant among the children and parents . . . no one knew if the person whose blood they were baying for was inside. The whole affair was based on rumour and speculation. In the end brute force brought all the answers.
> ('The day fury erupted on a city estate' *Aberdeen Evening Express*, 9 June 1997; see also 'Mob smashes up house in search of attacker' *Scotsman*, 9 June 1997)

As with all crowds, the motives for gathering and demonstrating are never clear-cut. Boredom and a search for action and 'something to do' could be as much a part of it as drunkenness and a desire to 'have a go' at authority, let alone demonstrate against sex offenders. Some journalists could see these traits running through the crowd:

> . . . their demonstrations have shades of political rallies, religious ceremonies, union meetings – all those group experiences which used to define people's sense of selves, and which are no longer available to them . . . now, people . . . organise against paedophiles. In a few years the cause will be something else.
> ('Paedophiles are one of the few groups you can respectfully hate' *Guardian*, 24 April 1998)

The theme of the crowd gathering against the sex offender has many precedents (see Chapter 3). The ambivalence of the crowd has also been noted before. At the 1965 trial of Myra Hindley and Ian Brady, for the assault and murder of children in what the press called the 'Moors Murders', Jeff Nuttall recalled the reaction of a friend of his:

> A press photographer I know had to be taken off the case, not on seeing the face of Hindley or hearing the tapes but on forming the impression that the crowd stood outside the court . . . stood there in envy rather than indignation.
>
> (Nuttall, 1970, p. 130)

Phrases like 'lynch-mob' and 'witch-hunt' were used in the reporting of crowd reactions. Paddy Ashdown (then leader of the Liberal Democratic Party) described the crowd in his Yeovil constituency as a 'lynch-mob' when they demonstrated outside a police station at the presence of the released paedophile Sydney Cooke. The crowd were happy to take on the label: 'So? What's wrong with that? We used to burn witches and it worked' (quoted in 'Paedophiles are one of the few groups you can respectfully hate' *Guardian*, 24 April 1998).

Demonstrations against the same man outside the Broadway Road police station in Bristol deteriorated into violence which had to be contained by police using riot gear; reports suggested petrol bombs had been used. Home Secretary Jack Straw condemned the violence:

> I understand the concern that people have about paedophiles. But there is no excuse for this kind of disgraceful behaviour, particularly when it's directed against the police who . . . are there to protect the public from paedophiles.
>
> ('Straw Pledges Action on Paedophiles'
> *Guardian*, 27 April 1998)

Presumably Straw was less than pleased when later evidence revealed the police themselves to have leaked details of 'high profile sex offenders . . . to the media and others' and in one case 'disorder [had] occurred resulting in injuries to many police officers' (HMIC, 1999, para. 5.30).

When the crowd did get hold of a known sex offender, the term 'vigilante' started to be used. An early example had occurred just outside Edinburgh, when 37-year-old Lawrence Leyden was identified by neighbours as having a record of sex offences against children. Leyden was subjected to verbal harassment, had his car vandalised and the words 'die' and 'beast' written on his front door in excrement; a petition was started to have him re-housed. Leyden himself also requested a move, but it was all too late. He was stabbed to death by unknown assailants who broke into his home. The community was reportedly not very keen to help police with their inquiries ('Closed doors on murder' *Guardian*, 28 February 1995).

The *Manchester Evening News* ran a front page picture of a sex offender named by them a few days earlier sitting in his vandalised car, and ran an editorial in the same edition justifying its actions:

> Once a paedophile always a paedophile . . . we are well aware that our action creates a civil rights problem, but we believe the safety of young children overwhelmingly outweighs the rights of a convicted paedophile . . . there have been far too many cases in recent years of perverts obtaining jobs working with children.
>
> ('Why we did it' *Manchester Evening News*,
> 30 August 1996)

Later the same editor explained the demands being put on him by members of the public:

> The only time we have named individuals is when the public come to us and tell us they have serious concerns about a person living near them . . . they were absolutely livid and they contacted us.
>
> (quoted in Potter, 1997)

Frances Duffy, aged 67, was mistakenly identified as a paedophile after another man had had his photograph in the *Manchester Evening News*. Duffy suffered a broken wrist, broken finger and severe bruising. A *Sunday Times* investigation into vigilantism estimated Duffy to be just one of about '30 cases where men wrongly suspected of abusing children have been beaten and humiliated by gangs bent on driving them out of their homes' ('Child abuse vigilantes terrorise the innocent' *The Sunday Times*, 2 November 1997).

A unique feature of the situation in Northern Ireland was the backdrop of sectarian violence that was present throughout most of the 1970s and 1980s. The police and security forces, of necessity, had to give priority to 'the troubles' which meant that 'normal' policing activities, including the policing of sex offenders, sometimes received a low priority. In turn, the paramilitary groups in the province were able to move into the resulting vacuum left by the police and operate parallel unofficial criminal justice systems and mete out violent reprisals on suspected sex offenders; as one witness told an inquiry:

> . . . a lot of it's about the paramilitaries making themselves indispensable within the community. Sex offenders is a popular issue. In the past, Sinn Fein would go to another organisation to have the RUC called. Now, the paramilitaries are more successful at driving sex offenders out because it's very popular with the local community.
>
> (HRW, 1997, p. 110)

Not only was the vacuum filled, but the paramilitaries gained goodwill and kudos within their neighbourhoods.

Elsewhere, protest was more low key. On the Seacroft estate in Leeds, a woman distributed leaflets and sent an open letter to residents giving details of a local man's address and conviction record. The protest was triggered by the man receiving a community sentence for indecent assaults on children: 'as far as his sentence goes the word justice no longer exists to the people of Seacroft . . . we feel betrayed' ('Police called in as mum shames paedophile' *Yorkshire Evening Post*, 27 June 1997).

Some spontaneous protests became more formalised and turned themselves into campaigning 'action groups'. At national level, the 'Parents Against Child Abuse', 'Mothers Against Murder and Aggression', 'Scottish Parents Against Child Abuse' and 'People Power' were formed; at local level there was the 'Child Protection Action Group' (Wakefield), the 'Unofficial Child Protection Unit' (Glasgow), the 'Peterhead Campaign Against Paedophiles', 'The White Ribbon Campaign for Justice' (Milton Keynes), and the 'Council for the Protection of Children' (Bradford), to name but a few. Many of these were short-lived but they demonstrate the degree of concern that was being felt.

Although the police had been in the direct firing line of some of the demonstrations, the long-term effect of the press coverage and communal activities of 1997–98 started to have a more direct impact on the activities of practitioners trying to work with sex offenders. In high profile cases it was impossible for police, probation officers and social workers to do anything that was not in the glare of the media's spotlight. Hostels refused to take sex offenders for fear of hostility from the local community and housing authorities started to do the same. For their part, sex offenders – high profile or not – were fearful of coming forward for help and, at worst, were being 'driven underground' where no-one knew their whereabouts. A spokesperson for the Association of Chief Officers of Probation said:

> there is firm evidence that real damage is being done to innocent children and adults by people taking the law into their own hands. Existing vital and effective supervision and surveillance operations are being destroyed.
> (quoted in 'Vigilantes "putting children at risk"'
> *Daily Telegraph*, 25 April 1998).

and the Chief Inspector of Probation added that hostels were refusing to take offenders 'not because they can't handle them but because of the consequences from the local community doing something very stupid and silly to the hostel and staff there' (quoted in 'Hysteria toward paedophiles "may increase the risk"' *Daily Telegraph*, 29 April 1998).

In August 1998, the Association of Chief Officers of Probation (ACOP) announced its intention to meet with the Press Complaints Commission.

A spokesman for ACOP said:

> We want to get some sort of guidelines and reach more of an understanding with the press so that journalists can cover the stories without scuppering the arrangements made by police and probation services to supervise offenders.
>
> ('Call for Media Curb on Paedophile
> Releases' *PA News*, 13 August 1998).

Gill Mackenzie, ACOP Vice Chair said:

> We must keep pressing for a more sophisticated debate to keep things in proportion. We must have a constructive dialogue with community groups without constantly finding ourselves deadlocked in stand-offs and threats of mob action.
>
> (*ibid*; see also 'Press gag sought to stop paedophile
> lynch mobs' *Independent*, 14 August 1998)

Discussions with the Press Complaints Commission did take place, but the Commission really needed someone to bring an actual complaint to them for consideration. Nonetheless, these background talks do appear to have made some impact.

Incidents continued to occur. A crowd of 100 people stoned a 68-year-old man out of his home in Kirkcudbright in Scotland after his prison release in May 1999 ('Mob forces paedophile out of home' *Daily Telegraph*, 17 May 1999) and demonstrations took place outside Nottingham prison against plans to build accommodation for sex offenders in the prison ground ('Prison blockade attempts to stop paedophile unit' *Guardian*, 16 June 1999). But the reporting was subdued and the editorials appeared to hold back; the high point of 'paedophile panic' in 1996–97 seemed to have passed.

The public, the media and the politicians have a view of sexual offending and have expressed that view to varying degrees. Other views, which we might call the 'expert' views, can be juxtaposed against it without necessarily saying that one should predominate over the other.

'Expert' explanations and responses

The term 'expert' has been used here to encompass different disciplines, including medical, penal, psychological and feminist. As already suggested, there is a struggle going on between the 'experts' and the more 'populist' explanations of sexual offending; each lays a claim to define the truth. To whom should we give credence? We can only say that the 'populist' explanations appear more subjective and prone to propagating 'mythologies' of rape about victims who 'ask for it' and 'strangers who lurk in shadows' like 'monsters', compared to the –

hopefully – more informed and objective research that comes from the various 'expert' disciplines.

The doctors

The general medical profession has a forensic role in helping the police to gather evidence following a sexual assault, but has otherwise made only a limited contribution to understanding why some people commit sexual crimes. Psychiatry is the branch of the profession that might have been expected to throw light on sexual deviance and behaviour, and to some extent it has fulfilled this role. On the other hand there is growing consensus that sexual offending is more often unconnected to mental illness.

Some people with a mental illness and in need of treatment may commit sexual offences, but the treatment is for the illness and may or may not remove the propensity to offend. The distinction may not always be clear to a public still confused about the nature of mental disorder and there is still talk of 'sex maniacs' and 'dangerous' people, plus the fact that sometimes mentally ill people do commit sexual offences (see e.g. 'Schizophrenic rapist given five life sentences' *Independent*, 8 February 1996).

The Mental Health Act 1983 appeared formally to disconnect psychiatry from sexual offending with its provisions in section 1(3) that state that the Act does not apply 'by reason only of promiscuity or other immoral conduct, [or] sexual deviancy'.

In the debate which started in 1997, about people with 'severe personality disorders' who commit sexual offences, the doctors felt they were not well placed to take on these people as patients:

> . . . the training and experience of many psychiatrists, which is focused on treating people with other mental disorders, leaves them poorly equipped to manage this group. Admission to mental health services for crisis intervention can be very problematic.
>
> (Home Office, 1999b, para. 12)

Even if it could not offer explanations, psychiatry still felt able to offer some treatments, and psychiatric skills in 'risk assessment' were still taken into account by courts and parole boards when it came to decisions on a person's civil liberties.

Treatments could include a general medical approach to organic or genetic factors that were in turn leading to sexual offending. Some patients with a 'hormone imbalance' could be helped by being given 'suppressants' to minimise their sexual drive (see e.g. Fennell, 1988). These treatments needed the consent of the patient. If there was going to be a surgical implant of a suppressant under the Mental Health Act, a second doctor needed to approve it, even if consent had been given (Mental Health Act 1983, s. 57).

Castration or 'de-sexing' was, according to Meyers, introduced to England by the Normans, who used it as a punitive measure for rapists (Meyers, 1970, p. 26). It has not become a regular feature of modern policies on criminal justice in this country, but is permitted in a number of states in the US.

In the 1920s and 1930s, castration became confused with sterilisation as part of the eugenics debate that, at its extreme, wanted to control the reproduction of people with mental impairments (see King, 1999, Chapter 3). Fennell recounts the story of actual castrations carried out in the Public Assistance Institution in Gateshead in 1930. A Ministry of Health inspection found three people to have been operated on, including a 14-year-old boy charged with indecent assault. The Ministry warned Gateshead that, even with the consent of the boy's mother, these castrations were illegal and could result in prosecution; the medical officer confirmed that there would be no more operations of this kind (Fennell, 1996, p. 86). King cites evidence that illegal sterilisations were not uncommon at this time (King, 1999, p. 92) and in 1923, in Derbyshire, the County Council wanted changes in the law 'to empower a court to order the sterilisation of mental defectives convicted of sexual offences' (Fennell, 1996, p. 81).

The confusion surrounding castration generally has been succinctly clarified by Meyers:

> the cause of, and answer to, the sexual psychopath's abnormal urges lies in his cranium, not in his scrotum. Castration, like sterilisation, ensures neither a reduction in libido nor in sexual act capability. The only certainty of the operation is that its effects are 'very variable'.
> (Meyers, 1970, p. 46; see also Heim and Hursch, 1979)

In the past, psychiatrists have involved themselves with 'treatments' such as aversion therapy or covert sensitisation, but, more recently, have left such techniques to the psychologists.

The therapists

Aversion therapy techniques depend on ideas of 'classical conditioning'. A person is exposed to evidence of the deviant behaviour or sex offending at the same time as an aversive stimulus is applied. Thus, a child sex offender would be shown pictures of children to induce sexual arousal and receive an electric shock or chemically-induced nausea by way of association.

Covert sensitisation is a form of aversion therapy, but without the external aversive stimulus. The technique depends upon a purely cognitive approach, whereby the patient or offender is asked to produce his own aversive thoughts whenever the deviant or sexual offending thoughts come into his head. Some therapists have suggested a simple elastic band around the wrists which is pulled and released as a sharp reminder whenever deviant sexual thoughts occur.

If aversion therapy seeks to reduce undesired behaviour, other techniques seek to positively increase desired behaviour. Thus, 'aversion relief' builds upon aversion therapy by giving positive reinforcement to benign or socially desired images and thoughts. A further variation is known as 'fading' or 'shaping', whereby deviant images are slowly replaced by more socially acceptable ones to change the subject's erotic fantasies. 'Orgasmic conditioning' relies on the subject learning to switch the theme of his fantasies from deviant to acceptable at the point of masturbatory orgasm (for an overview of these and other behavioural approaches see Hawton, 1983).

These crude behavioural approaches fell out of fashion in the 1980s and 1990s, and the treatment method now most favoured is that known as the 'cognitive-behavioural' approach. This approach draws on a variety of social and psychological explanations.

Psychological explanations of sex offending also locate the problem with the individual. Personality traits of the individual, such as an extrovert personality that seeks to dominate others, or a lack of social skills to contain anger and violence, all contribute to the development of a person prone to sex offending. Problem-solving skills with adults are poor or non-existent in these offenders.

Alternative personality traits could be a lack of self-esteem and a poor self-image, which leads on to, once again, poor problem-solving skills with adults and a preference for relationships with children who are seen as 'weak' and 'non-threatening' by comparison. The presence of so-called disinhibitors like alcohol or drugs, or the presence of 'stress' in various forms, then become facilitators of the propensity toward sexual offending.

These personality traits are seen as developing slowly through childhood and are linked to inappropriate parenting or theories of the 'dysfunctional family'. Associated features would include a 'distortion' of thinking that sees offending behaviour as not really offending at all, as well as an accompanying 'denial' of a problem.

The 'cognitive-behavioural' approach to treating male abusers appears to work best with those who offend against children. It is an eclectic approach, drawing on a variety of 'treatments', including some of those we have just looked at as 'behavioural approaches'. 'Cognitive-behavioural' work can be carried out by probation officers, prison officers, social workers and psychologists and can be delivered in either an individual 'one-to-one' format, tailored to the particular offender, or on a group work basis. It has been posited that a multi-agency approach to this work has the positive advantage of drawing in various perspectives and skills. Beckett has summarised the essentials of cognitive-behavioural treatment:

> . . . these interventions focus on altering patterns of deviant arousal, correcting distorted thinking, and increasing social competence, with educational input assisting offenders to gain knowledge in sexual matters, the effects of sexual abuse and sexual assault cycles.
>
> (Beckett, 1994)

The sessions with the offenders, whether individual or group work, are linked together by intervening 'homework' sessions which have to be completed: sometimes these programmes are called 'personal change programmes'. We should also note that, although we are looking at treatments here, practitioners such as probation officers and prison officers have other roles to perform in the containment and punishment of sex offenders (see Chapter 6).

'Cognitive-behavioural' approaches take the starting point that the offenders know what they are doing and are making a conscious decision to commit sexual offences. This decision-making is, however, qualified by the fact that the offender bases it on distorted thinking ('cognitive distortion') that becomes 'hardened' into 'fantasies' and 'anti-social personalities'. In the end, they may believe they have done no wrong, or that the victim 'led them on', or they are in total denial about the crimes.

The starting point for 'cognitive-behavioural' treatment is that the offender is willing to accept that an offence has taken place and is willing to enter into a 'contract' with the therapist to uncover the true motivation for the offending and to start confronting some of the distorted thinking that has formed around that offending. Once that has been achieved, an input of 'avoidance' and 'coping' mechanisms can be attempted, as well as general 'social skills training' to improve social competence, and also the developing of an understanding and empathy with the victim of the crimes (Beckett *et al.*, 1994; Clark and Erooga, 1994).

One technique of 'cognitive-behavioural' treatment is to introduce offenders to the idea of the 'model of change' developed by Prochaska and Di Clemente. Within this model, the offender is seen to move through various phases with respect to their behaviour:

1 Pre-contemplation: the offender is unaware of their 'problem'; in denial; defensive.
2 Contemplation: the offender decides to change.
3 Action: the 'rehearsal' of the change.
4 Maintenance: sustaining the new behaviour.
5 Relapse: giving up and returning to old behaviour.

The model, first developed with alcoholics and drug-users, invites the offender to place himself in one of the various phases with a view to understanding their progress. As relapse is built into the model, it can be anticipated and foreseen by worker and offender (Prochaska and Di Clemente, 1986).

Another frame of reference used by therapists with a 'cognitive-behavioural' approach is that of the 'pre-conditions' for child sexual abuse identified by Finkelhor. The starting point for this analysis is a person who is motivated to offend against children, but is prevented from doing so by 'internal' and 'external' obstacles. The 'internal' are personal to the offender and, once they are overcome, he looks to circumvent whatever 'external' obstacles exist by way of parents or other adult carers or guardians. If the 'external' obstacles are successfully overcome, there is only the child's own 'resistance' to be worked on before abuse takes place (Finkelhor, 1986).

The big question remains – does 'cognitive-behavioural' treatment work? The popular argument is that nothing changes these men and, as we have seen, 'once a paedophile, always a paedophile'. Evaluative studies would suggest otherwise, albeit with caution. The consensus appears to be that sexual offending behaviour can be controlled and contained, if not completely removed:

> . . . whilst no treatment approach is 100 per cent effective for all offenders all of the time, certain offenders do appear to benefit from particular types of intervention, as indicated by reduced recidivism.
>
> (Beckett, 1994)

For Beckett, those 'particular types of intervention' favoured a 'cognitive-behavioural' approach (see also Beech et al., 1998).

Part of the process of treatment has involved the categorising and 'labelling' of offenders into various types. In Scotland, for example, researchers classified child sex abusers into four categories using the acronym RAPID (Random Abusers, Paedophiles, Incest and Deniers) (Waterhouse et al., 1994, Chapter 4). Others have categorised paedophiles as 'fixated' or 'regressed'.

The 'regressed' paedophile is described as the less serious offender, who 'drifts' in and out of a desire to have sexual contact with children. The 'fixated' paedophile, on the other hand, is the more dangerous offender, being described by Wyre as 'highly addicted' in a way 'similar to a gambling or drug addiction'. Wyre goes on to explain how these paedophiles molest large numbers of children by being seductive towards them and their parents over a long period of time, in order to impose their distorted thinking on their victims to make their behaviour appear 'normal'. Part of this distortion is the idea that children can actually consent to what they are being induced into. For Wyre, the concept of the 'fixated paedophile' 'helps explain why there are some paedophile offenders who really do want to stop but find it impossible' (Wyre, 1996).

The feminist analysis

A feminist analysis of sexual offending, however, finds the labelling of a man as a paedophile unhelpful. Feminists argue that the label obscures the normality of the male perspective, which sees young girls as attractive and desirable, and overlooks the 'normality' of sexual offending being almost wholly a male activity, and one in which they choose to engage.

Cameron and Frazer, in their book on sexual murder, also indict criminology for overlooking and obscuring the gender-specific nature of murder:

> . . . there are various social constraints on who is a killer and who gets killed. One of these is, quite simply, gender: killers are mostly male, victims mostly female.
>
> (Cameron and Frazer, 1987, p. 30)

Cameron and Frazer have been criticised for overstating their case (Jenkins, 1994: Chapter 7), but the statistics are on their side. A large study of 500 known child sex abusers in Scotland found 99 per cent of them to be male and three quarters of the abused children female (Waterhouse et al., 1994), and in Northern Ireland, an estimated 95 per cent of serious assaults categorised as 'domestic' were by men (McWilliams and Spence, 1996, p. 49).

Kelly has put forward the idea of male violence and sexual assault as being on a 'continuum' from so-called normal behaviour through to generally recognised deviant and criminal behaviour. Forms of male behaviour at one end of the continuum are just a different version of behaviour to be found at the other end, and the idea of 'types' of sex offender becomes redundant. Male domination of women thus becomes normalised in all areas of life, as does the expectation of women's subordination and the requirement that they 'fall into line' almost as 'property' of men.

These cultural expectations are supported by patriarchal norms that are to be found in institutions, language and customs wherever we look (Kelly, 1988).

The 'continuum' idea explains how women experience male violence in various forms and as being all-pervasive. Male expectations of women are backed up by attitudinal, verbal and actual violence in all areas of life. Thus, women experience violence and domination in the home, in the work-place through limited career opportunities, sexual harassment and actual violence, and on the streets in generalised hostility toward women and the idea that some public places are safer than others. Many of these activities may fall short of being sexual offences as defined by a criminal court, but the 'continuum' provides a cultural context that circumscribes sexual offending.

If women are male 'property' they can be 'objectified' and in turn become 'dehumanised', making offending more likely. As the women's movement has analysed this phenomenon and challenged it, the very challenge has 'threatened' male dominance and led to a renewed effort – including violence – on the part of men to reassert their position.

Within the idea of a 'continuum' of sexual violence and assault, the very word 'paedophile' becomes unhelpful. As Kelly has pointed out, the labelling of a man as a 'paedophile' – invariably by male 'experts' – takes him outside of the continuum by focusing on the person rather than the behaviour and marks him out as being intrinsically 'different' from other men. This difference then gets elaborated to suggest that the paedophile never has sex with adult partners, invariably prefers boys and usually operates outside of the family. All of this is distracting us from the 'normality' of men targeting young girls, acting within the family and having adult relationships at the same time. Kelly quotes a worker with child prostitutes in Bradford:

> What is a paedophile anyway? As far as we can see on this project, he's over 30, drives a nice car and has a wife and kids.
> (Kelly, 1996)

An inquiry into safeguards for children in Scotland (see Chapter 8) had a similar experience. The committee of inquiry received various submissions on how to identify 'the paedophile', mostly in the form of 'check lists'. The committee was sceptical:

> There are checklists in existence which would probably allow every adult in Scotland to be seen as a potential paedophile.
> (Kent Report, 1997, para. 6.6.7)

The use of the word 'paedophile' implies that the man cannot help his behaviour and actually needs 'treatment' of some kind. The feminist analysis challenges this 'need for treatment' by emphasising the normality of the behaviour and by insisting that men could control it if they chose to. This challenge is also made to the 'cycle of abuse' concept – victims of abuse go on to become abusers – when it is pointed out that most victims of abuse are girls, and yet it is the men who are said to suffer most from being abused, when they go on to become child abusers (Kelly, 1996).

The devaluing of treatment in this analysis has gained some support from a recent study of treatment programmes of rapists where the victim has been an adult rather than a child. Cognitive-behavioural treatment programmes were found to be less successful with this group of offenders and 'current research . . . offered no clear indication of the most effective approach' (HMIP, 1998a, para. 3.21)

In this way the position of all women becomes one of vulnerability if they allow it to be; as one worker in a Rape Crisis Centre has put it:

> Whether or not we have been raped ourselves, we all share the experience of the threat of male violence, the sense of smallness and powerlessness constructed by the ideology of male authority, and the actualities of male social and economic power.
>
> (Anna, 1998)

Along the 'continuum', specific forms of sexual violence are thus connected to more common everyday aspects of male behaviour that include abuse, intimidation, coercion, intrusion and threat. The continuum is not about the relative seriousness of male activities or the idea of a hierarchy of abuse, but more an illustration of the prevalence of the phenomena (Kelly, 1988). In turn it is suggested that:

> Society does not want to hear what women have to say about this subject, and men have a vested interest in keeping definitions of sexual violence as narrow as possible. It is vital that women continue to speak, to tell their stories.
>
> (Hague and Malos, 1998, p. 8)

Radford and Kelly have elaborated on the experiences of women when 'nothing really happened' to show how women's minimising and discounting of their experiences is effectively a 'silencing' exercise by the mainstream society, which they rename as 'malestream' society:

> Men, who as the perpetrators of sexual violence have a vested interest in women's silence have in a range of ways and in a range of contexts, constructed 'knowledge' about sexual violence, crime and women's sexuality; through institutions such as the law, medicine, psychiatry as much as the 'common sense' that is promoted by the media, including pornography.
>
> (Kelly and Radford, 1990–1)

All the time, women's experiences are coming up against the ascendancy of the male perspective.

Drawing on information from the Equal Opportunities Commission, Gregory and Lees have quantified the male perspective:

> A mere 14% of police officers are women, mostly concentrated in the lowest rank . . . a total of 71% of solicitors on the Law Society's roll are male as are 78% of barristers and 94% of Queens Counsel (QCs) . . . the judiciary is 90% male and those women who are employed as judges are working mainly as assistant recorders, district judges, deputy district judges or stipendiary magistrates . . . the House of Lords judges and

32

the Heads of Divisions are all men. There is one women Appeal Court Judge (out of 35) and seven High Court Judges (out of 96).

(Gregory and Lees, 1999, pp. 203–4)

Whether women take this ascendant position or men actually relinquish it, the difficulties of establishing that actually 'something did happen' in terms of a sexual offence are starting from this initial imbalance.

Summary

In this chapter we have sought to find explanations for sexual offending that have been offered by the press, the public and the politicians on the one hand, and by 'experts' such as doctors, therapists and feminist scholars and activists on the other. The former have offered us a simplistic model of 'monsters' and 'beasts' that has sometimes led to direct action to identify and deal with these offenders. The latter has attempted to offer a more considered and scientific look at the phenomena, although the 'experts' inevitably disagree amongst themselves.

3

Social responses to the sex offender: an historical perspective

The idea of sex offending as we know it today has evolved slowly over the course of history. The definitive history of sex offending has probably still to be written, and this chapter attempts only an outline of developments to define and counter the sex offender, and the culture, mores and legal provisions put in place at the time. The chapter tries to highlight those provisions from the past that have a continuing resonance today; the perceived need to identify, label and regulate the 'dangerous' person, the competing definitions put forward by the popular crowd, the press and politicians and the later arrival of the medical and penal 'experts' and the move towards public protection. For more general histories of crime and the response to it, the reader is referred to Beattie (1986) and Radzinowicz and Hood (1990).

Pre-industrial times to 1800

Criminal behaviour that was apprehended in thirteenth-century Britain was brought before either the secular courts or the church courts. In general terms, the former examined crimes against property or public order, the latter crimes against morality, including sex offences. We should remember, however, that married women and children were often formally considered as 'property' in those times and marital separations, for example, might not necessarily end up in the church courts. The laws to be implemented were a mixture of common law, statutory law and church law.

The emerging ideas of 'the market' and private ownership of property, to replace that held in 'common', fed into the notion that sex offending was not just rape or sodomy and the crimes we know today, but could also include adultery, fornication, sex outside of wedlock and bigamy. One form of regulation was the parish register of births, deaths and marriages. This early form of registration could help decide subsequent property transactions and, according to the historian Christopher Hill:

> . . . declared who had and who had not a 'settlement' in any
> given parish, and so prevented false claims to poor relief . . .

> [and so] the discipline of parish registers and parochial assumption of control over the marriage of the poor complemented the discipline of the market.
>
> (Hill, 1996, p. 202)

The Statute of Westminster 1285 had made rape an offence punishable by death and put the 'age of discretion' (consent) at 10. Children aged 10 to 12 were given some protection, but claiming consent had been given was a valid defence for a man. The age of consent rose to 12 in 1576 (see also Jackson, 2000, pp. 12–14).

Incest was historically an ecclesiastical offence, triable before a church court and incestuous marriages could be declared null and void. Offenders – or sinners – 'were forced to do penance either by public confession in the parish church or in the marketplace . . . in bare feet, clothes in a white sheet and clutching a white wand' (Bailey and Blackburn, 1979). Excommunication from the church could be added. Parents who sexually abused their own children might be similarly punished, but, given the poor levels of housing and accommodation and lack of 'policing', such offences rarely came to light.

Sodomy, or anal intercourse, was made an offence by an Act of 1533 and persons – male or female – convicted were sentenced to death. It has been reported that such harsh sentences were reinforced by the belief that sodomy was associated with witchcraft and was, in fact, the way in which witches had communion with the devil 'who with his forked penis committed sodomy and fornication at the same time' (Bancroft, 1974, p. 8).

There is evidence to suggest that women were less in fear of sexual attack and rape than in fear of straight violence in these pre-industrial times. Historians have found few writings expressing such fears, and the conclusion has been drawn by some feminists that male domination was so clear-cut that men had little need to employ the threat of rape to maintain their dominance (Porter, 1985).

The natural hazards of life meant that children were always at risk from illness and disease, as well as injury from accident. Risk from adult offenders outside the family seems to have been relatively rare. One early example of a recorded abduction of a child is related, by Heywood, of one Alice de Salisbury:

> . . . who in 1373 stole Margaret Roper, the little daughter of a London grocer, carrying her away and stripping her of clothes so that she might not be recognised by her family.
>
> (Heywood, 1959, p. 6)

The abduction was to use the child for begging purposes, but the offender was caught and spent one hour per day in the stocks. In 1645, Parliament was informed that 'divers lewd persons do go up and down the city of London and elsewhere, and in the most barbarous and wicked manner steal away many little children'. Constables were to apprehend anyone stealing, buying or receiving stolen children (Laurence, 1994, pp. 84–85). The state of policing through the local constables and 'night watch' was, of course, primitive, and prevention and detection of crimes was difficult. An Act of 1604 required the whole community to assist, when necessary, in the apprehending of criminals.

It is probably at this time also that the spectre of the individual dangerous person – as opposed to groups – first appears as a nomadic figure which could threaten communities anywhere. The vagrant was a particular demonised figure of the times. A figure that blends in with mythical tales of demons, werewolves and those, like the 'raggle taggle gypsies', who would steal your children.

Vagrancy Acts were introduced to impose some order and improve public protection. The Vagrancy Act 1714 identified the mentally disordered person – 'the furiously mad and dangerous' – as requiring restraint as a matter of urgency to protect the community. The Vagrancy Act 1744 allowed for restraint of the mad, along with an element of 'curing' in such establishments as the emerging county workhouses. Children as well as adults could end up in workhouses, where their treatment was quite miserable. Many children in these early institutions 'were the victims of murder, manslaughter, assault and rape' (Heywood, 1959, p. 19).

The mid-eighteenth century saw the vagrancy problem worsen with the influx of many Irish people on to the British mainland. One proposal for dealing with them included in 1748 the idea of a register:

> Vagrants released from the county workhouses should be made to appear at the Quarter Sessions to be 'registered and recorded' so that their offending might be more easily convicted, which Register, and proving the identity of the Persons, shall be sufficient Evidence for convicting such Vagrant in order for Transportation.
>
> (cited in Radzinowicz, 1948, p. 19)

Other suggestions of the time included the need to require 'servants and labourers' to have a certificate signed by a magistrate, minister or churchwarden should they wish to move from their place of residence (*ibid*, p. 20).

The earliest attempts at policing, as we know it today, also thought the idea of a register was a positive one. Henry Fielding, the Chief Magistrate of Bow Street (1748–54), started his reform of the police in London in the 1740s with the creation of the Bow Street runners, which included the innovation of the post of 'Register Clerk'. This particular register was to be a record of crimes reported, goods lost and names and descriptions of people both suspected and convicted. Sir John Fielding, Henry's brother, later suggested that one of its purposes was to help identify those who should be shown mercy, instead of being executed:

> Wisdom, policy and humanity dictate that the most abandoned, dangerous people and incorrigible offenders should be pointed out for this melancholy purpose, the knowledge of which cannot be obtained with any degree of certainty but from the valuable register of offenders.
>
> (Radzinowicz, 1956, p. 47)

A variation on this use of a register for helping to detect crime and for influencing sentencing was the early idea of a register to assist with pre-employment screening. In 1749, the Fieldings established the Universal Register Officer 'as a labour exchange where employers might examine prospective servants and study their character references', and published a bulletin called 'The Public Advertiser' providing information on the servant labour market (Linebaugh, 1991, p. 252).

Later developments from the Fielding brothers included dissemination of information through the 'Weekly Pursuit', the 'Quarterly Pursuit' and 'Lists of Offenders at Large' (Radzinowicz, 1956, p. 48). Later still, another 'founding father' of early policing, Patrick Colquhoun, developed the register idea and organised 'a continually expanding inventory of all that was noxious in society, so as to serve the purposes of his General Police Machine' (*ibid*, p. 295).

1800 to 1900

The start of the nineteenth century found the UK still without a regular police force yet with an emerging working class being 'created' from the Industrial Revolution, living in rapidly growing cities and in housing that was insanitary and squalid. Criminality was considered endemic amongst the dispossessed 'dangerous classes', where it went hand in hand with the immorality of 'de-moralised' communities.

New prisons were being built to complement the Bridewells, and the Houses of Correction and the old Debtors Prisons were being overhauled after the reforming interventions of such as John Howard, the Sheriff of Bedfordshire, and the Quaker, Elizabeth Fry; the aim was to introduce order into the prison system, which previously seemed to only offer chaos. By the end of the century, the prison system had been reformed, an organised police force was in place and laws protecting children and defining sexual offending had been passed.

Forms of detention for the criminal lunatic were limited. Madhouses, licensed houses or Poor Law establishments existed but this seemed insufficient. The 1808 County Asylum Act permitted the building of local asylums to increase the number of beds for these patients. Later amendments to the law allowed for the transfer of the criminally insane from prisons to hospitals. In 1862, building started on Broadmoor as a special institution to hold the dangerous criminally insane. One novel feature of the laws at this time was the power to fine hospital staff who allowed patients to escape.

The second event to shake complacency in the early decades of the century was the so-called Wapping murders, when two whole families in London were murdered *en masse* in 1811. Some of the local watchmen were summarily dismissed and special armed patrols appointed to protect the neighbourhood. Neighbouring parishes sent volunteers in for additional night patrolling to take place (Critchley, 1967, pp. 40–41).

The ruling class was slowly coming round to the idea that new forms of public policing were needed. People with money might buy their own private policing protection, but it was clear that more was needed. The Peterloo killings in Manchester had shown the shortcomings of the military's ability to keep public order, and the increased vagrancy from soldiers returning from the Napoleonic Wars suggested that new measures were needed. The Metropolitan Police Act 1829 brought into being the first regularised police force on mainland Britain for the London area, to be followed by enactments to create provincial forces across the country. A police force for Ireland had already been established in 1786.

These early forms of policing would inevitably involve the collation of information on people, but it was to be some time before a formal national collection of criminal records was started. There is evidence that employers were already looking to the police for information on the trustworthiness of potential employees, perhaps prompted by the early experiments of Fielding with his Universal Register Office. Emsley reports that:

> In 1857 the Chief Constable of Bedford gave confidential information to a local employer about one of his workmen (and) . . . in 1863 the Chief Constable of Lincolnshire protested that his men were 'constantly receiving letters from private enquiry offices seeking information as to the character, respectability, and money value of persons residing in the towns and villages'.
>
> (Emsley, 1991, p. 107)

It is probable that the screening out of sex offenders was not a priority for these employers, but it was clear that in some quarters, at least, police records from an early age were seen as not just being for the police to use for policing purposes, but were legitimate information for others who had to weigh up risks about people.

In 1857, an Obscene Publications Act was passed and the Metropolitan Police formed an Obscene Publications Squad in 1863. The advent of photography had brought a new dimension to this particular 'art' and the term 'pornography' was passing into common usage. In 1870, the

Obscene Publications Squad mounted a joint operation with a voluntary organisation called the Vice Society against the sellers of obscene material, but not long after the Squad was disbanded until its re-emergence in the late 1880s in response to public demand (Bristow, 1977, p. 47).

Police progress against brothels remained notoriously uneven. Prostitution had yet to be conceived as a form of economic violence against women and was seen rather as a crime without a victim. Bristow reports that the slow progress was due to 'a vexed tale of Home Office delay, badly drafted legislation, unfavourable judicial rulings and police corruption' (ibid, p. 57). By the late 1850s, a concerted effort was made for action when the Vice Society joined forces with other campaigners, rescue houses and local authorities in London to press for better policing of the brothels. Together, they formed what later would be loosely called the 'Social Purity' movement.

Part of the continuing problem with regulating prostitution in all its forms was the Victorian double standards surrounding sexual matters, and the latent belief that prostitution might even enable 'the family' to exist in a more perfected form. In practical policing terms, there was the problem of obtaining evidence and the overall hostility to the police, especially when they entered brothels. Added to this was an age of consent of 12, which was only raised to 13 in 1875 (objections were raised that young men would be entrapped and blackmailed by girls if the age was raised any higher) (ibid, p. 91).

It was the outraged mob who also still saw it as their role to let the perpetrators of sex crime know exactly what they thought of them. In working class communities in Wales, we are told:

> ... generally the community, embodied in the mob, intervened on the side of women, up-braiding wife beaters and punishing adulterers.
>
> (Jones, 1982, p. 111)

In Dowlais, a man who lived off immoral earnings had a crowd of some 500 put his doors and windows through (ibid, p. 111) and when two men were publicly hanged for killing their wives because they suspected infidelity, 'it needed all the efforts of the constables . . . to keep the angry spectators at a distance' (Jones, 1992, p. 74).

Behind many Victorian reforms of this period were the organisations of the 'Social Purity' movement. The Vice Society, formed in 1802, was a central agency of this movement, but so too were organisations like the London Society for the Protection of Young Females, the Guardian Society, the Rescue Society, the Midnight Meeting Movement and a host of others. Their rise should be seen against the declining influence of the church courts and the desire for something to replace them. Towards the end of the century, they would be complemented – or replaced – by such as the National Vigilance Association, the White Cross League and the Social Purity Alliance (see Bristow, 1977, passim) and, ultimately, by the rise of the authority of the academic hierarchy and the professional 'experts'.

The 'Social Purity' movement saw their role as being to ameliorate the worst excesses of Victorian high liberalism and laissez-faire, and saw immorality and criminality being closely entwined, with the former usually a precursor to the latter. They campaigned for tighter laws on pornography, prostitution and brothel keeping and sought to enforce the law through private prosecutions or in tandem with the police. For their part, the police seemed happy with this arrangement and to leave these aspects of law enforcement to these vigilant – 'vigilante' – groups who could only enhance the efforts of the police. Bristow offers further explanation:

> Officials left the initiative for law enforcement as well as legal reform to the vigilantes. Did the State acquiesce with a cunning understanding of the function obscenity played in the social system, as was the case with prostitution? Perhaps more relevant in explaining official reticence was the availability of a strong voluntary effort, the tradition of private initiative, the unpopularity of using the police to entrap people and the very magnitude of the task.
>
> (*ibid*, p. 45)

The Vice Society, for example, saw a number of legislative initiatives taken which they had campaigned for. The Vagrancy Act 1824, for example, included for the first time 'streetwalking' as an offence; the earlier 1744 version of the Act had left out streetwalkers.

Previously, the prison had been a 'secondary' arm of penal policy that 'held' people for short periods in local debtors prisons, Bridewells and Houses of Corrections; the more serious offenders were 'held' on a temporary basis to await transportation or execution. The loss of transportation and the accompanying reduction in the use of capital punishment caused the Victorians to re-think the role of the prison. Now, the prison would move to centre stage as a 'primary' arm of penal policy and as penitentiaries in their own right; it would no longer be the place where you waited for punishment but would now be that punishment.

The period between 1780 and 1850 had already seen reforms and experiments in prison design and regimes. Sophisticated systems of surveillance were designed, such as Jeremy Bentham's panopticon, which allowed the prisoner no privacy or escape from the all-seeing warders; an actual paropticon style prison was never built in the UK but the ideas were taken on board (Ignatieff, 1978, pp. 109–13).

As the prison became more central to penal policy, the Victorians started to worry about what happened when prisoners came out and went back into the community; a worry that never existed with high levels of capital punishment and transportation for the serious offender.

Within the prisons, a new rising class of prison administrators also saw the need for systems of remission and early release to help control the conduct of individual prisoners and to regulate the growing size of the prison population:

> ... a remission of sentence was a standard device for securing
> the co-operation of prisoners during confinement by holding
> out a promise of early release. Those who administered prisons
> knew how important such a policy was. But to both penal
> reformers and advocates of deterrence, this policy looked like
> a dangerous relaxation of penal discipline.
>
> (McGowen, 1995)

The Penal Servitude Act 1853 increased prison sentences and created a system of licensing for discharged prisoners, known as 'ticket-of-leave'. Despite amendments to the law in 1857, the 'ticket-of-leave' system never really worked and the public had little faith in these new arrangements. The press blamed ticket-of-leave men for all manner of crimes and the general feeling was that they were dangerous and had been discharged too early. Letters to *The Times* described them as 'creating terror in the public mind' and said the public was 'becoming thoroughly frightened' (Bartrip, 1981, p. 164).

In 1862, a wave of 'garottings' hit London as a form of street attack that left victims half strangled and robbed; the garotting epidemic was blamed on the ticket-of-leave men (*ibid*, p. 166). In the same year, the failings of the system were revealed most starkly when the Home Office asked the Commissioner of the Metropolitan Police for a report on the ticket-of-leave men; the Commissioner had to acknowledge that 'the police could not find or produce a single man of them' (Radzinowicz and Hood, 1990, p. 249).

The Government reviewed the whole system of penal servitude with a Royal Commission in 1863. The report came down in favour of continuing the system, but with a more rigorous supervision of ticket-of-leave men by the police. The new, enhanced supervision was to be based on systems developed in Ireland by Sir Walter Crofton; the argument ran that if it worked on the Irish, it would work on the British (HL Debs, 7 June 1864, col. 1339). The Penal Servitude Bill was published in 1864.

Essential to the new system was the requirement for ticket-of-leave men to report to the police within three days of leaving prison, and thereafter on a monthly basis or within 48 hours if they should change address. The system was immediately criticised as an infringement of civil liberties and for being 'un-British':

> ... to make it a misdemeanour for a discharged criminal not
> to report himself to the police was a regulation far better

adapted to the police systems of other countries than of our own.

(HL Debs, 7 June 1864, col. 1342)

Others disagreed. Lord Cranworth thought protection of the public was paramount and he:

> . . . had no sympathy with those who advanced the argument, that to require a convict to place himself under supervision would interfere with the rights and liberties of the subject. The matter properly to be considered was, what system would answer best for the public.

(HL Debs, 7 June 1864, col. 1345)

In practice even with the new Penal Servitude Act 1864, the ticket-of-leave arrangements did not work. The police found it hard to communicate between themselves and had no central register they could refer to. In 1869, Parliament heard that the system verged on 'absolute failure' (HL Debs, 5 March 1869, col. 691ff.; see also Bartrip, 1981).

The Habitual Criminals Act 1869 repealed the ticket-of-leave arrangements except for those with two felony convictions who had been given absolute prison discharge; police supervision continued for them. The major innovation of the 1869 Act, however, was to be the compilation of a national register of offenders – the Habitual Criminal Register – to assist the police in general matters relating to crime detection and prosecution, as well as supervising those remaining hard core ticket-of-leave men.

Within the Parliamentary debate on the 1869 Act, cautious voices were raised:

> A man watched at every step and moment of his existence, and becoming more notorious, as he is sure to be before long by the action of the police, and a thousand other circumstances, will find the door of ordinary employment shut against him, and will be driven to the choice between violence and starvation.

(HL Debs, 5 March 1869, col. 697)

Such arguments were lost and the Habitual Criminals Act 1869 introduced a national register of criminals (England, Wales and Ireland) to be held at Scotland Yard and to be regularly added to and updated by contributing forces. According to one MP, it was to be nothing less than 'a wholesale system of police surveillance, so that another considerable portion of the people would be in a state of out-door imprisonment, tied, as it were, by the leg to the police' (HC Debs, 4 August 1869, col. 1261). The Prevention of Crimes Act 1871 extended the system to Scotland. Ticket-of-leave men were rarely charged for failing to report, although most did, in fact, do so; the strictness of the supervision was always 'greater on paper than in practice' (Bartrip, 1981, p. 172).

The Metropolitan Police were amongst those forces having difficulty with their supervisory role. In 1880, attempts were made to try to remedy the position by the creation of a specialised Convict Supervision Office, made up of a Chief Inspector and three sergeants. The new office improved the maintenance of the register and dissemination of relevant information to other officers, and also improved the efficacy of home visits to ensure compliance. It also worked more closely with the emergent Societies for the Aid of Discharged Prisoners. The new arrangements were generally considered successful by the police, although offenders at the time could still point out that 'if a man is determined to do wrong all the supervision in England will not prevent it. They cannot always watch a man' (cited in Petrow, 1994, p. 80).

This particular form of police supervision was effectively dismantled in 1910 by the Home Secretary, Winston Churchill. Had it been successful? Some think not:

> On balance police supervision, while theoretically valuable, had been practically useless. It helped the police manufacture a criminal class, without really deterring criminals or diminishing crime.
>
> (Petrow, 1994, p. 82)

The Victorians passed laws to help protect children from the worst excesses of child labour and to give them rights of elementary education. The 1889 and 1894 Prevention of Cruelty to Children Acts were also passed, but their implementation was left largely in the hands of voluntary agencies like the NSPCC, formed in 1889, or the Waifs and Strays Society, founded in 1881; the latter later became the Childrens Society of the Church of England (see e.g. Ferguson, 1990). Other notable 'rescue' organisations included Dr Barnardo's Childrens Homes, which started in 1870, and the Charity Organisation Society (COS) in 1869. Later, these 'casework' experts would evolve into the child care officers and social work experts of the new century (see also Bartley, 2000, for an account of rescue work with women prostitutes). Looking back, one of the founders of the COS, describing London in the late 1860s, saw only:

> . . . a confused mass of poverty, crime, and mendicancy living side by side with the independent wage earners under conditions of overcrowding and insanitation, and baffling all the efforts of authority and benevolence.
>
> (Bosanquet, 1914, p. 17)

Mrs Bosanquet also noted that one of those involved in the discussions to start the COS was Sir Walter Crofton, the architect of the ticket-of-leave supervision policy (*ibid*, p. 18).

In 1885, the position of children as victims of sex offending was to be given massive publicity by what became known as 'The Maiden Tribute of Modern Babylon'. This was a series of special editions of the *Pall Mall Gazette*, edited by William T. Stead, which highlighted the extent of prostitution that existed in London and the large numbers of young girls being drawn into it. By the third edition in July, 'mobs were rioting at the *Pall Mall Gazette* offices in an attempt to obtain copies' (Bristow, 1977, p. 110), and although other newspapers and publications were slow to follow, Stead could eventually boast that his revelations had been printed 'in every capital of the Continent, as well as by the "purest journals in the great American republic"' (Walkowitz, 1992, p. 82). (Stead himself was later drowned in the *Titanic* disaster.)

Stead had been briefed in advance of publication by campaigners in London and it was they who continued the agitation in the post-publication phase; the Salvation Army was reported to be particularly active at this time. Overflow meetings were addressed throughout the country. At Manchester Free Trade Hall, for example, the campaigner James Wookey was heard by a crowd of 6,000 when he spoke on 'The Massacre of the Innocents'; Wookey 'harangued against the privileged who abused poor girls but whose own daughters were protected by footmen' (Bristow, 1977, p. 111).

The result of all this public pressure and campaigning was the Criminal Law Amendment Act 1885. The Act, amongst other things, raised the age of consent to 16, and made illegal acts of gross indecency between males (the law had previously only covered acts of buggery and sodomy). To ensure the Act was implemented, 'vigilance committees' started to appear across the country and were ultimately absorbed into the newly formed National Vigilance Association (NVA), which took over the mantle of the Vice Society. The Act was most (in)famously used to prosecute Oscar Wilde.

In 1888, the serial murder of five women prostitutes in the Whitechapel area of London was taken up by the press and public to cause a wave of panic throughout the capital and beyond. The police failure to solve these so-called 'Jack-the-Ripper' murders only added to the sense of awe and mystery.

As the press reporting of the murders intensified, a picture emerged of the squalid conditions of the housing in Whitechapel and the contrast and similarities with other parts of London. The ineptitude of the police in being unable to find a suspect was reported, alongside the grisly nature of the sexual mutilation carried out and the facts of why women had to resort to prostitution as a means of income. The press speculated on possible suspects and one, John Pizer, named by the *Star*, had to turn himself into the police to escape the fury of a mob (Walkowitz, 1992, p. 203).

The respectable citizens of Whitechapel organised themselves into self-protection patrols, and called for the closure of brothels and common lodging houses, described as 'nurseries of crime'. Walkowitz suggests these activities were not just about self-protection but about 'surveillance of the unrespectable poor and low-life women in particular':

> ... by designating themselves 'vigilance committees' the male patrols in Whitechapel explicitly modelled themselves on similarly named social purity organisations already active in the area.
>
> (Walkowitz, 1992, p. 213)

The un-respectable poor of Whitechapel contented themselves with violent rioting and the victimisation of Jewish immigrants and doctors (both considered possible suspects, according to the press) as well as police officers (for their inability to find the killer). The funerals of the victims produced large crowds and outpourings of sympathy (*ibid*, pp. 216–17).

Cameron and Frazer (1987) have pointed out that a Robert Louis Stevenson story published in 1886 may have fed into the hysteria of this time. *The Strange Case of Doctor Jekyll and Mr Hyde* is the story of a respectable doctor who is transformed by various medications into an evil monster. The story has taken a hold on popular imagination to this day, to support the idea that there is, within us all, an evil side that may come through at any time.

Meanwhile, within the hospital systems, further changes were taking place in the care of the criminally insane. The new profession of psychiatry, having got a foot in the door in 1845 to detain people, was anxious to try and treat as many as possible as early as possible. Arraigned against them were the lawyers, upholding principles of Victorian liberty and due process of law, and conscious that the public was somewhat alarmed at the ease with which people could be detained in hospitals (Unsworth, 1979).

The lawyers won out and the doctors had to stand back. The Lunacy Act 1890 eventually put legal safeguards above the doctors' desire to treat. Coercion and therapy did not have to go hand in hand and even the medical journal the *Lancet* agreed that 'no single power is needed by physicians engaged in the medical treatment of the insane which the common law does not give every citizen' (Editorial, 7 February 1885).

Violence towards women – including sexual violence – was endemic throughout Victorian times. The philosopher John Stuart Mill joined the campaign to highlight the extent of the problem and, in the 1870s, the feminist campaigner Frances Power Cobbe published her pamphlet 'Wife Torture' (republished 1992). Men who raped their wives could not be prosecuted following a rule laid down as early as 1736 by Sir Matthew Hale, which stated that a wife gave a general consent to all future sexual intercourse when she married him; this common law ruling was only abandoned in 1992. As late as 1915, a London magistrate was still able to say that 'the husband of a nagging wife . . . could beat her at home provided the stick he used was no thicker than a man's thumb' (Wilson, 1983, p. 84–86; see also Ross, 1982).

The position of children was not much better:

> Until late in the nineteenth century, both Parliament and the national press were largely unconcerned with the way in which parents treated their children, regarding even the most barbarous cruelty as beyond public intervention since children were not then regarded as citizens in their own right.
>
> (Pinchbeck and Hewitt, 1973, p. 611)

It was known that sex offending against children did take place within the home, and references to it start to emerge at this time. Andrew Mearns, who would go on to be a founder of the National Vigilance Association, had produced in 1883 his 'Bitter Cry of Outcast London', drawing attention to the poverty, overcrowding and the moral corruption that inevitably went with it; amongst it all Mearns reported that 'incest is common' (Mearns, 1883). Apart from protection in the public sphere, children appeared to need protection in the private sphere of the home (Jackson, 2000).

In 1885, the Royal Commission on Housing reported that incest appeared to be all too common in overcrowded accommodation (RCHWC, 1885, p. 267) and, in 1890, William Booth produced similar findings in his report, deliberately entitled to mock the then fashionable explorers of Africa, *In Darkest England and the Way Out*. According to Booth, 'incest is so familiar as hardly to call for remark' (Booth, 1890, p. 65).

There is also evidence to suggest that, however much campaigners might be offended by incest, the same feelings were not always experienced by those who had been victims of it. Beatrice Webb recalls talking to:

> Young girls, who were in no way mentally defective, who were, on the contrary, just as keen witted and generous-hearted as my own circle of friends [yet] could chaff each other about having babies by their fathers and brothers.
>
> (cited in Wohl, 1978)

Webb could only attribute this to the general debasing effect social environment could have on personal character and family life.

In terms of legalities, incest was in the anomalous position of being outside the criminal law. Incest was an offence against morality and as such had, in the past, been dealt with by the ecclesiastical courts or bawdy courts and politicians appeared in no hurry to change this situation:

> . . . legislating authority in the home was entirely different from legislating public morality and perhaps if the official

policy was to let sleeping siblings lie, it was because 'laissez-faire' was preferable to state intervention.

(Wohl, 1978)

The NVA turned its attention to putting this anomaly to right and, in doing so, 'found a valuable ally in the NSPCC' (Bailey and Blackburn, 1979). Their continued efforts were to take them into the new century.

1900 to 1970

Moving into the modern era, this narrative divides into: (1) the policy area we now know as criminal justice studies or penal policy; and (2) what starts out as child care policies and becomes a more generalised public protection exercise.

Criminal justice

At the start of the century, the NSPCC and the NVA continued their efforts to get incest made a criminal offence and supported unsuccessful Bills in 1900, 1903 and 1907. MPs referring to 'this rather disagreeable subject' thought the policing of the new proposals constituted the main stumbling block (see e.g. HC Debs, 5 March 1903, col. 1683). A better approach might be through education or moral instruction rather than law enforcement, because even if one caught the offenders one 'might thrash and imprison people, but [still] not make them good' (HC Debs, 26 June 1908, col. 288).

The Home Office was eventually won over by the arguments that 'it was exceedingly necessary to add to the law . . . [as] the offence was by no means rare' (HC Debs, 26 June 1908, col. 284). A secondary consideration hovering in the background was the eugenics argument that inbreeding led to degeneration and weak mindedness, although these arguments did not come to the fore (Bailey and Blackburn, 1979); in 1908 the Punishment of Incest Act became law for England and Wales. Scotland continued to use the common law until the passing of the Incest and Related Offences (Scotland) Act 1986.

Putting a law into place was one thing; enforcement of that law was another. The British police, arguably, only got to grips with sexual offending against children and adults in the last quarter of the twentieth century. No doubt investigations and prosecutions took place in the years following the 1908 Act, but throughout this period sexual offending was perceived more as prostitution or homosexual activities. Even with this focus, police interventions were often seen as callous or indifferent.

A 1928 parliamentary report on soliciting and other street offences had gone out of its way to mention the need for police tact, especially when there was the chance of wrongly accusing innocent people:

No class of crime requires more tact and discretion on the part of the police and any failure in this respect on their part in dealing with such cases is visited with public condemnation.
(Report on the Street Offences Committee, 1928, para. 53)

The comments of one police officer writing in the 1930s makes the point:

Now and again they brought in a Nancy-Boy as they were then called, and treated him as though he were an inanimate object without feeling. They rubbed his face with toilet paper to procure evidence of make-up, joked and laughed about him as if he were not present and always found the same sized tin of Vaseline in his pocket.
(Daley, 1986, p. 101)

Or consider the following reflections in a training manual for the Scottish Police, published as recently as 1980:

the terms 'sodomy', 'indecent exposure', 'lewd and libidinous practice' and 'gross indecency' etc. which are used in law give but little indication of the nature of these offences; the manner in which they are usually committed, and the veils they are liable to bring in their train . . . the movements of persons of manifestly lewd disposition should always be closely watched as many and varied are the artifices employed by these persons to achieve their evil objectives.
(quoted in Crane, 1983, pp. 41–42)

Crane gives a number of examples of poor policing practice against homosexual activities that still breach the law despite the Sexual Offences Act 1967, which largely de-criminalised such acts in the UK. These varied from forms of police entrapment, to abusive behaviour toward gay men – 'queer bashing' – or a refusal to take seriously their reports of crime.

At the turn of the century, the police shared concern with the public that all classes of offenders were getting more mobile and more anonymous with the growth of public transport and the expansion of urban conurbations. The spectre of the invisible sex offender moving around at will took up the mantle of the dangerous vagrant.

One response was the merging of the Habitual Criminals Register, the Convict Supervision Office and the new Fingerprint Registry into a national Criminal Record Office; in 1901, the Fingerprint Registry had started using the Henry System of Classification. The *Police Gazette*, which circulated to all forces lists of wanted men, was revamped and re-launched by 1910 with supplements on 'travelling criminals' and details of 'expert criminals' recently released from prison (Petrow, 1994, pp.

99–101). The Criminal Record Office remained more or less unchanged until its merger into the National Identification Bureau (NIB) in 1980: the NIB subsequently became the National Identification Service in 1995, by which time the whole national collection of criminal records was being transferred to the Police National Computer.

The Probation of Offenders Act 1907 introduced the modern Probation Service to take over the earlier work of the Court Missionary Service; supervision of offenders to keep them out of prison was a new item on their agenda. The Prevention of Crimes Act 1908 brought in separate custodial facilities for young offenders, named after a pilot scheme in the Kent village of Borstal, and included the new idea of supervised after-care on a compulsory licence basis, with the possibility of recall for any breach of supervisory requirements.

After-care supervision was not totally novel and we have earlier described the ticket-of-leave system, whereby ex-offenders from prison had to report monthly to the police and notify the police whenever they changed address. The new arrangements for young prisoners leaving Borstal combined this straight policing role with a general helping role from probation officers. Any help that the old ticket-of-leave prisoners got did not come from the police, but might come from such voluntary organisations as the local Discharged Prisoners Aid Society.

The Prevention of Crimes Act also introduced the idea of Preventive Detention (PD). This was to be a measure for tackling the 'habitual' offender – including the sex offender – by not just punishing them for what they had done, but by recognising their previous convictions and to give them longer prison sentences in order better to protect the public (PCA, 1908, s. 10(1)). The courts were not really sure about PD and it seems to have had an uncertain start in life. In 1911, the then Home Secretary, Winston Churchill, said it should only be used for the older offender (over 30) who had already had one sentence of penal servitude and had now committed another serious offence. It was not for the public nuisance but for the persistent dangerous criminal.

Despite this guidance, there was variation in the use of PD and arguments emerged that perhaps it was not such a good idea after all. Some judges hardly used it, as it seemed to contradict the principle that an offender be sentenced for the charge on which he or she came to court. After the Second World War, the Criminal Justice Act 1948 restricted the use of PD to the serious persistent offender only, and it was eventually abolished by the Criminal Justice Act 1967 (see also Home Office, 1963).

A new sentence was created by the 1967 Act, which had a resonance with PD, and this was the 'extended sentence' which could be passed on people who already had three or more previous convictions. In practice, 'extended sentences' were hardly used and the Government decided to repeal the power to pass them:

. . . to the extent that [an extended sentence] may have been useful for dealing with persistent violent or sexual offenders and protecting the public, it will be replaced by [a] new Crown Court Power.

(Home Office, 1990a, para. 3.17)

The Criminal Justice Act 1991 duly repealed the extended sentence.

Penal policy had started to receive an input from the medical and psychiatric services from the 1930s onwards, premised on the idea that offenders could be 'treated' rather than just punished (see e.g. East and Hubert, 1939). The idea of treating prisoners in 'therapeutic communities' found its fullest form at the prison opened in 1962 at Grendon Underwood in Buckinghamshire. Grendon took sex offenders and other prisoners who suffered from various neuroses or personality disorders; the inmates were transferred there from within the prison service rather than going directly from the courts (Parker, 1970).

For all prisoners on discharge from prison, there has always been a tradition of helping the offender and his or her family. This has included voluntary arrangements through the Discharged Prisoners Aid Societies. The concept of the Borstal Licence introduced an element of control and sanctions into custodial after-care, and these two dimensions of both helping and controlling the ex-prisoner have always rested uneasily alongside each other.

The licence system applicable to young men leaving Borstal was eventually adapted for adult prisoners leaving prisons. The Criminal Justice Act 1948 brought in the new sentence of corrective training to run alongside preventive detention, and along with it came new arrangements for release on licence after two-thirds of the sentence or five-sixths of a PD sentence. Further reforms in the 1960s saw the Probation Service move more centrally into the after-care of prisoners field, and a merging of the care and control elements.

In due course, the Criminal Justice Act 1967 replaced the 1948 Release on Licence arrangements with the concept of parole. As Parsloe put it:

Licence is a right – or an obligation – for certain prisoners but is in almost all cases unavoidable. Parole, however, is widely held to be a state which a prisoner can earn.

(Parsloe, 1979)

The Criminal Justice Act 1967, Part III established the Parole Board to consider the discretionary release of 'Life' prisoners for post-custodial supervision; the formulation of parole policies has to be seen in the light of the abolition of capital punishment for murder which preceded it (see Coker and Martin, 1985). Life prisoners, however, could also encompass serious sex offenders and not just murderers.

Protecting children and the public

The Children Act 1908 consolidated what law there was on child protection and was a public indication that children were important and that their care and protection should be taken seriously, but enforcement of the law at this time was often left to voluntary agencies, such as the NSPCC, when not left to the police.

A parliamentary report in 1925 looked specifically at sexual offences committed against children and young persons, and noted the high number of acquittals that seemed to take place. Overall, it reported a decrease in sexual crime accompanied by violence, but an increase in such crime committed against children under the age of 16 (Departmental Committee, 1925, para. 18). The report also noted the wide variety of male offenders who came from all classes of society (*ibid*, para. 75) and recommended long prison sentences as the best punishment for them; probation was an alternative to be used with 'caution' and probably worked best with young offenders (*ibid*, para. 87).

The report suggested that the police or the courts should notify schools when a pupil had been the victim of sexual abuse. This was to facilitate the teacher giving assistance to a child who was 'unsettled' by the experience and to 'prevent contamination of other children' by the possible spreading of 'debased tendencies' (*ibid*, paras. 110 and 114). As for the very young child, it was thought that the experience would be 'quickly forgotten' (*ibid*, para. 93).

A similar report the following year on sex offences against children in Scotland came to similar conclusions, but made the wider comment on sex offending generally that it was:

> . . . no more than the surface manifestation of the irregular habits and secret moral standards of a considerable section of the community – a mere symptom of a larger disorder.
> (Departmental Committee, 1926, para. 141)

As such the real answer was to raise the moral tone of society.

The civil law on child care and protection was consolidated in the Children and Young Persons Act 1933. The Act introduced its Schedule 1, which would pass into the everyday language of child protection workers for the next 60 years and more, being the list of offences it is possible to commit against a child and which, in due course, has led to various prohibitions on activities that can be engaged in by 'Schedule One Offenders' if those activities should bring them into contact with children (see Chapter 6).

In the same year, the Children and Young Persons (Boarding Out) Rules prohibited anyone from becoming a foster-parent if they had offences which rendered them 'unfit', and this was upheld a few years later in primary legislation by the Public Health Act 1936, section 210(c), which prevented anyone being a foster-parent who had:

... been convicted of any offence under Part I of the Children and Young Persons Act 1933, or Part 2 of the Children Act 1908.

Presumably, some form of criminal record information disclosure existed to ensure these requirements were met.

Hospital confinement remained an option for sex offenders who were also assessed as being mentally disordered. The Lunacy Act 1890 and the Mental Deficiency Act 1913 provided the legislative framework for compulsory detention, and for those considered the most 'dangerous', there was Broadmoor 'criminal asylum' (opened in 1863), Rampton Hospital (built in 1910) and Moss Side Hospital (built in 1914, but only taking mentally disordered patients after 1933). These three hospitals – later designated 'special hospitals' – would be joined by a fourth, Park Lane Hospital in Lancashire (in 1974), and in Scotland by Carstairs State Hospital. Ultimately, Moss Side and Park Lane – physically adjacent to each other – would amalgamate and form Ashworth Hospital in 1990.

The Mental Health Act 1959 introduced some new sexual offences; it made it an offence for a male member of staff at a hospital to have sex with a woman under treatment for a mental disorder and a similar offence was introduced for a male guardian (s. 128). In the case of *R v. Goodwin* (unreported, 19 May 1994) a male nurse who developed a sexual relationship with a patient that continued after her discharge received two years in prison. The court held 'this was as gross, deliberate and wicked breach of trust as one might regret to see' (Hill and Fletcher-Rogers, 1997, para. 11.14). The 1959 Act also amended the Sexual Offences Act 1956 by making it an offence for any man to have sex with a woman he knows is 'defective' or mentally impaired (s. 27).

Mental health legislation received a further overhaul in the 1980s. In England and Wales the new law was the Mental Health Act 1983, in Scotland the Mental Health (Scotland) Act 1984 and in Northern Ireland the Mental Health (Northern Ireland) Order 1986. Common to them all was a focus on the rights of hospital in-patients and improved training for those empowered to take away the right of freedom to live in the community. In England and Wales, the 1983 Act introduced a right of after-care for previously detained patients and new supervisory arrangements for those who had been detained on a Hospital Order with added restrictions (Home Office/DHSS, 1987). Later, the after-care of former mental health patients would be strengthened by a new 'supervision register' for those still 'at risk' (Department of Health, 1994a) and, in 1995, amendments to the 1983 Act allowing for more formal supervision in the community.

Sexual deviance was marked out as no longer constituting a mental disorder in its own right, and what hospital treatments there were would have been a mixture of medication and individual and group therapeutic work. Experiments with various forms of aversion therapy were falling into disuse by this time (see Chapter 2).

The post-war years saw the enlargement of the personal social services to be 'administered' locally by health and local authorities. Community mental health services employing mental welfare officers (MWOs) came under the health service, and local authorities had charge of welfare departments for elderly and disabled people and children's departments for children and families. The war years had created a greater awareness of the conditions of city life, when thousands of child evacuees had been relocated to rural areas and fostering had become a way of life for the children and their host families. Ultimately, the Children Act 1948 created local authority children's departments in England, Wales and Scotland which were centrally accountable to the Home Office.

In 1971, children's departments were incorporated into the new social services departments along with the mental health departments and welfare departments. The rationale was to have a more integrated service, meeting all personal needs under one roof through the 'generic' social worker, who replaced the child care officer, welfare officer and mental welfare officer. The Social Work (Scotland) Act 1968, based on the Kilbrandon Report (1964), had made similar arrangements for north of the border, with the added embellishment of including the probation service into their social work departments.

In terms of law, the Children and Young Persons Act 1963 had defined the circumstances whereby a child might need 'care, protection or control', and those circumstances would include the presence in a child's household of someone convicted of a 'Schedule One offence', including sexual offences against a child. The 1963 Act was replaced by the Children and Young Persons Act 1969, with its 'grounds' for care including a child being in 'moral danger' (s. 1(2)(c)) or being harmed by a 'Schedule One offender' joining the household (s. 1(2)(bb)).

Summary

In this chapter, we have considered a selective outline of historical aspects of sexual offending and the social response to it. Certain themes can be seen to have a resonance with contemporary preoccupations. The keeping of registers on certain criminals and the requirement for ticket-of-leave offenders to report to the police have a clear link to our current sex offenders register (see Chapter 7); we have also noted early attempts at pre-employment screening by reference to conviction records and the attempts by the police to enhance the quality of their record keeping. Populist agitation against the sex offender also has a long history, and the sensationalising of such offenders by the press is also a well-established phenomenon, as witnessed in the 'Ripper' murders of 1888.

Current concerns to find a way to incarcerate the 'dangerous' person before he or she offends (see Chapter 6) also have earlier attempts at 'preventive detentions' to guide their deliberations.

4

Policing sex offenders

The police are the initial 'gateway' for all criminals coming into the criminal justice system. The police receive reports of new crimes, investigate and detect who is responsible and, when satisfied, pass their work on to the Crown Prosecution Service for prosecution. For present purposes, all these police activities are considered on three levels – local, national and international. The police approach to sexual offending on all three levels is outlined, and the emerging importance of 'personal information' on offenders for purposes of policing is drawn out. The final part of the chapter examines the work of the Forensic Science Service and especially its creation of a National DNA Database to assist the police in the identifying of offenders.

Local policing

Reports and investigations

Initial crime reports of sexual offending are made to the local police for them to investigate and put together a case for possible prosecution in the courts. The way in which the police received these reports and acted upon them has, in the past, been clumsy and insensitive, and the number of reports never getting beyond the police has been a cause for concern. Critics started to talk about an unacceptable 'attrition' rate to describe the way in which the police failed to act, decided there was no case to answer or found other reasons to file cases rather then ensure they went forward for prosecution. In turn, the attrition rate was blamed for making many victims of sexual assault decide not to bother reporting it to the police in the first place.

The general feeling in the 1970s was that the police did not take reports of sexual assault as seriously as they should have done. Investigating officers were often unsympathetic men who had little empathy with the 'stories' they were hearing; 'stories' they believed the women made up to get themselves out of various scrapes they should never have got into in the first place. The apocryphal police approach seemed to be 'listen to the story, then drive a coach and horses through it'. Some police surgeons actively tried to research the number of false rape allegations they came across because 'innocent men must be protected against baseless allegations' (MacLean, 1979; see also Geis *et al.*, 1978).

The end product of attitudes like this was the police decision not even to record a crime having taken place – the practice of 'no-criming'. If they did record it as a crime, it still often resulted in 'no further action' being taken. Either way, it led in turn to an under-reporting of sexual crimes once women realised what they had to face when they did report. Two national events contributed to a challenge to these attitudes.

The spotlight first fell on West Yorkshire police and their search for the serial killer the press called the 'Yorkshire Ripper'. From 1975 onwards, this unknown assailant had started to murder women at regular intervals, with the police seemingly inept and unable to detect him. The early victims were women acting as prostitutes in red light areas, but in 1977, the chosen victim was Jayne MacDonald, described by the police as an 'innocent' teenager (Burn, 1985, p. 181). The clear upgrading of the investigation after this date, with its blatant message that the murder of the earlier women did not matter as much, was not lost on the British public. After a massive police effort, the 'Ripper' – Peter Sutcliffe – was eventually caught in 1981, almost by accident, by the South Yorkshire Police.

The Thames Valley police were the second police force to find the spotlight of the national media falling on them. Where the West Yorkshire Police were reluctantly in the glare of the lights, the Thames Valley Police had invited a television documentary crew in to film them at work. The series of programmes that resulted were shown in January 1982, and included insensitive police handling of a woman reporting a rape to them. The impact of the film was all the greater because the police obviously knew they were being filmed, but had not thought to change their approach or temper their attitudes of disbelieving the woman. The impression given was that this was a perfectly normal policing technique. The police did not help themselves when stories came to light of the Metropolitan Police using pornographic films they had confiscated in the course of their duty for their own police station 'stag' parties (Cox *et al.*, 1977, p. 168).

Away from the media, more considered criticism was also coming from the women's movement that had emerged from the 1960s. A sophisticated analysis of male domination and oppression was being backed up by the stories told by women coming to the new network of refuges which were springing up throughout the 1970s (see Chapter 7). In academia, women researchers started to make inroads into a male dominated criminology to throw light on the poor quality of the policing of sexual assault.

Research commissioned by the Home Office would later find that only 25 per cent of cases of rape reported to the police in 1985 resulted in a conviction. The key points of attrition were identified as the practice of 'no-criming', which helped the 'clear-up' rate because the police could not be accused of failing to clear up a crime that had not happened; the practice of 'no further action' and therefore not proceeding to prosecution; and the down-grading of charges to lesser offences by the time they got to court (Grace *et al.*, 1992). Earlier research in Scotland had confirmed a dismal lack of sensitivity and similar levels of decision-making (Chambers and Millar, 1983).

The research also clarified the different categories of rape which the police were now identifying and the break-up of the idea that rape was a monolithic form of crime. In practice the police now recognised:

- 'Stranger' rape, where the assailant was unknown to the victim.
- 'Acquaintance' rape, where the complainant and the suspect knew each other casually.
- 'Intimate' rape, where the persons concerned were in a relationship or even married.

Critics argued that this was an artificial categorisation and that the essential element of rape – the lack of consent – was the same whatever the circumstances.

The Home Office responded to the criticisms with two circulars giving advice to Chief Constables. The first, in 1983, called for an improvement in the investigation of rape allegations, including more sensitive interviewing and the need for early medical examinations to allow the victim to get washed and changed more quickly (Home Office, 1983). The second, a few years later, addressed the wider crimes of violence toward women and recommended better training for officers, systems to keep the victim informed of the progress of the investigation and the need for separate examination suites for women away from police stations; no-criming was to be exceptional and only when a woman completely retracted a complaint (Home Office, 1986a).

The problem with Home Office circulars was that they were just circulars, and were aimed at Chief Constables. They did not have the status of substantive law and their impact had to trickle down through a male-orientated organisation, which had other priorities to consider and was not always sympathetic to such crimes.

The Police and Criminal Evidence Act 1984 was substantive law (for England and Wales) and did carry provisions that the police could use in tackling violence against women. Section 17 of the Act empowered an officer to enter premises for purposes of saving life and limb, and to arrest for an arrestable offence such as assaults or wounding; however, there is some evidence that the police have not used section 17 very much (Brown, 1997, p. 36). Section 24 gave the powers for an arrestable offence, which are offences attracting a five-year sentence or more but also includes indecent assault on a woman, and section 25 introduced the so-called 'protective arrest', where the officer thinks it necessary to prevent injury to another person or to protect a child or other vulnerable person.

The Police and Criminal Evidence Act also introduced new powers to compel a woman victim of violence or sexual assault to give evidence in court against her husband. The new section 80 promised a way to reduce the number of women who chose to withdraw their complaints, leaving the prosecution high and dry. Later legislation enabled a woman's police statement to be used as evidence in court as an alternative to her attendance (Criminal Justice Act 1988, s. 23).

The police were given further circular advice in 1988 on how they should investigate sexual offences against children. The police had been participating members of local child protection arrangements since 1974, but the new advice came after the Cleveland affair of 1987 and called for better training, joint investigations with social workers where appropriate and, once again, for the provision of separate examination suites away from police stations (Home Office, 1988; see also Chapter 8).

The effect of these circulars led some forces to form specialist teams of officers: Domestic Violence Units came into being for investigating offences against women, and Child Protection Units for offences against children. The actual names of the units might vary (e.g. Family Support Unit) and sometimes the two were joined together (e.g. in Northern Ireland, the RUC's CARE Units (Child Abuse and Rape Enquiry Unit)). Some units had uniformed officers, some had non-uniformed detectives or a mixture of both. When another Home Office circular appeared on domestic violence, it was able to note that 'some forces [had] dedicated domestic violence units with specially trained officers', and all Chief Constables were 'urged to consider setting up such Units where it is practicable and cost effective to do so' (Home Office, 1990b, para. 10).

The 1990 domestic violence circular recommended that each force draw up a policy statement to help influence the attitudes and behaviour of officers who are called on to deal with cases of domestic violence. The policy statement was to emphasise the duty to protect victims and children, treat the crime seriously, use powers of arrest, be wary of trying for reconciliation and keep good records to assist policy evaluation. (Home Office 1990b, para. 11; see also Scottish Office, 1990).

Early reports have suggested that adult women victims of sexual assault and violence are happier with the new initiatives taken by the police (see e.g. Adler, 1991), but later research suggests there is still work to be done (e.g. Temkin, 1999). Domestic Violence Units had improved the knowledge and skills of officers, but they still often felt marginalised by 'mainstream' policing. Separate examination suites and the move of some officers out of police stations had exacerbated this problem, but cultural attitudes of senior managers were also said to be part of the problem:

> We all do our own thing in this position. Nobody would have a clue if I was doing nothing. As it is I'm tearing my hair out
> . . .

> There is no credibility in dealing with domestic violence as far as my colleagues are concerned . . . the uniformed officers just don't want to get involved . . .

> I talk at divisional meetings to inspector rank and below to raise awareness of domestic violence. I still get comments like 'didn't you used to be a policeman?' . . .
> (Plotnikoff and Woolfson, 1998, pp. 11–12)

More recent research (Harris and Grace, 1999) has shown that the reporting of rape has increased threefold between 1985 and 1996, and a more receptive attitude on the part of the police has doubtless contributed to this increase. In terms of the categorisations of rape, the main increase was in 'acquaintance' and 'intimate' rape, with the figures for stranger rape staying roughly the same; some researchers have suggested male rapists may deliberately 'find out' details about their victims to actively get themselves into these categories to help any defence they may need (Gregory and Lees, 1999, p. 100). Of more concern was the finding that conviction rates were not keeping up with this increase, and the attrition rate in terms of police decisions was still high (Harris and Grace, 1999).

Child Protection Units (CPUs) suffered the same feelings of marginalisation by their colleagues in 'mainstream' policing. Officers within them might be fully committed and have raised their levels of skill and knowledge, but outside the CPU the allegations continued that it was the 'Andy Pandy Squad' and 'not real police work'. Researchers at the University of Manchester identified possible reasons:

- CPU work was seen as 'a cushy number' because staff worked a 'days and lates' system;
- CPUs were mostly staffed by women officers;
- within CPUs women officers dealt with the victims, and male officers with the suspects; and
- work with children was low status and 'unskilled' insofar as 'anyone can talk to children, can't they?'
  (Hughes *et al.*, 1996, p. 13)

CPUs could become isolated and demoralised. One unit worker expressed the lack of interest shown by the senior management, who never came near them: 'It shows in who visits you. We've never had a commander at the Unit, ever. But he visits other places' (*ibid*, p. 16).

The Manchester research summarised a common management view:

> They applauded the creation of . . . Units as an important advance in the policing of child sexual abuse but most felt that more senior management now believed that 'child protection is sorted' and the Units . . . therefore, receive little attention 'as long as a wheel doesn't come off'.
>
> (*ibid*, p. 11)

CPUs have, nonetheless, continued to progress and develop, albeit with ups and downs. Comprehensive record systems of children and families can be developed and used to complement the mainstream systems of the local force. A Department of Health investigation heard complaints that the 'police [were] not always taking this work seriously . . . sometimes appearing to sympathise with alleged perpetrators' (the Department of Health 1994b, para. 3.25), and others have criticised the over-deployment of women police officers to CPUs, leading to the 'feminisation of policing' within child protection (Adams and Horrocks, 1999). But, overall, they have become an institutionalised feature of current policing organisation, work closely with social workers, undertake evidence videoing (see Chapter 5) and are here to stay.

One innovation the police appear to have imposed on social workers is the practice of the 'dawn raid'. If children had to be compulsory removed from a home because of alleged sexual abuse, an early morning visit might secure evidence that would otherwise be disposed of, and even reveal unacceptable sleeping patterns. Social workers – not, perhaps, known for their early start to the working day – went along with the practice despite misgivings ('Fury over dawn raid' *Social Work Today*, 13 September 1990).

A later ruling of Mr Justice Hollings in the Family Division warned against the practice:

> Early morning removals of children from their home, by police, even though in conjunction with social services, should only be effected when there are clear grounds for believing significant harm would otherwise be caused to the children or vital evidence is only obtainable by such means.
>
> (*Re A (Minors)* [1992] 1 FLR 439)

Later evaluations of police child protection work have noted continuing progress, but have still called for more consistent training and possibly a new core national curriculum for all police child abuse investigators (Davies *et al.*, 1995). A report by HM Inspectorate of Constabulary, which pointed out the variation in provision between forces, has recommended that the Association of Chief Police Officers produce a standards-based service to ensure more consistency (HMIC, 1999, para. 3.20).

Police Child Protection Units have also often found themselves excluded from investigations into sexual assault on women and children which takes place outside the home. Extra-familial abductions and assaults by strangers acting in public places continue to be the province of the CID or vice-squad. If anything, a national response is looked to rather than a local CPU one. The archetypal mobile sex offender striking anywhere in the country was the case of Robert Black, convicted in 1994 for a series of abductions and murders of young children in England and Scotland (Clark and Johnston, 1994).

The deficiencies of the 'Ripper' inquiries in the 1970s included the realisation that the police, in large-scale investigations, had often been 'overloaded' with information and been unable to see the wood for the trees. An inquiry by HM Inspectors of Constabulary recommended better use of information technology in such investigations (Ackroyd *et al.*, 1992, pp.150–56). The result was HOLMES (Home Office Large Major Enquiry System), a computerised system brought into play for large-scale police investigation involving serious crime (Maguire and Norris, 1992, pp. 57–59).

The HOLMES system has been particularly used by the police when investigating serious sexual crimes committed in institutions such as children's homes and residential schools. These investigations can involve many victims and many abusers ('networks' or 'rings') over a long period of time: many of the victims may now be adults and living miles away from the scene of the crime.

Complex cases of institutional abuse, sometimes involving organised criminal activities, can take up months of police time as trawls are made through old records of children and staff, links made and victims and suspects tracked down. Investigations of this kind took place during the 1990s in Leicestershire, Castle Hill School, Shropshire, North Wales children's homes and Cheshire (see Oates, 1998, for an account of the latter). At the time of writing, Operation Clyde had been going on in Kirklees for the last few years.

The Waterhouse Report into physical and sexual abuse in the children's homes of North Wales devoted three chapters (Chapters 50 to 52 and Appendix XII) to the way in which these police investigations were best carried out. The report emphasised the importance of police training to ensure 'appropriate sensitivity' in investigations and the need for 'close liaison between the police and other agencies, particularly social services departments' (Waterhouse Report, 2000, para. 5.38). In view of the number of police investigations, it recommended:

> . . . an inter-agency review of the procedures followed and personnel employed in these investigations . . . with a view to issuing practical procedural guidance for the future.
>
> (*ibid*, recommendation 22)

The report thought this guidance should particularly look at the safeguarding and preservation of records and files by both social services departments and the police where there have been earlier investigations, and at how police are to have access to social services' files. The guidance might also usefully look at the sharing of information generally for criminal investigation and child protection purposes (*ibid*).

In 1995, the NSPCC had set up the first of its Regional Investigation Units (RIUs) to help the police make sense of the world of residential child care and the circumstances in which this sort of sexual offending is taking place. The local authorities as the main employers in these investigations have to agree to the NSPCC workers coming in and having access to the records (Gallagher, 1998).

These police investigations into serious allegations in children's homes do give cause, nonetheless, for continuing concern. One criticism is that the retrospective police investigation is actually producing the allegations rather than collecting them:

> Police forces normally spend their time collecting evidence in relation to crimes whose reality no-one doubts. They embark on retrospective investigations, however, without knowing whether the crimes they are investigating have taken place at all.
>
> (Webster, 1998, p. 22)

Add to this the possibility of victims making false allegations because they believe there may be financial compensation on offer, and we have 'one of the most dangerous developments in methods of police investigations which has ever taken place' (*ibid*, p. 33; see also Webster, 1999). The Waterhouse Report found little evidence to support the accusation that compensation was a motivating factor (Waterhouse Report, 2000, para. 57.31)

Arrest, detention and cautions

As a police criminal investigation proceeds, the actual holding of a suspect at a police station is governed by the time limits set down in the Police and Criminal Evidence Act 1984 (ss. 42–45). The custody officer at the police station ensures that the time limits are kept to, that evidence exists for charging and that the general welfare of the prisoner is seen to. The custody officer will also be instrumental in decisions to charge a suspect and bring them before a court, or to release them with or without a charge being made; if a charge has been made the release on police bail can have conditions attached to it.

Conditions of police bail of relevance to the suspected sexual offender might be a curfew to remain indoors after a specified time in the evening until a specified time in the morning; an exclusion zone to, for example, stay away from a witnesses home or place of work; a requirement not to associate with named people; or a condition of regular reporting to the police station (Bail Act 1976, s. 3, as amended; Police and Criminal Evidence Act 1984, s. 47, as amended). Local authority social services departments are empowered at this point to offer assistance to help a man move out of accommodation where children are still living who have been his suspected victims (Children Act 1989, Sch. 2, para. 5) and, since 1996, courts have also had powers to add 'exclusion requirements' to an Emergency Protection Order granted to a local authority (Children Act 1989, s. 44A(2); see also Children (Scotland) Act 1995, s. 76).

Once a police investigation is completed, the 'case file' has to be prepared by them for submission to the Crown Prosecution Service (CPS) for furtherance of the prosecution. This work is normally carried out by the police Administrative Support Unit (ASU), who are responsible for liaison with the CPS and can consult them for advice on whether or not they have sufficient evidence or what is the 'best' charge. One thing the police should not be doing at this stage is taking 'no further action' because they have tried to 'second guess' whether the CPS will take it on to court and decided it is not going to be worth it. 'Gatekeeping' only adds to the police attrition rate and recommendations have been made that they should always pass it through if there is any 'case to answer' (Harris and Grace, 1999, p. 24).

One alternative for the police is for them to issue their own caution as an alternative to a prosecution and necessity of going to court; the use of cautions for sexual offending has sometimes been queried ('Police forces allow rapists to go free with a caution' *The Sunday Times*, 18 February 1996).

The police caution has been an administrative device for the police to deal with the less serious offender who was, perhaps, a first time offender and seemed unlikely to re-offend. It has been a formal affair delivered by a senior officer and could be brought up and cited in court if there was later re-offending. Sexual offenders have been the subject of police cautioning, but the most recent Home Office guidance on how the police should caution offenders has warned against such practices.

> Cautions have been given for crimes as serious as attempted murder and rape: this undermines the credibility of this disposal. Cautions should *never* be used for the most serious indictable-only offences such as these . . .
> (Home Office, 1994a, para. 5; emphasis in original)

In the past, cautions have been available for adult and juvenile offenders, but the Crime and Disorder Act 1998, sections 65–66 introduced statutory 'reprimands' and 'warnings' for juveniles to replace the administrative caution; draft guidance on the new provisions repeated the advice that they should not be used for offences such as rape. The old-style cautions remain an available disposal for the police if the offender is an adult, and the Sex Offenders Act 1997 accepts that cautions will still be given to sex offenders and that cautions will result in their registration. A special form of caution can be administered to women committing street offences (Home Office, 1959).

National policing

British policing has always prided itself on being local policing. Local communities had their own forces in what became known as the Anglo-Saxon model of policing. If anything more were needed, the police could assist each other through the doctrine of 'mutual assistance'. Centralised policing was otherwise best left to other countries.

This position has been changing slowly. In 1974, a lot of small police forces disappeared by amalgamation into larger regional units and various national units have come into being. The Police National Computer (PNC), which came on-line in 1974, is the obvious example of a national unit, jointly financed by all 52 local forces to their common benefit. It is an apocryphal story that the PNC was not named the 'National Police Computer' deliberately to downplay the word 'national' by hiding it in the middle.

In 1992, the National Criminal Intelligence Service (NCIS) was formed and in 1997, the National Crime Squad (NCS). These initiatives were to take on 'serious organised crime' and the impetus for them came very much from the UK's involvement in Europe and the need for a 'national voice' to 'talk' to other countries on matters of policing. The National Criminal Intelligence Service from its inception has had a Paedophile Section.

The NCIS Paedophile Section inherited a national database that had been kept by the Metropolitan Police ('3000 names on Yard paedophile register' *Guardian*, 28 July 1990). By 1997, this database held 25,000 items, including names and other intelligence of related interest, with most of it having been contributed by local police forces (HC Debs, 25 February 1997, col. 132 WA).

The sort of information held by NCIS has been described as 'soft' information or intelligence, as opposed to 'hard' verifiable information such as criminal conviction histories. Soft information invariably includes speculative suspicions that cannot necessarily be verified, and does not necessarily relate to any current crime under investigation. Local forces hold similar soft information as intelligence.

This information is controlled and regulated by the Data Protection Act 1998 and the police's own Code of Practice (ACPO, 1995). The police are also bound by the provisions of a Council of Europe Recommendation, signed by the British Government in 1987, and including the requirement that information on people's sexual behaviour should not be held by the police unless connected to a particular inquiry:

The [police] collection of data on individuals solely on the basis that they have a particular racial origin, particular religious convictions, sexual behaviour or political opinions . . . which are not proscribed by law should be prohibited. The collection of data concerning these factors may only be carried out if absolutely necessary for the purposes of a particular enquiry.

(Council of Europe, 1988, para. 2.4)

The British Government, having signed up to this Recommendation, then entered a 'derogation' which effectively gave it an exemption from having to abide by paragraph 2.4. When questioned about this in the House of Commons, the Government was quite clear that in its view the paragraph:

Restricts police activities in collecting data on particular groups such as suspected paedophiles [and] could seriously inhibit the police in preventing and detecting crime.

(HC Debs, 15 October 1990, cols. 721–22)

Whatever the rights or wrongs of holding information on sex offenders or people's sexual behaviour when no particular crime is being investigated, the relationship between NCIS and local forces has not always been harmonious. When local forces have had to contain vigilante crowds, field national press inquiries and offer protection to unwanted child sex offenders, many have wondered where the NCIS Paedophile Section was. In their daily work, CPU officers have asked similar questions:

NCIS is a waste of time. We need a proper national intelligence system to assist in tracking paedophiles.

The paedophile index? Where is it? Can someone give me the 'phone number?

(Hughes et al., 1996, p. 31)

The introduction of the sex offender 'register' in 1997 (see Chapter 7) answered some of these criticisms but, arguably, left the NCIS Paedophile Section even further out on a limb, because local CPUs could have access to the register without any reference to NCIS. The HM Inspectorate of Constabulary found many forces now compiling their own local paedophile index which, in turn, 'minimised their incentive to update the NCIS database' (HMIC, 1999, para. 4.15).

A final criticism of the NCIS Paedophile Section has been made by HM Inspectorate of Constabulary, which found the database being held to be mainly on individual offenders. This presented something of a problem because the NCIS terms of reference require it only to be dealing with 'serious organised crime', which involves two or more participants.

On balance the Inspectorate decided to turn a blind eye (HMIC, 1997, p. 20).

One other national database available to all forces is operated away from NCIS by the Derbyshire Constabulary. This is the system known as CATCHEM (Centralised Analytical Team Collating Homicide Expertise Management), which holds data on more than 3,000 child murders committed since 1960, whether solved or unsolved. New entries are made on a pro-forma document with over 200 questions on it, and the idea is to check the probability of the murder being part of a series of crimes (Gibbons, 1997).

International policing

Policing is by definition restricted to a given nation state and police officers are not allowed to operate outside their authorised jurisdictions. In practice, they often have a need to work across national borders with their counterparts in other countries, but this work has to be largely restricted to the communication of personal data on individuals or groups wanted or suspected of crimes.

Increasingly, the dialogue between police forces has become the subject of international treaties and conventions to improve the efficiency and effectiveness of the communications, and the police have formed permanent Transnational Policing Networks (TPNs) to formalise these communications. The two best known TPNs are Interpol (The International Criminal Police Organisation) and Europol (The European Police Office).

The origins of Interpol can be traced back to 1914 and a meeting in Monaco. The organisation has always been non-governmental and strictly by the police and for the police. In 1997, Interpol had a global membership of 177 countries, each with its own Interpol office – known as the National Central Bureau (NCB) – and a head office in Lyon, France. In the past, Interpol has suffered from a poor image, but of late has transformed itself and now has:

> . . . one of the most sophisticated automated search and image transmission systems in the world. It enables rapid reliable and secure exchange of information. NCB's will have access to an enormous store of data.
>
> (Benyon *et al.*, 1993, p. 226)

The UK's Interpol NCB is located at NCIS in the same building as the NCIS Paedophile Section. At international level, Interpol has a 'Standing Working Party on Offences Against Minors', which has in turn produced a handbook of best practice in investigating crimes against children ('Concerns and division over tackling global child abuse' *International Police Review*, 1997, pp. 24–25; Interpol, 1997).

Europol has political origins in the European Union and emerged from the 1991 Maastricht Treaty. As a TPN, it operates just between the 15 EU member states and only deals with serious organised crime from its headquarters in The Hague; in contrast, Interpol will deal with any sort of crime. Europol is 'governed' by the Europol Convention, which came into force on 1 October 1998 and includes within it a mandate to deal with organised trafficking in human beings defined as:

> [The] subjection of a person to the real and illegal sway of other persons by using violence or menaces or by the abuse of authority or intrigue with a view to the exploitation of prostitution, forms of sexual exploitation and assault of minors or trade in abandoned children
>
> (Europol Convention, 1995,
> (as amended) Annex to art. 2)

This mandate was added to the Convention after the events of 1996 in Belgium when 200,000 people had demonstrated in the streets of Brussels on 20 October against the crimes of child sex offender Marc Dutroux and the apparent ineffectiveness of the criminal justice system to stop his activities.

In London, Europol's UK office is also located at NCIS headquarters alongside the Interpol NCB and the Paedophile Section. Such proximity gives the UK a direct link into policing directed against sexual offending that has an international dimension to it; sexual offending that includes so-called 'sex tourism'.

'Sex tourism' was the term coined to describe the practice of men from developed industrialised countries, such as the US, Japan and Western Europe, travelling to less developed countries, such as Thailand, Sri Lanka and the Philippines, to use prostitutes – including child prostitutes. Sometimes these men were taking advantage of permissive legislation in these countries and sometimes the law was simply not enforced as it should have been. Non-governmental organisations such as ECPAT (End Child Prostitution, Pornography, Trafficking) and the Preda Foundation started to raise international awareness, culminating in the 1996 Stockholm World Congress against Commercial Sexual Exploitation of Children (Kane, 1998).

In the UK, a private Member's Bill promoted by Lord Hylton in 1995 sought to enable prosecution of men in this country for crimes against children committed abroad. The Government appreciated the 'admirable aim' of the Bill, but felt unable to support it because it failed to recognise the difficulties of British police investigating crime abroad and the inability of courts to compel foreign witnesses to appear before them. As a first step, the Government preferred the approach of trying to prevent men going overseas for purposes of sex tourism, but did produce an extensive consultation paper to see what further options existed (Home Office, 1996b).

In 1996, the Government supported another private Member's Bill, which sought to allow the prosecution in Britain of people who conspired, or incited others, to commit sexual offences against children abroad. The Sexual Offences (Conspiracy and Incitement) Act 1996 was aimed at the organisers of travel arrangements for purposes of sex tourism; the Act was implemented from 1 October 1996.

Interpol had by this time already formed its own Standing Working Party on Offences Against Minors (Interpol General-Secretariat, 1995). Sex tourism was high on its agenda, and when London hosted one of the Working Party's regular meetings in November 1995, police officers from Sweden explained how they had successfully prosecuted a man in Sweden for sexual offences against children committed abroad (NCIS, 1995; Home Office, 1996b, Annex D).

When the Sex Offenders Act 1997 was implemented on 1 September 1997, most of the attention was on the introduction of the 'sex offenders register' in Part I of the Act (see Chapter 7). Part II of the Act, however, gave UK courts jurisdiction to prosecute those who travel abroad to commit sexual offences against children; the offence had to be a crime in both countries, and the Act applied only to British citizens or people resident in the UK, but the penalties for a crime would be the same as if the offence had been committed in the UK.

The police are developing their expertise to act under the 1997 law, and NCIS paedophile section officers have visited the Philippines to improve practical police co-operation (Drew, 1997). In 1998 some of this work came to fruition in Operation Osprey, an inter-agency exercise led by the British Customs and Excise Service involving Belgium, Canada, Finland, Germany, Ireland, Luxembourg, Netherlands and the US. A reported ten arrests were made and a further 37 individuals became the subject of further investigation (Collins, 1999). The first prosecution under the Act was against a man who had offended in France ('Camp site owner jailed for sex assaults on girls' *Independent*, 22 January 2000).

The Forensic Science Service

The UK's Forensic Science Service offers a support service to the police with a staff of over 1,200 scientists and their assistants at six regional laboratories. The service has traditionally analysed the content of drugs and other evidence from scenes of crime, including the analysis of body fluids such as blood and semen.

One scientific development to help police investigations of sexual offending has been the use of DNA (deoxyribonucleic acid) to help identify and detect offenders. The technique had been pioneered by academics at the University of Leicester in the mid-1980s, but early attempts to apply the findings in practice were hampered by the need to get an optimum size of sample and a means of storage; police were also lacking any powers to compel suspects to give a suitable sample that could be then matched with samples found at a scene of crime or on a victim (Dovaston and Burton, 1996).

The Government moved to take these obstacles out of the way of the police. The Criminal Justice and Public Order Act 1994, Part IV made amendments to the Police and Criminal Evidence Act 1984 to give the police powers to take samples from suspects for DNA analysis in the course of investigations. The same amendment allowed the police to take DNA samples from offenders who had been convicted of a 'recordable offence' from 10 April 1995 onwards (a 'recordable offence' is an offence punishable with imprisonment or is otherwise specified in law, and 10 April 1995 was the day that the UK's National DNA Database opened for business). Similar police powers were introduced north of the border by the Criminal Procedure (Scotland) Act 1995.

The National DNA Database was based in Birmingham as part of the Forensic Science Service. All DNA samples were to be recorded on a computer for rapid search and retrieval. The database was set up in record-breaking time, which the Director of the Forensic Science Service described as:

> . . . a tribute to the dedication, drive and expertise of the staff
> of Birmingham who have produced an operational service in
> five months.
>
> (Home Office, 1995a)

The 1996 Home Office Consultation Document on the 'Sentencing and Supervision of Sex Offenders' saw the National DNA Database as a prime means of detecting sex offenders, and also of deterring them from committing crime in the first place. The document proposed building up the database by taking samples from convicted sex offenders currently in custody (Home Office, 1996a, paras. 39–40).

The scientific accuracy of DNA tests had by now, already been questioned (see e.g. McLeod, 1991; Brown, 1993) and various rumblings were coming from the police about their dissatisfaction with the existing service they were getting from the national database (see e.g. 'Police anger over database disorder' *The Times*, 10 September 1996), with some even wanting to break away and use a private company for DNA testing ('Police back rival DNA tests after Home Office delays' *Observer*, 14 April 1996). Despite these difficulties the consultation document proposals were accepted, and the civil rights group Liberty did not even mention it in its response to the document (Liberty, 1996). Legislation duly followed to allow the taking of DNA samples from sex offenders in custody in the form of the Criminal Evidence (Amendment) Act 1997 and the Crime and Punishment (Scotland) Act 1997, section 48 (see also Bagshaw, 1997).

The taking of DNA samples in other circumstances remained a voluntary affair, and in particular where the police wanted to take samples from, perhaps, hundreds of men in a given area to help resolve a local sex crime (see e.g. 'DNA checks for 200 in hunt for rapist' *Yorkshire Post*, 18 April 1998). The police have usually described this as 'eliminating' large numbers of men from their inquiry, with the men who choose not to 'volunteer' inevitably becoming the subject of a different and more intensive form of investigation.

The popularity of DNA testing to identify criminals has given it a momentum of its own. By January 1997, the National DNA Database held more than 112,000 samples (HC Debs, 20 February 1997, col. 1029) and by 1999 this had risen to over 600,000 ('FSS clears DNA backlog' *Policing Today*, 5(2) June 1999, p. 7); reports suggested that scientists will soon be able to produce pictures of a criminal's face from a DNA sample ('DNA to provide face-fit pictures of criminals' *Independent*, 3 July 1997). The Council of the European Union wants all EU member states to develop their own National DNA Database within a standardised format to facilitate international exchange, and cites action against child sexual exploitation as a reason for doing this (Council of the European Union, 1997). The Police Superintendents' Association of the UK has even suggested that we start talking about a National DNA Database for the entire population ('Police urge talks on DNA database for whole nation' *Guardian*, 6 May 1998).

Summary

Most policing activities in the UK, whether for action against sex offending or any other form of crime, take place at a local level. Criticisms of police attitudes towards the investigation of sexual crime (especially by women criminologists) have caused them to rethink their approach to this work over the last 20 years. Specialist units have been developed to improve the level of intervention required and to make the police more sensitive to the needs of women and child victims of sexual offending.

What has also become increasingly important to the policing of sex offenders – at local, national and international levels – is the obtaining, collating and analysis of 'personal information' on sex offenders. This increased importance of the database has been facilitated by the advances in information technology and the ability to retrieve or exchange data in 'real time', and by the specific advances in the use of DNA sampling technology in order to identify more easily the person to whom 'personal information' should be attached. These advances bring with them critical issues of civil liberties which will be returned to later.

5

The search for justice – at court

When the police have completed their investigations and they believe they have a case to present to court, that case is passed to the Crown Prosecution Service (England and Wales), the Procurator Fiscal (Scotland) or the Director of Public Prosecutions (Northern Ireland). In turn, these prosecuting agencies make their own decisions, based on the evidence given to them, as to whether a prosecution is worthwhile in terms of a likely conviction or whether it is in the 'public interest' to prosecute.

Prosecuting

The Crown Prosecution Service came into being following the recommendation of the 1981 Royal Commission on Criminal Procedure that the investigation of crime should be separated from the prosecution of offenders; the aim was to end the system of police prosecutions that had been in place almost since the origins of police forces. The Prosecution of Offenders Act 1985 created the Crown Prosecution Service (CPS), which started work in October 1986.

From the outset the new CPS had a rocky ride. Police resentment at the loss of their prosecuting role and the new demands the CPS was putting on them led to allegations of police obstruction. A 1992 Parliamentary Select Committee inquiry into what was going on aired some of the grievances and, by the mid 1990s, the CPS was more established as a part of the criminal justice system. Further reform was recommended by the Glidewell Report, which called for greater decentralisation, better liaison arrangements with the police and the ending of the division of work into magistrates' and Crown Court work (Glidewell Report, 1998).

Aside from organisational problems has been the CPS's seeming inability successfully to prosecute sex offenders. A critical report from two women's groups accused the CPS of regularly failing to prosecute rape crimes, and stated that the chances of justice for women and children who were raped or sexually assaulted was unacceptably low. The report also highlighted what it saw as the reluctance of the CPS to get involved in sex offending where there was a 'domestic' context or the alleged attacker was known to the women:

> Those who have been convicted of a crime they didn't commit are not the only victims of a 'miscarriage of justice'; so are those who have suffered a crime and are denied justice.
>
> (WAR/LAW, 1995)

Others picked up on the fact that the first version of the Code for Crown Prosecutors had a clear statement that:

> . . . sexual assaults upon children should always be regarded seriously, as should offences against adults, such as rape, which amount to gross personal violation. In such cases, where the Crown Prosecutor is satisfied as to the sufficiency of the evidence there will seldom be any doubt that prosecution will be in the public interest.
>
> (CPS n.d., para. 8(vi)(b))

Yet in the revised (and still current) edition, this statement had been deleted (CPS, 1994). The CPS felt obliged to put out a further explanation that 'sexual assaults . . . are always serious offences and the service is committed to making sure that appropriate action is taken' (CPS, 1996, para. 5.2).

At the heart of the criticism was the CPS practice of 'downgrading' charges in order to improve the chances of a successful prosecution, or the outright 'discontinuance' of proceedings because there was insufficient evidence, irregularities in its collection or it was not, somehow, in the public interest. It all added up to a continuation of the process of attrition started by the police.

Research examining possible reasons for discontinuance has found 'evidential difficulties' to be a prime reason for the CPS not taking a case to court. Evidential difficulties include:

- victims who are vulnerable in terms of age or learning disabilities;
- the victim's previous sexual history;
- a prior relationship between victim and offender which can test the victim's willingness to give evidence – if the victim pulls out, the prosecution has no case;
- when the case turns on the issue of 'consent' it is often one person's word against another.
  (Harris and Grace, 1999, p. 26; see also Sone, 1995, on the particular problems of people with learning disabilities)

The CPS's instructing of barristers has been favourably commented upon by researchers, with perhaps only the need for more case conferences between them, and involving the police, to seek out any evidential weaknesses (Harris and Grace, 1999, p. 36). The CPS maintains that it always tries to proceed to court and only 'discontinue' with 'very good reason' (*ibid*, p. 25); court proceedings were more likely to take place when the victim was slightly older or very young (*ibid*, p. 27).

One continuing problem for the CPS and the police was the sex offender's access to witness statements or video recordings (see below) which made out the case against him. Any accused person is entitled to know what that case is, and the accused sex offender, therefore, has a right to see statements, videos, medical reports or photographs. The problem arose when the offender then chose to distribute this evidence amongst his friends as a form of pornography in its own right; an action that not only diminishes the seriousness of the offences, but also reasserts the defendant's position as being not so deviant after all.

In response to reports that this was happening (see e.g. 'Rape Statements "used as porn"' *Guardian*, 26 October 1989; 'Violated by prying prison eyes' *Independent*, 3 August 1990) the Home Office produced a consultation document suggesting a regime of supervised access to statements, photographs and videos that could not be removed (Home Office, 1991). The Royal Commission on Criminal Justice recommended that instructing solicitors should take the lead in safeguarding the confidentiality of those disclosed documents (RCCJ, 1993, p. 129), but reports that the Law Society was having to investigate its own members for hanging on to them were not encouraging ('Solicitor failed to return sex tape' *Daily Telegraph*, 17 September 1996).

The Home Office's jointly produced guidance on the video-recording of children's statements had advised that defendants should be supervised when viewing them and sign an undertaking not to show them to other people (Home Office/Department of Health, 1992, para. 4.12), but its 1996 Consultation Document went further and proposed making it a criminal offence to misuse victim statements (Home Office, 1996a, paras. 78–86). Liberty responded by reminding the Home Office of the part non-disclosure had played in recent miscarriages of justice and cited the Prison Rules and the Criminal Justice Act 1988, section 160, covering possession of indecent photographs, as possible alternative existing measures (Liberty, 1996, paras 60–65).

An unsuccessful attempt was made to amend the Criminal Proceedings and Investigations Bill (HC Debs, 12 June 1996, cols. 328–41) but later a private Member's Bill was supported by the Government, and the Sexual Offences (Protected Material) Act received its Royal Assent on 21 March 1997. In future, defendants could only view disclosed documents through their legal representatives and under supervised conditions; if they were not represented, supervision would be by the police or a prison governor; offenders against these conditions could be fined or imprisoned for a maximum of two years.

The court hearing

The conduct of court proceedings involving sexual offenders has been the subject of much debate. Women victims have felt more on trial than defendants, and the problem of an adult court hearing evidence from a child victim has been equally fraught. In the adversarial criminal justice system that we have, with the presumption that the accused is 'innocent until proved guilty', the onus is on the prosecution to prove the allegations made and on the defence to mount a reasonable opposition to the allegations.

Before we reach the point of conviction and sentence, however, the court will probably require an adjournment whilst the case against the accused is put together and, similarly, a defence is mounted. At this point, the court must make decisions about whether or not to remand on bail or remand in custody until the case is ready to proceed.

The Bail Act 1976, section 4 gives the defendant a 'presumption' of bail unless circumstances dictate otherwise. Bail is not, however, available to a man charged with rape or attempted rape if he already has previous convictions for similar offences (Criminal Justice and Public Order Act 1994, s. 25). If he has no previous convictions but still faces the same charges, any court granting bail, where the prosecutor has raised objections, must state the reasons for giving bail in open court (Bail Act 1976, Sch. I, Part I, para. 9A).

In non-rape cases, bail may be refused if the court is satisfied that there are substantial grounds for believing further offences would be committed, witnesses would be interfered with, the defendant was already on bail when the new allegations occurred or the offence is considered to be particularly serious (see Bail Act 1976, Sch. I for a complete list of the exemptions to the right of bail).

If a remand on bail is granted over a remand in custody, conditions may be attached to that bail. As with police bail, this might include a condition of residence, a curfew, an exclusion zone which the defendant must not enter, a condition of non-association or the regular reporting to a specified police station (Bail Act 1976, s. 3, as amended). Research does exist from South Wales on how bail conditions were imposed, and the findings suggest it is a haphazard process that is sometimes used excessively; at worst it has been described as 'a pre-conviction punishment' (Hucklesby, 1994).

In 1975, the much publicised case of *R v. Morgan* ([1975] 2 All ER 347) generated a wider debate on the definition of rape and the defence of the man believing he had consent; questions were also raised about the extent to which a woman's previous sexual behaviour could be admitted as a defence. A committee of inquiry was formed to look into these questions and recommended accordingly (Heilbron Committee, 1975).

The Sexual Offences (Amendment) Act 1976 duly followed, with a clarification of the definition of rape and the meaning of consent; in future, juries were to consider whether there were reasonable grounds for a man to *believe* he had consent. Section 2 of the Act prohibited any references to the woman's previous sexual conduct being used by a man in his defence; judges could still allow such references on application if they considered it might reveal previous similar conduct to the present proceedings.

The implementation of section 2 in the courts has been criticised as still failing to protect a woman and making her feel that it is she who is actually on trial. Lawyers find ways round it and judges seem too ready to give exemptions (see e.g. Adler, 1987; Temkin, 1993; Lees, 1997). An unsuccessful attempt was made to strengthen section 2 with amendments to the Criminal Proceedings and Investigations Bill; the opposition spokeswoman accused the Government of 'indifference, and [refusing] to do anything about one of the most serious problems besetting women in the criminal justice system' (HC Debs, 12 June 1996, col. 363). In Scotland, there was a change to the law in the Criminal Procedure (Scotland) Act 1995, sections 274–275. In time, the Youth Justice and Criminal Evidence Act 1999, which received its Royal Assent in July 1999, did tighten up section 2 and, in future, the intention is that evidence of the complainant's sexual behaviour will only be introduced when relevant to the alleged offence.

The Sexual Offences (Amendment) Act 1976, section 4 had introduced anonymity into rape proceedings for the first time for both complainant and defendant. The press could still report proceedings, but not identify any of the parties involved during the trial. The 1992 Sexual Offences (Amendment) Act extended these provisions on anonymity to sexual offences hearings other than rape. Reporting restrictions may be lifted by the judge if, for example, the accused wants publicity to encourage witnesses to come forward.

Some defendants in rape cases have been known to dismiss their defence lawyers and conduct their own defence. This move has been permissible in British law, but has been criticised in rape cases because it puts the alleged offender in a face-to-face confrontation with the victim for purposes of cross-examination. Much publicity was given to the defendant Ralston Edwards in 1996 when he cross-examined his victim for several days, causing her great distress and taking her through the ordeal a second time; Edwards reportedly wore the same clothes in court as he had worn during the attack ('Inquiry into rape victim's court ordeal' *Daily Telegraph*, 23 August 1996).

A subsequent Home Office Interdepartmental Working Group recommended a mandatory prohibition on unrepresented defendants personally cross-examining the complainant in cases of rape and serious sexual assault (Home Office, 1998a, para. 9.39); such a prohibition already existed where the victim was a child (Criminal Justice Act 1988, s. 34A). The Youth Justice and Criminal Evidence Act 1999 in due course introduced measures that prohibited a defendant from personally cross-examining a witness who was the victim of an alleged sexual offence; powers were given to the court to appoint a legal representative to 'test the evidence' if the defendant refused to be represented.

The same Act also allowed an adult complainant in a sexual offence case to give evidence from behind a screen, or through a live TV link, or to have the public gallery cleared before giving evidence. Evidence could also be pre-recorded on a video tape. The Act gave a presumption in favour of all these 'special measures' in sexual offences should the victim ask for them.

On a non-statutory level, adult complainants could also be helped by the Witness Service; this is a service offered by Victim Support. It is a voluntary service to help vulnerable witnesses through the ordeal of appearing in the Crown Court and there are plans to extend the service to other courts. The Witness Service helps people before, during and after their attendance at court, explaining the layout of the court, going on 'familiarisation' visits and talking though the experience afterwards (see Home Office 1998a, Annex G).

Children's evidence

The Youth Justice and Criminal Evidence Act 1999 brought in new protection for child witnesses. Child witnesses had first received special provision when the 1987 Criminal Justice Bill brought in clauses to introduce 'live' video-links, allowing the child to speak to the court from a room removed from the court environs.

At the same time, the Home Office published a short briefing on the subject and invited comments on 'live' links and pre-recorded video tapes, whilst still holding that it is:

> . . . an unfettered right to cross-examine by counsel of the defendant's choice [and this], is an indispensable part of our system of justice
>
> (Home Office 1987, para. 27)

The balance that had to be struck was between the needs of children in court as witnesses and the traditional safeguards afforded the accused by English criminal procedure. The resulting Criminal Justice Act 1988, section 32 introduced live video links for children under 14 to give their evidence to court. The same Act (s. 34) also abolished the need for a judge to give a warning when a child's uncorroborated evidence had been heard; section 34 did not extend to sexual offences, but the later Criminal Justice and Public Order Act 1994, sections 32–33 did make that extension. The Government held back from introducing any pre-recorded tapes being used as evidence in court.

Chelmsford Crown Court achieved the distinction of being the first UK court to hear evidence on a live video-link from a 13-year-old victim in a rape case; the judge reportedly tried to put the girl at ease with the words 'What's it like being on the telly, not too bad?' ('Girl gives evidence by video link' *Independent*, 10 January 1989).

Other experiments to improve the taking of evidence from children were more problematic. The use of 'anatomically correct' dolls in order that children could demonstrate what had happened to them were one device that had a short reign of fashion. The judiciary urged caution in their use when it was pointed out that children who had not been sexually abused might be just as interested in undressing the dolls and showing interest in their genitalia. In the same vein, social workers were warned not to refer to children's statements about sexual abuse as 'disclosures' because of its connotations of being 'factual' when the statements clearly might not be.

The arguments for and against pre-recorded testimony continued. The Children's Legal Centre was in favour ('CLC calls for legal reform to end trauma for child witnesses' *Childright*, October 1987) and the Cleveland Report considered the question, but made no recommendation other than to comment that 'not all the judiciary are in favour of video recording' (Cleveland Report, 1988, para. 12.47). The chair of the Criminal Bar Association was clear that the defence lawyer's right to cross-examine a witness must be preserved, and challenged what he described as the 'dangerous climate of opinion that children virtually never lie about sexual abuse' ('Warning on child video evidence' *Guardian*, 2 October 1989).

Meanwhile, the Home Office had decided to convene an advisory group, to be chaired by Judge Thomas Pigot, to look more closely at the practical implications of allowing pre-recorded video statements. The resulting Pigot Report came down in favour of pre-recording and even the possibility of pre-recording a cross-examination (Pigot Report, 1989). In Scotland, the Scottish Law Commission had recommended that trials be adjourned to enable a child's evidence to be obtained using a video-recorded deposition procedure; it preferred this idea to any live links.

The Criminal Justice Act 1991 allowed the use of pre-recorded video interviews of children in the Crown Court and Youth Courts of England and Wales, by amending the Criminal Justice Act 1988 with a new section 32A; for sex offences, 'children' were defined as under 17 and live links were also extended from under 14s to those under 17. The Act did not implement the Pigot Report recommendation of pre-recorded cross-examination and, even with the present pre-recorded provisions, a child had to be available for follow-up cross-examination. Other new departures included allowing a child to give unsworn evidence and a faster 'transfer' system from magistrates' to Crown Court without lengthy committal proceedings.

The Home Office and the Department of Health jointly produced a Memorandum of Good Practice for police officers and social workers who would be conducting the video sessions. Advice was given on the need to go at the child's pace, and to avoid leading questions and other interventions that might render the tape inadmissible as evidence (Home Office/Department of Health, 1992). In practice, the police, with their understanding of criminal evidence and the needs of the criminal courts, invariably took the lead over social workers when it came to videoing, and today the taking of recordings is a standard part of the investigation of sexual offences against children, even if many of them never get used in court (see e.g. Davies *et al.*, 1995). The Pigot Report recommendation that cross-examinations could be pre-recorded remained unimplemented, despite continuing proposals that it should be (see e.g. CPSI, 1998, Recommendation 45).

The NSPCC led a campaign in 1996 called 'Justice for Children', which sought to make it easier for children to give evidence in the intimidating atmosphere of the court. The following year, it produced a video entitled 'A Case for Balance', which demonstrated examples of good practice when a child is a witness; the video was distributed to courts across the country (Tsang, 1998).

Eventually, the Youth Justice and Criminal Evidence Act 1999 did introduce more 'special measures' for the child witness. As for adults, these included the screening of witnesses, the giving of evidence through live links and the giving of evidence (including cross-examinations) on a pre-recorded video-tape. The Act made such 'special measures' automatically available for children (under 17), who were also deemed competent to give evidence as long as they understood the questions asked and could give answers capable of being understood.

Reports to court

Following a conviction, the courts may read a Pre-Sentence Report (PSR) prepared by a probation officer or social worker before deciding on the appropriate sentence. In the 1960s, when the idea of reports to the criminal court started to take off, the reports were variously referred to as the Social Inquiry Report or simply Court Reports. The officers writing them had a relatively free hand in how they wrote them and what recommendations they made on possible sentences, but by 1990 the Government was clear that we needed to take 'a fresh look at the purpose, content and format of these reports' (Home Office, 1990a, para. 3.10).

When 'National Standards' were introduced in 1992, they gave advice on how to write PSRs. The focus was to be on the offence rather than the offender, and the views of victims were to be included in the report. The National Standards were revised in 1995, and again in 2000, when they stated that the report should:

... assess the consequences of the offence, including what is known of the impact on any victim, either from the CPS papers, or from a victim statement where available.

(Home Office, 2000b, B6)

Another addition to the PSR, made by the revised National Standards, was the inclusion of a risk assessment. Every PSR is now expected to:

- contain an assessment of the offender's likelihood of re-offending based on the current offence, attitude to it, and other relevant information;
- contain an assessment of the offender's risk of causing serious harm to the public;
- identify any risks of self harm.

(Home Office, 2000b, B8)

The PSR requirements to look at the victims' views and to include a risk assessment clearly have direct relevance for PSRs on sex offenders.

Sentencing

Following a finding of guilt (a conviction) and the reading of any reports to the court, a sentence has to be decided upon. Before moving on to the principles of sentencing, we cannot pass by without at least a reference to the sexist comments of some of our judges presiding over cases of sexual assault. Sampson, for example, cites the almost caricature comments of Mr Justice Wild in 1982:

Women who say no do not always mean no. It is not just a question of saying no, it is a question of how she says it, how she shows it and makes it clear. If she doesn't want it she only has to keep her legs shut and she would not get it without force and there will be marks of force being used.

(Sampson, 1994, p. 57)

and in 1993, the requirement in Newport Crown Court that a 15-year-old assailant be given three years' supervision and pay £500 compensation to the victim 'to give her a good holiday' (ibid, p.46; see also Pattullo, 1984, for a litany of similar pronouncements). Hopefully, such comments are slowly being consigned to history as enlightenment falls upon the judiciary. In any event, judges in the Crown Court must now complete a Serious Sexual Offences course and be authorised by the Lord Chief Justice before taking such cases; this is known as getting their 'sex ticket'.

In general terms, the principles of sentencing require a balance between the need for retribution and 'just deserts' against the need for reform and the reduction of future crimes. Unless the criminal law specifies certain sentences, the autonomy of the courts in passing sentences means that there is no such thing as a 'correct' sentence for a given offence, and the belief that the courts have got it 'wrong' yet again is the staple diet of our tabloid press. The principles of sentencing that we do have are based on the precedent of previous court judgments and especially those of the Courts of Appeal. Since 1980, the Court of Appeal has periodically produced what are called 'guideline' judgments, which go beyond the confines of the immediate case to guide other courts coming across similar cases.

A guideline judgment on the appropriate sentencing in cases of rape was made in the case of *Billam* in 1986. The judgment defined five types of rape, graded in order of seriousness, and laid down the initial sentence that could then be raised or lowered depending on aggravating or mitigating factors (*R v. Billam* (1986) 82 Cr App R 347).

1 The least serious was a rape in wholly exceptional circumstances and the sentence might be non-custodial.
2 A single rape with no aggravating factors should lead to five years' imprisonment.
3 A single rape with aggravating factors (e.g. two or more men acting together, a break-in to the victims home, etc.) should lead to eight years' imprisonment.
4 Multiple rape should lead to 15 years' imprisonment.
5 Multiple rape with 'perverted' or 'psychopathic' tendencies should lead to life imprisonment.

The aggravating factors that might raise these sentences included additional violence, use of a weapon, careful planning or a very old or very young victim; the mental or physical effect on a victim could also be taken into account. Mitigating factors would include a guilty plea, which reduced the victims' need to be in court.

The *Billam* guidelines were followed closely in 1987 during the sentencing of offenders in what became known as the 'Ealing vicarage rape'. The sentences were immediately picked upon by the press as being too lenient, and later research has revealed that the courts thereafter (until 1991) chose to depart from the guidelines in favour of their own heavier sentences. For the researchers, 'the Billam judgment is not shaping sentencing practice in the way intended . . . [and] raises the issue of the value of current guideline judgments' (Ranyard *et al.*, 1994).

The Criminal Justice Act 1988 had introduced to British law the concept of an appeal being made against a sentence considered too lenient, and the first use of this section was against a custodial sentence of three years for a man who had pleaded guilty to three counts of incest on one daughter and one count of incest with another daughter. The sentence was duly increased to six years, but at the same time, Lord Lane, the Lord Chief Justice now set out sentencing guidelines for similar crimes.

In summary, the maximum penalties were:

- incest by a man with a girl under 13 – life imprisonment;
- incest by a man with a girl over 13 – seven years;
- attempted incest by a man with a girl under 13 – two years;
- attempted incest by a man with a girl over 13 – two years;
- incest by a woman – seven years;
- attempted incest by a woman – two years.

(Attorney-General's Reference (No. 1 of 1989) [1989] WLR
1117)

The guidelines were not universally welcomed, as they suggested that differing ages meant the offender might see this as an 'excuse' for his own behaviour. The founder of Childline, Esther Rantzen, said they implied 'the offender is a victim and can be seduced by a child. It detracts from the fact that it is a man's responsibility not to abuse children, whatever the age' (quoted in 'Project to educate judges on handling child sex offenders' *Independent*, 25 September 1989).

Lord Lane responded later the same year with yet further guidelines, making the point that all incest cases varied and were often very complex; the sentencing judge was reminded that 'a rigid arithmetical approach' was not the best way to approach them. Aggravating factors might include threats and violence, psychological damage to the child and the frequency of offending; mitigating factors were a plea of guilty, otherwise good relationships, or where the girl had had previous sexual experience *(Attorney-General's Reference (No. 4 of 1989)* (1989) 11 Cr App R (S) 517). Two years later, this guidance was extended to cover non-incestuous sexual offending *(Attorney-General's Reference (No. 4 of 1991)* (1992) 13 Cr App R (S) 182).

The Government was approving of these guideline judgments but was now prepared to impose its will on the courts to ensure sentencing was based on the seriousness of the offence – the 'just deserts' approach took over from an earlier treatment-orientated approach which had become increasingly discredited. The 1990 White Paper explained the new way forward:

> The recent guideline judgements, such as those on rape [and] incest . . . have provided much clearer guidance on how sentencing decisions should be reached . . . To achieve a more coherent and comprehensive consistency of approach in sentencing, a new framework is needed for the use of custodial, community and financial penalties.
>
> (Home Office, 1990a, para. 2.3)

Part of this new framework was to give the courts new powers to sentence according to seriousness of offence, and, in so doing, to sentence persistent violent and sexual offenders to longer custodial sentences. The target was 'a small number of offenders who became progressively more dangerous and who are a real risk to public safety' (*ibid*, para. 3.13). The new sentencing provisions duly appeared in the Criminal Justice Act 1991.

The 1991 Act was clear that offences of violence or sexual offending could always result in a custodial sentence (s. 1(2)(b)) and that that sentence could be lengthened if necessary in order to protect the public from serious harm (s. 2(2)(b)); in the latter case the court had to explain in open court why it was of the opinion that section 2(2)(b) applied (s. 2(3)). The Act also defined what it meant by sexual offences (s. 31(1)) (see Table 1.1 in Chapter 1).

Before deciding on the length of a custodial sentence, the court has to consider a Pre-Sentence Report (1991 Act, s. 3(1)). There is no requirement in the Act that the court should consider medical reports, but the Court of Appeal has stated its opinion that 'if the danger is due to a mental or personality problem, the sentencing court should, in our view always call for a medical report before passing sentence under section 2(2)(b)' (*R v. Fawcett* (1995) 16 Cr App R (S) 53).

The just deserts approach to sentencing takes little or no account of 'treatment' approaches; the whole idea has been to replace the 'treatment' approach which begged too many questions about 'what works?'. The Criminal Justice Act 1991, however, coincided with the launch of the Prison Service, Sex Offender Treatment Programmes (see below); the problem occurred when the programmes turned out to be longer than the sentences. The more serious sex offenders got treatment because of their longer sentences, but the less serious did not (Henham, 1998).

In the light of mounting public disquiet about sex offending, and in keeping with the just deserts approach, the Government now moved forward with its most controversial proposals for sentencing. This was the idea for automatic life sentences for persistent violent or sexual offending, based on the American model of similar legislation, where it was known as 'three strikes and out' (a reference to the sport of baseball). For this country, the recommendation was that it be just 'two strikes and out' (Home Office, 1996c).

One of the underlying premises of the proposal was the oft-quoted policy slogan that 'prison works' and that public confidence in sentencing needed to be restored; treatment approaches had fallen into disrepute. The arguments against it were that longer sentences did not deter crime, prisons would become overcrowded, and sexual offenders who have already been convicted would now be more likely to kill their victims, either to avoid detection, or because they know they are going to get a life sentence whether or not they kill. Overall, the idea was seen as inconsistent with the interests of justice and the judiciary, which was having its discretion to consider individual circumstances taken away (Henham, 1996).

The Government view prevailed and the Crime (Sentences) Act received the Royal Assent on 21 March 1997. Section 2 of the Act requires a court to impose an automatic life sentence for a second serious violent or sexual offence, unless there are exceptional circumstances relating to either offence or offender which justify it not doing so. If a life sentence is not imposed, the court must state what the exceptional circumstances are in open court. These provisions were implemented from 1 October 1998.

Courts were also given a lesser power, when imposing a prison sentence, to direct offenders assessed as having a psychiatric disorder to be admitted to hospital for treatment. At the end of treatment, or if untreatable, the offender is then remitted to prison to serve the rest of his sentence. This became known as a 'hybrid' order because of its involvement of both prison and health services and was widely seen as being an acknowledgement that mental health community services were not working (Crime (Sentences) Act 1997, ss. 46–47).

Summary

Within the courts, the response to sexual offending has been another arena for male attitudes to predominate and, possibly, obstruct the course of justice. The Crown Prosecution Service and the judiciary have been criticised for their unhelpful attitudes and steps have been taken to try and improve matters.

The importance of information on the offence and the offender in the form of Pre-Sentence Reports has been enhanced to help sentencers make their decision; part of these reports should now make an assessment of the risk that the offender might pose in the future. At the same time as these measures have sought to help sentencers, the politics of 'law and order' have resulted in heavier sentences being made mandatory for some sexual offending and thereby at the same time reducing any discretion the courts might have.

6
The search for justice – after court

After a conviction and sentence has been made, the sex offender passes into the hands of those agencies of the penal system charged with dealing with him or her. These post-court services are the probation and social services and the custodial or prison elements of the criminal justice system. Together, they provide for community sentences, custodial sentences or a period of community supervision following a custodial sentence. One further option recently suggested is that of indeterminate sentence for those considered too dangerous to release.

Community sentences

In theory, the whole range of community sentences including community supervision orders, attendance centre orders, curfew orders, supervision orders and probation orders are available for sex offenders. Here we look at the two most significant orders – the probation order and the supervision order.

Offenders put 'on probation' in the 1970s and 1980s were supervised by probation officers very much according to their own professional judgments. Probation officers received a social work education that gave them various forms of 'intervention' or 'treatment' which they could apply. The offender had had to agree to be 'on probation' and was expected to report to his or her probation officer as required and to receive the officer on home visits. Failure to comply might lead to a reappearance in court for 'breach' of probation.

At the end of the 1980s, this relatively laissez-faire approach came under attack. The Government wanted probation orders to be community sentences of the court rather than – as they currently appeared – an alternative to sentence. It also wanted to promote probation as a form of 'punishment in the community' rather than just treatment, and for the probation service to work more collectively with other agencies in the community: 'one to one work with individual offenders will not usually be enough to turn [offenders] away from crime' (Home Office 1990a, para. 7.20).

The Criminal Justice Act 1991 introduced the probation order as a sentence of the court for the first time, and defined it as:

(a) securing the rehabilitation of the offender; or
(b) protecting the public from harm from him or preventing the commission by him of further offences.

(Powers of Criminal Courts Act 1973, s. 2(1),
as amended by the Criminal Justice Act 1991)

Accompanying these legal changes was the introduction of 'National Standards for the Supervision of Offenders in the Community' to challenge individual approaches of different probation officers; the National Standards appeared in 1992, but were updated in 1995 and again in 2000 (Home Office, 2000b). At the same time, the Government removed the necessity to receive a social work education to become a probation officer; for probation the age of professionalism was giving way to the age of managerialism (see Worrall, 1997, esp. part 2), and by the turn of the century, even the very name 'probation' was in danger of being replaced by the more punitive sounding Community Punishment and Rehabilitation Service (Home Office, 1999c); although by March 2000 this idea had been quietly dropped.

The Criminal Justice Act 1991 also allowed a range of 'additional requirements' to be attached to probation orders, including requirements as to activities to be undertaken, activities to be refrained from, attendance at a probation centre, a specified residence, or treatment for drugs and alcohol dependency. These additional requirements could last for a maximum of 60 days, but this could be extended in the case of the sex offender (Criminal Justice Act 1991, Sch. 1, Part II, para. 4): offenders could also be required to attend for psychiatric treatment.

The sort of 'additional requirements' a sex offender might expect to see were:

- not to seek or undertake employment which would bring the offender into direct contact with young people under the age of 16 years;
- not to receive visits at home from any child under the age of 16 years and not to visit the home of any child without prior permission from the supervising officer;
- not to undertake any leisure pursuit or hobby which brings the offender into direct contact with any child;
- to reside where approved by the supervising officer;
- to attend group work sessions to confront sex offending, and not to have any contact with group members between sessions etc.

(see HMIP 1998a, para. 4.31)

In Scotland, the system is slightly different because the local authority social work departments carry out probation order supervision as part of their criminal justice social work services. Orders last between six months and three years and can include any 'requirement' which is 'conducive to securing the good conduct of the offender or for preventing a repetition of the offence or the commission of a further offence' (Criminal Procedure (Scotland) Act 1995, ss. 228–229).

Supervision orders are, broadly speaking, the same as probation orders but for young offenders. In fact, they have in the past, arguably, been less structured than probation orders, requiring the supervisor only to 'advise, assist and befriend' the offender. Various additional requirements can be included in a supervision order (Children and Young Persons Act 1969, s. 12, as amended) and the expectation that supervisors will abide by National Standards have more recently increased the standing of the supervision order. Supervision orders have usually been the province of local authority social workers, and the probation service has taken on probation orders; the introduction of Youth Offending Teams has led to a legal relaxation of any clear-cut demarcation in this respect (Crime and Disorder Act 1998, s. 71(5)).

The purpose of a community sentence including both probation and supervision orders has been defined by the Home Office as being to:

- provide a rigorous and effective punishment;
- reduce the likelihood of re-offending;
- rehabilitate the offender, where possible; and
- enable reparation to be made to the community.

(Home Office, 2000b, C7)

Within that punitive framework supervision then seeks to:

- address and reduce offending behaviour;
- challenge the offender to accept responsibility for the crimes committed and their consequences;
- contribute to the protection of the public;
- motivate and assist the offender towards a greater sense of personal responsibility and discipline;
- aid re-integration as a law abiding member of the community.

(Home Office, 2000b, C8)

Achieving compliance and ensuring enforcement of orders and any additional conditions has become progressively more central to supervisory work over the last decade; probation officers, in particular, have been encouraged to be tougher and to return offenders to courts more readily if in breach of orders (*ibid*, D20).

Supervisors can carry out individual one-to-one work with the offender or, increasingly, can become 'case managers' who involve others in different parts of the work. Specialist workers with sex offenders carry out both 'direct' and 'indirect' work as advisers to colleagues.

Community-based treatment for sex offenders can be group-work carried out on an interdisciplinary basis by probation, social services and voluntary agencies (ACOP, 1996).

The Home Office has commissioned an independent evaluation of these community-based treatment programmes through its Sex Offender Treatment Evaluation Project (STEP) study.

Reports have generally been favourable, but variation between programmes has been noted, as well as their strong and weak points:

> While offenders became more able, after treatment, to admit to having planned their sexual offences and have an improved appreciation of their offence antecedents, there was little evidence that they had developed skills to cope with 'risk' situations in the future.
>
> (Beckett *et al.*, 1994; see also Barker and Morgan, 1993)

The use of hostels run by the probation service for housing offenders, including sex offenders, is seen as an extension of supervision arrangements rather than simply a form of housing. Staff there can monitor and make risk assessments which are constantly discussed with the probation officer. The problem has been, in recent times, the reluctance of hostels to take on sex offenders when they know it will cause public disquiet in their local community and ultimately could distract them from carrying out their work with other offenders (see e.g. HMIP, 1998a, paras. 4.67–4.73).

In 1997, public anxiety was heightened when the Home Office took the unusual step of releasing figures to show that a high number of people charged with serious crimes, including murder, were already under the supervision of the probation service. The figures were described as a 'damaging blow to the probation service' and as prompting 'fresh concern about the level of supervision carried out by officers' ('One in eight accused of murder is on probation' *The Times*, 2 July 1997). There has been subsequent speculation that this disclosure by the Home Office was deliberately engineered to embarrass the probation service and 'soften up' any resistance it might offer to the spreading use of electronic monitoring, or tagging, of offenders (Brownlee, 1998, p. 122).

Whatever the truth of the matter, HM Inspectorate of Probation was able to report more positively the following year with the publication of a Thematic Report on the supervision of sex offenders. High levels of 'rigour' and 'vigilance' were noted with just a few gaps, such as the lack of provision for adolescent sex offenders and a lack of integration with prison treatment programmes, to take away from the overall good impression (HMIP, 1998a). Home Office Minister Joyce Quinn said:

> This report is a testament to the dedication and professionalism of probation staff and sends a clear and reassuring message to

the public that sex offenders are being supervised to an excellent standard in the community.

(Home Office, 1998b; see also Home Office, 1999d)

Not that the probation service could now relax, as the Home Office now made its push towards more 'effective supervision' using 'evidence based' practice (Home Office, 1998c; HMIP, 1998b). Probation services were invited to nominate successful projects, including projects working with sex offenders, as 'Pathfinder Projects'. These were to be evaluated and approved by a new Joint Prison and Probation Accreditation Panel and the results of the successful projects disseminated across the country (Home Office, 1999e).

Another adjunct to supervision has emerged from technological innovations which allow for the electronic monitoring or tagging of offenders; from the start, sexual offenders were seen as candidates for tagging (see 'Rapists tagged for life' *Today*, 27 July 1989). When electronic monitoring originally became a possibility, there was talk of it being used in its own right as a stand-alone technique. Today, there is a consensus that it needs to be accompanied always by appropriate supervision arrangements (Whitfield, 1997).

Experiments with the electronic tagging of offenders had been tried in 1989–90 and again in 1995. Systems generally worked on the basis of a person being subject to a curfew requiring him or her to be at home during certain hours of the day, and this requirement could be confirmed by a monitor permanently attached to the wrist or ankle (the Personal Identification Device (PID)) and equipment placed in the home (the Home Monitoring Unit (HMU)), which 'reported' to a local control centre. The first experiments had proved problematic, but later experiments, in Reading, Manchester and Norfolk, looked more promising (Mair and Mortimer, 1996) and in late 1997, the Government announced plans to extend the use of tagging to Suffolk, Middlesex, West Yorkshire and Cambridgeshire. The same announcement foresaw an extension to its use from straight supervision to those on bail, fine defaulters, juveniles and persistent petty offenders; the legal arrangements were put into the Criminal Justice Act 1991, section 13 and the Crime and Punishment (Scotland) Act, section 5 (Home Office, 1997a).

Further developments for tagging might include using technology already in use for mobile phones to devise systems for tracking offenders across wider geographical areas, rather than just confirming their whereabouts at a given point. In the case of sex offenders, the piloting of so-called 'reverse-monitoring' systems might also offer new options. In the US, reverse-monitoring has been tried in domestic violence cases, giving the potential victim – usually a woman – a device in her home that is triggered off by the approach of a person who is tagged. It is not too fanciful to imagine, for example, a school having such a device to give warning when a tagged sex offender comes within a certain range of it (see Whitfield, 1997, pp. 111–12).

More recently, technology in the form of a combination of a pager, computers and voice recognition systems has been piloted by Kent Probation Service, to try yet another form of 'tracking' for sex offenders ('Big Brother system to track paedophiles' *Independent*, 10 January 2000).

Custodial sentences

Sex offenders in prison have traditionally been given a rough ride. For many years they were offered no particular treatment programmes, were widely despised by other prisoners and received open hostility if their victim had been a child.

Invariably, the prison service has had to class them as 'vulnerable prisoners', while other prisoners class them as 'nonces':

> . . . hostility towards 'nonces' from 'straight' prisoners is routine. It is usually expressed in straightforwardly vehement moral terms . . . to emphasise a sense of frustration at having to share their living space with men whose crimes they consider monstrous. By tradition 'nonces' are expected to know their place and to keep out of the way of 'straight cons'.
>
> (Sparks *et al.*, 1996, p. 179)

In more colourful language, Coggan and Walker have described how direct action may be taken against the 'nonce' with prison officer collusion:

> [the] sex offender runs considerable risk of being attacked with razor blades, hot fat or boiling water, invariably while prison officers are conveniently looking in another direction. . . in many instances it is the prison officers themselves who have provoked the assaults by passing on to the attacking prisoners details of the offence for which a newly arrived prisoner was sentenced.
>
> (Coggan and Walker, 1982, p. 119)

Faced with such a threatening environment, the sex offender, as a 'vulnerable prisoner', has often had to be 'removed from association' with other prisoners under Prison Rule 43 for their own protection; Rule 43 became Rule 45 under the revised Prison Rules introduced 1 April 1999 (S.I. 1999, No. 728).

No-one has been very happy with this need to segregate certain offenders, and the Home Office has been pursuing a low key 'integrationist' policy to try and keep them in normal locations or to develop Vulnerable Prisoner Units (see Sparks *et al.*, 1996, p. 205 and Chapter 6).

The propensity for the sex offender to turn in on himself in the face of constant harassment and bullying has also been noted. Suicides and self-inflicted injury have been a recurring factor of prison life. The prison service has tried to address the problem and has given guidance to officers on suicide risk indicators; one such indicator being 'a conviction for homicide, sexual offences or offences against a child' (HM Prison Service, 1989, para. 8).

What many in the prison service wanted was some systematic treatment programmes for sex offenders. Some programmes did exist, but it was all a bit hit-and-miss. The Home Office actually claimed as many as 60 programmes existed at the end of the 1980s, but 'they have failed to mention that "treatment" in this respect might simply mean the provision of social skills training by a part time teacher for an hour, once each week' (Seven, 1991). What was needed was a fully worked out strategy.

The prison service strategy for sex offenders, including their treatment, was unveiled in June 1991. The main features of the strategy were:

- to hold sex offenders in fewer prisons to enable consistency of approach, effective use of skills and resources in working with them and the promotion of a safe and supportive environment to counter the worst excesses of violence towards them;
- to provide Sex Offender Treatment Programmes (SOTPs);
- to give priority to treatment for those likely to represent the greatest risk to the community on their release; and
- to assess which prisoners are most in need of treatment in terms of previous offending patterns.

The SOTPs were to be of two kinds, with a 'core programme' for most offenders and an 'extended programme' for the more serious offenders. Both programmes were to be built around group-work based on cognitive-behavioural principles to reduce the risk of offending (HM Prison Service, 1991; Guy, 1992).

The prison service has put a lot of effort into its SOTPs to make them meaningful and practical. Teams of staff involving psychologists, probation officers, prison officers and others are carefully selected and trained, and the programmes are monitored for 'programme integrity' to ensure that they are delivered as designed.

Most work has taken place on the 'core programmes', which, in the light of experience, were revised in 1994 and are due for further revision at the time of writing. The core programmes were seen as a 'responsibility-building' strategy, which may not 'cure' sex offenders, but should develop their self-control and help them recognise situations where offending might take place. Men with a mental illness, insufficient intelligence or assessed as having 'severe personality disorders' were debarred from the programme (HM Prison Service, 1996, p. 2).

The extended programmes were for those who had normally completed the core programme, but needed extra help for, for example, an inability to control anger or manage stress. The extended programmes were seen as part of a resource-building strategy.

Other programmes have been added since the strategy was first drawn up. The 'booster programme' was a follow up to the core programme for prisoners coming into the last 12 months of their sentence and needing some revision of key treatment concepts and a rehearsal of their relapse prevention plan. An 'adapted core programme' has also been designed to help those prisoners with learning and communication difficulties (HM Prison Service, 1998).

Evaluation of the prison service SOTPs offered to child sex offenders has found evidence of success. As the prison service itself had predicted, an outright 'cure' was never a realistic possibility but the SOTPs did make some progress:

- there was an increase in the level of admittance of sexual offending behaviour;
- offending attitudes were reduced and there was more awareness of the impact on victims;
- overall levels of social competence were increased;
- 67% of the sample evaluated were judged to have shown a treatment effect; and
- longer-term treatment programmes produced better results.
  (Beech *et al.*, 1998).

One controversial element of work with sex offenders in prisons was the use of the device known as the penile plethysmograph (PPG).

Staff assessing sex offenders, either in advance of a treatment programme or during a programme, have sometimes used a PPG. This device consists of a loop of rubber tubing containing a mercury column which is placed around the subject's penis. Instruments monitor the electrical resistance of the mercury as the subject's penis volume increases in response to stimuli he is shown. The PPG had been used by medical staff at Wormwood Scrubs Prison between 1970 and 1981, when questions were asked about the ethics of its use. As with any medical interventions, prisoners are able to consent or withhold consent to its use and it continues to be used.

The Prison Reform Trust has described it as 'a degrading breach of human rights' ('Doubts cast on 'sex crime' tests in prisons' *Independent*, 24 August 1995; see also PRT, 1995).

Post-custodial supervision

Arrangements for leaving prison have long included an element of 'early release', accompanied by a form of continued supervision. Earlier, we noted the Victorian ticket-of-leave system and the Borstal innovation of licensed release. For most of the twentieth century prisoners were given 'remission' on their sentences and since 1967 'parole' arrangements allowed prisoners to be released 'early'. Not everyone has been happy with these arrangements and confusion has sometimes set in. The populist argument has been that prisoners are getting out 'too early' and that 'five years' or 'life' should mean what it says. These arguments become more forcibly expressed when a prisoner so released commits further offences.

The Criminal Justice Act 1991 tried to clarify the arrangements for England and Wales with its philosophy of a sentence being part custodial and part community-based. The offender was not getting out early, but was still having a form of 'punishment' in the community by having his or her freedom curtailed by continued supervision. For either an Automatic Conditional Release (ACR) or a Discretionary Conditional Release (DCR) prisoner, the period of post-custody supervision could be extended if the original offence was a sexual offence (Criminal Justice Act 1991, s. 44). The decision would need to have been made by the judge in open court, perhaps on the advice of a probation officer through a Pre-Sentence Report (Home Office et al., 1995, para. 2.33; see also HMIP, 1998a; paras. 4.14–17).

The Crime and Disorder Act 1998 amended section 44 of the 1991 Act because of worries that sexual offenders were not getting sufficient periods of time under supervision after being released from custody; it introduced arrangements for 'extended supervision'. The 1998 Act gave courts the power to impose extended sentences (other than life sentences) on violent and sexual offenders, with the sentence being conceived as an aggregate of two elements – the 'custodial term' and the 'extension period' of supervision under licence. The maximum length of the extension period is ten years for sex offenders and five years for violent offenders and is, therefore, a significant development of post-release supervisory arrangements for prisoners considered 'high risk' (Crime and Disorder Act 1998, ss. 58–66 (England and Wales) and ss. 86–88 (Scotland)). Discharge arrangements exist in Scotland to allow for the early release of short-term prisoners (under four years) with the possibility of a 'supervised release order' covering the last part of their sentence; the courts must stipulate the need for this order at the time of passing sentence.

Life sentence prisoners are subject to a different release system. Life sentences are classified as either 'mandatory' or 'discretionary'. A mandatory sentence is fixed by law and gives the judge no discretion; it applies in cases of murder and, since 1 October 1998 in England and Wales, when a person has committed a second serious violent or sexual offence (Crime (Sentences) Act 1997, s. 2). Scotland has a similar mandatory life sentence for a second serious offence in the Crime and Punishment (Scotland) Act 1997, section 1. A discretionary life sentence is usually given for serious violent or sexual offences.

Both mandatory and discretionary life prisoners may be liable for early release and follow-up licence or supervision in the community. Whatever the precise legal circumstances of a prisoner's release, it falls to the probation service – or in Scotland the social work department – actually to fulfil the supervision. All prisoners may also be liable to 'extra-licence conditions' being added on to their supervision arrangements.

The imposing of extra-licence conditions is made after discussion between the supervising authorities and the prison governor or Parole Board.

The 1995 edition of the National Standards listed the sort of conditions that could be insisted on, and these included conditions of particular relevance to sex offenders:

- not to engage in any work or other organised activity involving a person under a given age, either on a professional or voluntary basis;
- not to reside in the same household as any child under a given age, or
- not to seek to approach or communicate with family members including children without permission of the supervising officer.

(Home Office *et al.*, 1995, s. 7, Annex A)

Particular note was to be taken of child protection issues during these discussions (*ibid*, paras. 7.20–21, 7.24). The 2000 edition of the National Standards is less specific on the conditions and the child protection issues.

The decision to add on extra-licence conditions for sex offenders is made after an assessment of the prisoner's progress in custody and the likelihood of any continuing risk they may pose. The decision also takes into account the views of the offender's victim or victims.

In the late 1980s, pressure was starting to build that victims should know when an offender was due for release from prison, and should have their views taken into account regarding any post-custody conditions imposed on the offender. The aim was to remove any possibility of the victim accidentally bumping into the offender in the same street when they did not even know he had been released. In 1993, a 14-year-old boy had committed suicide in Mid Glamorgan when he found out that his sexual assailant was coming out of prison ('Boy hanged himself over fear of sex offender's release' *The Times*, 11 November 1993).

An unsuccessful attempt was made to amend the Criminal Justice and Public Order Act 1994 to make it a statutory requirement to notify victims of release dates (HC Debs, 28 March 1994, cols. 747–56). Instead, reformers had to content themselves with administrative guidance that this should be done.

Victims were to be contacted during the initial part of an offender's prison sentence and given general information about likely timescales of custody and release considerations. Nearer to the time of release, they were to be contacted again and invited to comment on any conditions of release which might be imposed. The victim had to accept that a prisoner was entitled to know the grounds on which release conditions are decided, but in exceptional circumstances the victims' concerns could be withheld (Home Office, 1995b; see also Home Office, 2000, C3 and ACOP/Victim Support, 1996).

Before a child sex offender leaves prison, a check is made on the home address he says he will be going to live at to ensure the safety of any children who may be living there. The system whereby this is done applies to anyone who has committed *any* offence against a child and not just sexual offences. In effect, the systems cover any offence against a child listed in Schedule 1 to the Children and Young Persons Act 1933, giving the offender the shorthand name of being a 'Schedule 1 offender'. A similar list in Scotland, started by the Children and Young Persons (Scotland) Act 1937, is now contained in Schedule 1 to the Criminal Procedure (Scotland) Act 1995, and for Northern Ireland in Schedule 1 to the Children and Young Persons Act (Northern Ireland) 1968 (see Tables 6.1, 6.2 and 6.3).

The origins of these checks on home arrangements can be traced back to the 1960s, when a Home Office circular confirmed that the police would notify local authorities when a person was convicted of incest, a sexual offence from the list of 'Schedule 1 offences' or any offence involving cruelty or ill-treatment of a child, whenever it was believed a child at risk was still living in the household; the notification took place whether or not the sentence was a custodial one.

The circular also revealed that it had been the practice 'for many years' to notify local authorities when people convicted of incest offences were leaving prison; the circular now widened the categories of offenders and extended the provisions to those receiving non-custodial sentences (Home Office, 1964, para. 6–7).

Offences listed in Schedule 1 to the Children and Young Persons Act 1933 ('Schedule 1 Offences') in England and Wales

Common law offences:
• The murder of a child or young person under 18
• Common assault and battery

Offences Against the Person Act 1861:
s. 5 Manslaughter of a child or young person under 18
s. 27 The abandonment or exposure of a child under two so as to endanger its life or health

Infant Life (Preservation) Act 1929:
s. 1 Child destruction

Children and Young Persons Act 1933:
s. 1   Cruelty to (including assault, ill treatment or neglect) a person under 16
s. 3   Allowing a person under 16 to be in a brothel
s. 4   Causing or allowing a person under 16 to be used for begging
s. 11 Exposing a child under seven to risk of burning
s. 23 Allowing a person under 16 to take part in a dangerous performance

Infanticide Act 1938:
s. 1   Infanticide

Sexual Offences Act 1956:
s. 1   Rape (or attempted rape) of a girl aged under 18
s. 2   Procurement (or attempted procurement) of a girl under 18 by threats
s. 3   Procurement of a girl under 18 by false pretences
s. 4   Administering drugs to a girl under 18 to obtain or facilitate intercourse
s. 5   Intercourse (or attempted intercourse) with a girl under 13
s. 6   Intercourse (or attempted intercourse) with a girl between 13 and 16
s. 7   Intercourse (or attempted intercourse) with a mentally deficient girl under 18
s. 10 Incest (or attempt to commit incest) by a man against a female, where the victim is under 18
s. 11 Incest (or attempt to commit incest) by a woman, where the victim is under 18
s. 12 Buggery (or attempt to commit buggery) with a person under 18
s. 13 Indecency between men where one or both is under 18
s. 14 Indecent assault on a girl under 18
s. 15 Indecent assault on a male under 18
s. 16 Assault with intent to commit buggery
s. 19 Abduction of an unmarried girl under 18 from parent or guardian
s. 20 Abduction of an unmarried girl under 16 from parent or guardian
s. 22 Causing (or attempting to cause) prostitution of a girl under 18
s. 23 Procuration (or attempted procuration) of a girl under 18
s. 24 Detention of a girl under 18 in brothel or other premises
s. 25 Permitting a girl under 13 to use premises for intercourse
s. 26 Permitting a girl between 13 and 16 to use premises for intercourse
s. 28 Causing or encouraging prostitution of, intercourse with, or indecent assault on, a girl under 16

Indecency with Children Act 1960:
s. 1   Indecent conduct towards a child under 14

Suicide Act 1961:
s. 2   Aiding, abetting, counselling or procuring the suicide of a person under 18

Other Offences:
Any other offence involving bodily injury to a person under 18

Table 6.1

Offences listed in Schedule 1 to the Criminal Procedure (Scotland) Act 1995 ('Schedule 1 Offences') for Scotland

Criminal Law (Consolidation) (Scotland) Act 1995:

s. 1   Incest
s. 2   Intercourse with a step-child
s. 3   Intercourse of a person in position of trust with a child under 16
s. 5   Unlawful sexual intercourse (or attempted intercourse) with a girl under the age of 16 years
s. 6   Indecent behaviour towards a girl aged between 12 years and 16 years
s. 7(1)   Procuring unlawful sexual intercourse or for the purpose of prostitution
s. 7(2)(3) Procuring by threats etc.
s. 8   Abduction of a girl, or unlawful detention with the intent to have sexual intercourse
s. 9   Permitting a girl under the age of (a) 13 and (b) 16 to use premises for sexual intercourse
s. 10   Causing or encouraging the seduction or prostitution etc. of a girl under the age of 16 years
s. 12   Allowing a child (aged between 4 years and 15 years) to live in a brothel
s. 13   Procuring or being party to the commission of a homosexual act in certain circumstances (i.e. person under 16)

Children and Young Persons (Scotland) Act 1937 (as amended by the Sexual Offences (Scotland) Act 1976):

s. 12 Cruelty to a child or young person under the age of 16 years
s. 15 Causing or allowing persons under 16 years of age to be used for begging
s. 22 Exposing children under 7 years of age to risk of burning or scalding
s. 33 Prohibiting of persons under 16 years of age taking part in performances endangering life or limb

Any other offence involving bodily injury to a child under the age of 17 years

Any offence involving the use of lewd, indecent, or libidinous practices or behaviour towards a child under the age of 17 years.

Table 6.2

Offences listed in Schedule 1 to the Children and Young Persons (NI) Act 1968 ('Schedule 1 Offences') for Northern Ireland

Common law offences:
- The murder of manslaughter of a child or young person
- Infanticide
- Aiding, abetting, counselling or procuring the suicide of a child or young person

Offences Against the Person Act 1861:
s. 27 Abandoning a child. Exposing a child whereby life is endangered
s. 55 Abduction of a girl under 16 years of age

or if a child or young person is involved:
s. 42 Common assault or battery
s. 43 Aggravated assault on females and boys under 14
s. 52 Indecent assault on a female
s. 61 Sodomy, which is intercourse by rectum
s. 62 Attempted sodomy, assault with intent to commit same, or any indecent assault upon a male, which is attempting the intercourse described above and includes the indecent assault for that purpose

Criminal Law Amendment Act 1885:
s. 2(1) Procuring – taking a female being a child or young person away against her will for the purpose of sexual intercourse with any person anywhere
s. 2(2) Procuring – taking a female being a child or young person away against her will for the purpose of making her a prostitute
s. 2(3) Procuring a child or young person to leave UK to become an inmate of a brothel
s. 2(4) Procuring a child or young person to leave place of abode to become an inmate of a brothel
s. 3(1) Procuring as described at above by threats or intimidation
s. 3(2) Procuring as described at above by deceit, false pretences etc
s. 3(3) Procuring as described at above by using drugs
s. 4 Sexual intercourse with a girl under 14 years
s. 5 Sexual intercourse with a girl under 17 years
s. 6(2) Inducing a girl under 17 years to resort to premises for sexual activity
s. 7 Abducting a girl under 17 years for the purposes of sexual intercourse
s. 8(1)&(2) Unlawful detention for sexual purposes of any girl under 17 years in any premises or in a brothel. Taking away victim's clothes or other property would amount to detention
s. 11 A male committing an act of gross indecency in a public place with another male under 17 years or assisting in the commission of that act
s. 20(4) Assault, ill treatment of a person under 16 where the person convicted is interested in any sum of money payable in the even of the death of the person under 16

Punishment of Incest Act 1908:
s. 1   Male person having sexual intercourse with granddaughter, daughter, sister, half-sister or mother in respect of a child or young person
s. 2   Female person of 16 years and over allowing a person of the relationship mentioned at (1) above to have intercourse with her, where the person is a child or young person
s. 3   Attempts to commit any such offence
s. 4   Upon conviction before any court of any male of an offence under this section to attempt to commit same against any female under 17 years the court has the power to divest the offender of all authority over such female

Mental Health (NI) Order 1986:
Art. 122   Having unlawful sexual intercourse with a girl or woman suffering from severe mental handicap
Procuring a child or woman for the purpose of above
Causing or encouraging prostitution of any girl or woman suffering from severe mental handicap
Inducing or suffering a girl or woman to be on premises for the purposes of the above
Making or causing to be taken a girl or woman out of possession of parent or other person having lawful care for the purposes of the above
Art. 123   An officer on the staff of a hospital or nursing home or a guardian appointed under the Mental Health Order:
   – having unlawful sexual intercourse with a girl or woman receiving treatment for a mental disorder; or
   – committing a homosexual act with or in relation to a boy or man receiving treatment for a mental disorder

Children and Young Person (NI) Act 1968:
s. 20   Cruelty to a child or young person under 16 by a person that age or over
s. 21   Causing or encouraging seduction or prostitution of a girl under 17 years by a person having custody or care of her
s. 22   Acts of gross indecency with a child or young person or inciting a child or young person to commit acts of gross indecency
s. 23   Allowing a child or young person of 4 years or more in a brothel.
s. 24   Causing or allowing persons under 16 years to be used for begging.
s. 29   Exposing children under 12 years to risk of burning

Children (NI) Order 1995:
Art. 147(2) in respect of a contravention of Article 141 of that Order:
Prohibition against persons under 16 years taking part in performances endangering life or limb.

Any attempt to commit against a child or young person an offence under:
Offences Against the Person Act 1861 (sections 61 or 62)
Criminal Law Amendment Act 1885

Punishment of Incest Act 1908
Mental Health (NI) Order 1986
    Articles 122 and 123

Any offence under:
Child Abduction (NI) Order 1985

Table 6.3

These systems were reviewed in 1975 after the death of another child at the hands of her parent. John Auckland from South Yorkshire had served time in Durham Prison after killing his 15-month-old daughter in 1968. On his release, Auckland had gone on to kill a second daughter, only nine weeks old, in 1974. One feature that bothered the committee of inquiry set up to examine what had happened was the lack of communication between the prison and community-based services, which could have alerted practitioners that a child was potentially at risk; the committee recommended:

> when a prisoner is discharged who has been serving a sentence for an offence against a child we would like to see more information passed to agencies outside the prison so that they may be aware of any potential risk and take steps to guard against it.
>
> (DHSS, 1975, para. 251)

The new arrangements now entered into consisted of a triangular exchange of information between prison, probation service and social services department to identify any possible child protection questions arising from the address at which a prisoner says he is going to live on release; a parallel exchange of information was to go from the prison medical officers to the offender's GP. The new system was just for prisoners who had offended against children in the home but covered all offences and not just sexual offences (DHSS, 1978); the Scottish Office issued similar guidance to cover its prisons and Departments of Social Work (Scottish Office, 1979) as did Northern Ireland's Department of Health and Social Services (1978).

These arrangements were revised again in 1994 for England and Wales. The centrality of the Schedule 1 list was made clear and the list duly reproduced in Annex A of the new guidance. The age of the victims was raised from 17 to 18, and there was a new emphasis on telling prisoners that they had been identified and classified as 'Schedule 1 Offenders'. Notification systems to local authorities and the probation service were more or less unchanged, but the notification system to GPs seemed to have disappeared from consideration (HM Prison Service, 1994).

One change from the 1978 circular was the widening of the class of offenders by dropping the requirement that the offence had to have been committed in the home. The new arrangements reflected the widening concerns of the time to cover all offences against children, irrespective of where those offences were committed. The prison service said this was simply to implement more fully the recommendations of the Auckland Report published 19 years earlier (*ibid*, para. 2), but the 1991 inquiry report into the Staffordshire 'pindown' affair had recommended such widening (Levy and Kahan, 1991, para. 16.33) and in many areas the change was just ratifying what was already happening in practice.

Similar arrangements exist in Scotland, where liaison is between the prison and the local authority social work department (Scottish Office, 1994). A joint initiative in Glasgow between the City Council's Housing Department and Social Work Department has led to the placing of a housing caseworker in Barlinnie Prison to help prisoners on discharge to find suitable accommodation at the same time as minimising the risk to public safety. In Northern Ireland, the release arrangements for Schedule 1 offenders are now to be found in a 1996 circular (DHSS (NI), 1996a) which has been revised once and is currently being revised again for inclusion in their wider manual on the assessment and risk of sex offenders.

Despite the guidance and the National Standards, reports still singled out the supervision of sex offenders as a group who gave 'particular concern' (HMIP, 1995, para. 5.4). From the public point of view it was the spectre of the sex offender under supervision who chose to re-offend that caused anxiety.

Further Home Office thinking on supervision came in the 1996 Consultation Document's suggestion for post-custody 'extended supervision' periods and even indefinite supervision for the rest of an offender's life (Home Office, 1996a). Liberty wanted clear statutory provisions outlining when it might be imposed in order to avoid its arbitrary imposition; essentially, this should only be when it was necessary to protect the public from serious harm (Liberty, 1996, paras. 72–94). More fundamentally, NACRO asked why people needing lifetime supervision in order to protect the public had been given determinate sentences in the first place and not life sentences (NACRO, 1996a, p. 4).

One further attempt to manage the release of prisoners back into the community in a structured way was the decision to use electronic monitoring to allow prisoners to complete their sentences in the community. Until now, electronic monitoring had been restricted to a condition of bail or as an enforcement of curfews. The idea now was to use it on prisoners in custody in England and Wales to help them out of prison.

The use of electronic monitoring in this way was known as the Home Detention Curfew (HDC) scheme, and provisions for it had been included in the Crime and Disorder Act 1998, sections 99–105. Three private companies provided the service covering the North, the South and the Midlands and Wales respectively. The scheme was launched on 28 January 1999, with all prisoners being first subject to a risk assessment and a home circumstances report by the Probation Service (HC Debs, 28 January 1999, col. 353 WA).

Sex offenders required to register under the Sex Offenders Act 1997 could be eligible for HDC but only in 'exceptional circumstances'. Any such offenders were to be subjected to a 'rigorous enhanced risk assessment' and would only be released following authorisation by the Director General of the Prison Service (HC Debs, 25 February 1999, 72369 WA).

Indeterminate sentences

Some offenders leaving prison, with or without post-custody supervision, have been considered to be still dangerous and liable to re-offend. Policy makers have started to look at the possibility of 'indeterminate sentences' for those people, which would result in their release only when the risk they pose has been reduced and they are no longer considered dangerous.

When Graham Seddon, a 48-year-old convicted sex offender, was released from prison, he was found wandering the streets of Liverpool with a teddy bear, toys and colouring pencils and reportedly stalking children. Here was a seemingly dangerous person who fell outside of the remit of the Mental Health Act because psychiatrists said he was not treatable and yet the police could not intervene because he had not actually committed an offence ('Shunned child-sex attacker cannot be held' *The Times*, 5 July 1997).

The spectre arose of the sex offender leaving prison at the end of his sentence just as dangerous as when he went in, and openly telling prison officers of his criminal intent toward children when he left. In the case of Seddon, the matter was raised in the Commons:

> Mr O'Hara: [the sex offender] can be released into the community under mental health law and be beyond the reach of the forces of criminal law until he commits an offence – not any old offence, but a sexual offence against a child. In other words, until he ruins a child's life, ruins a family and blights a community.
>
> (HC Debs, 7 July 1997, col. 748)

For the Home Office, Minister of State, Alun Michael, acknowledged the seriousness of the problem and said the Government 'was looking closely at the scope for further action on mental health and the criminal law to safeguard the public from people with apparently untreatable psychopathic disorders, particularly in relation to sexual offences' (HC

Debs, 7 July 1997, col. 749); a few months later it was reported that a working party from the Home Office and the Department of Health was actively working on plans to introduce indeterminate sentences for specified sex offences and later, that the same working party was also looking at possible changes to mental health legislation and how agencies could better respond to the release from prison of dangerous sex offenders ('Worst paedophiles may never go free as loopholes targeted' *Scotsman*, 6 May 1998).

The problem with mental health legislation was that the Mental Health Act 1983 for England and Wales allowed for compulsory detention of patients only if they were 'treatable' and their mental disorder made the Act applicable. The Act applied to those with a 'psychopathic disorder' (Mental Health Act 1983, s. 1(2)), but whether the disorder was treatable was open to debate. The courts had looked at the question and laid down 'principles of treatability' for the psychopath, which included the prevention of deterioration, the stabilisation of the patient and the general provision of care under medical guidance, but the debate continued (*R v. Cannons Park Mental Health Review Tribunal, ex p. A* [1994] 3 WLR 630).

In Scotland, the provisions of the Mental Health (Scotland) Act 1984 were similarly worded and were tested by a man held in Carstairs secure hospital. Alexander Reid claimed that his detention should be stopped because he was receiving no treatment. This case went as far as the House of Lords, which again took the line that the word 'treatment' has a very wide definition and could include prevention of deterioration (*Reid v. Secretary for Scotland* (1998) Independent, 8 December); Reid was not released.

During 1998, the terminology changed somewhat and instead of 'psychopaths' some sex offenders were now termed as having 'severe personality disorders'.

Tony Butler, Chief Constable of Gloucestershire and spokesperson on sex offending for the Association of Chief Police Officers, explained the problem:

> The assessment of these people is that they have a severe personality disorder which isn't treatable, therefore they don't fall within the terms of the Mental Health Act, therefore they can't be detained under current provisions in mental hospitals . . . we need a new law.
>
> (cited in 'Police seek new powers to hold freed paedophiles'
> PA Report, 3 June 1998)

'Personality disorders' and 'anti-social personality disorders' had been around for some time, but the addition of the word 'severe' now found favour, and not least when applied to sex offenders. The dilemma was that those with severe personality disorders might not be detained for mental health treatment and might not be arrested because they had committed no crime, although, given time, they almost certainly would commit a crime – including possibly a sexual crime. Although it meant anticipating crimes before they were committed and taking action against people who had not actually done anything, the search was on for a 'third way' to deal with people with severe personality disorders.

Various States in the US had introduced 'civil confinement' laws to achieve this end. Sexual offenders, known as 'sexual predators', coming to the end of a prison sentence but still assessed as potentially dangerous and continuing to pose a risk, could be detained by civil confinement when their prison sentence had ended. Washington State had been amongst the first to pass such laws in 1990 (Greenlees, 1991), but in 1997, when Kansas appealed to the Supreme Court for a test of the legitimacy of what they were doing, some 38 other States joined them in the Appeal. The Supreme Court duly ruled in their favour in a narrow decision ('Sex offenders in the US face being locked up for life' *Guardian*, 26 June 1997; see also Janus, 1996).

In the UK, the debate was spurred on by the problematic release from prison of Robert Oliver and Sydney Cooke amidst popular protest that had deteriorated into mob violence, and by the conviction of Michael Stone in 1998 for the killing of Lyn Russell and her daughter Megan. It was claimed that Stone had sought psychiatric in-patient treatment days before he attacked his victims, but had been refused admission because he was 'untreatable'.

Home Secretary Jack Straw announced his decision to legislate to introduce indeterminate sentences comparable to the Americans' civil confinement in February 1999. Straw explained that:

> There is . . . a group of dangerous and severe personality disordered individuals from whom the public at present are not properly protected, and who are restrained effectively neither by the criminal law nor by the provisions of the Mental Health Acts. The propensity of such people to commit the most serious sexual and violent acts may be well known and well recorded . . . the Government propose that there should be new legal powers for the indeterminate but reviewable detention of dangerous personality disordered individuals.
> (HC Debs, 15 February 1999, cols. 601–02)

Straw said he would be producing a consultation document jointly with the Secretary of State for Health outlining the options for a new legal framework.

The statement of the Home Secretary was greeted with a wave of concern at the idea of locking up people indefinitely when they had not done anything, and simply on the evidence of medical experts (see e.g. 'Psychopaths plan will hit "the innocent"' *Independent*, 16 February

1999; Valios, 1999; Donnelly, 1999). The social work journal *Community Care* warned that the proposals should not be dismissed out of hand, 'but his consultation had better be good' ('A protection racket' *Community Care*, Editorial, 18–24 February 1999).

Meanwhile, Scotland headed out on a similar path with the formation of its own committee, chaired by the Hon. Lord MacLean, to look into the sentencing and treatment of serious violent and sexual offenders, including those with personality disorders. The MacLean Committee was formed in March 1999 (see Scottish Office, 1999).

The Home Office consultation paper duly appeared in July 1999, and set out two broad options. Option A built on existing arrangements by amending the Mental Health Act 1983, extending the use of discretionary life sentence and introducing new powers of compulsory supervision. Option B involved new laws on indeterminate detention in new facilities separate from mainstream prison and hospital facilities; a new specialist service would be needed to manage these offenders who by now had their own new acronym – DSPD or Dangerous Severely Personality Disordered People (Home Office, 1999b).

The urgency of the debate took on a new dimension when an investigation was ordered into the release of Noel Ruddle from Carstairs secure hospital in Scotland. This time the courts had ruled that Ruddle could not be detained because he was not receiving effective treatment, although he had previously killed a person and was considered dangerous ('Inquiry ordered into release of rifle killer' *Guardian*, 3 August 1999). In February 2000, the Home Office announced the first pilot assessment procedures for dangerous and severely personality disordered prisoners would start at Whitemoor Prison (Home Office, 2000c).

Summary

The court has the choice of custodial or community sentences for sex offenders and the amount of 'personal information' available on the offender and any risk assessment based on that information will determine which form of sentence is appropriate; mandatory custodial sentences are now prescribed for the more serious sexual offender. The probation service is the agency responsible for ensuring that community sentences are completed and that any conditions attached are complied with; the same agency has responsibility for any post-custody period of supervision in the community and, again, for ensuring that any conditions are met. Within a custodial prison sentence, Sex Offender Treatment Programmes are well established and a degree of continuity is now required between the practitioners within the prison walls and those outside to ensure that positive work is carried out. The efficient exchange of 'personal information' on the offender is a critical part of ensuring compliance, preventing relapse and protecting the public.

The continuing fear of the 'dangerous' person in the community has led politicians to look for new ways of containing such people, whether or not they have committed an offence, in order to protect the public. At present, proposals have been put forward for so-called indeterminate sentences for those considered 'dangerous'; how this risk will be assessed and by whom will be a critical factor for this new 'third way'.

7

A sex offender 'register'

The 1996 Home Office Consultation Document on the 'Sentencing and Supervision of Sex Offenders' proposed that convicted sex offenders should be required to notify the police every time they change address. In effect, a register of all convicted sex offenders would be compiled and kept up to date by the offenders themselves (Home Office, 1996a, paras. 41–62).

Origins of a policy

The idea of a register of sex offenders or paedophiles had been circulating in social work and police circles for some time. The British Association of Social Workers had proposed one at its AGM as early as 1988 ('Controversy of Motions on Registers' *Social Work Today*, 13 March 1988). In 1991, it was reported that a small number of local authority social services departments were already keeping their own local registers of known offenders against children in their area; the departments were warned about the limitations of such lists or registers, especially in terms of keeping it up to date, and were specifically told that lists of suspects 'should not be held' (Home Office *et al.*, 1991, paras. 6.52–6.54).

At this time, it was also becoming apparent that the traditional division of labour between social workers (concentrating on the child) and the police (concentrating on the abusing adult) was breaking down. Social workers were increasingly viewing child protection in wider terms and looking at the perpetrators of the abuse as the starting point for child protection. The Children Act 1989, Schedule 2, paragraph 5, for example, had introduced powers to enable Social Services departments to help adults leave households, rather than the children, following incidents of suspected abuse. The Department of Health reported many local authorities and other child protection agencies expressing concern about the lack of an offender register and the difficulties they had tracking known and suspected child abusers. The London Borough of Brent, for example, wondered 'why the police have no Borough based register of (Schedule 1) offenders' (Department of Health, 1995, para. 23.2 and paras. 49–49.4).

The police, for their part, had increasingly to look at children and the child's perspective in their work. The police have long had powers to remove children from households if necessary, and joint child protection work had been given an impetus by the 1987 'Cleveland affair' and subsequent inquiry report (see Chapters 4 and 8). The introduction of specialist 'Child Protection Units' and joint arrangements for videoing children's testimony had drawn the police yet further into this area of work. The creation of the Paedophile Section at the National Criminal Intelligence Service had confirmed a national dimension to this work, but the police were still self-critical about their inability to collate and use intelligence on child sexual abuse and sex offenders as effectively as they would wish (Hughes *et al.*, 1996).

Meanwhile, the American experience of sex offender registers was beginning to filter across the Atlantic to both police and child care practitioners. The general public also picked up on it and its associated ideas of letting the community know where these offenders lived. The father of Sophie Hook, a seven-year-old sexually abused and killed in North Wales, voiced his support for the idea of a register when it emerged that the police had kept a 'close eye' on the man who had attacked his daughter for a number of years before the abduction and murder ('Murdered girl's father supports register plans' *Independent*, 20 July 1996).

Within police circles, it was the Police Superintendents' Association which was the most vocal in calling for a UK sex offender register, and after two unsuccessful private Members' Bills had been introduced to the House of Commons, the Government proposed a register in its 1996 Consultation Document.

The idea of registration itself was premised on three arguments:

• it would help police identify suspects after a crime;
• it could help prevent crimes; and
• it might act as a deterrent.

(Home Office, 1996a, para. 43)

The 1996 Consultation Document put forward other ideas apart from that of the register. It proposed the extended supervision of sex offenders on leaving prison (see Chapter 6); the extension of DNA testing (see Chapter 4); the prohibiting of sex offenders seeking work with children (see Chapter 8); and the prevention of witness statements being used as pornography (see Chapter 5). The consultation period ran from June to August 1996, and the Home Office received some 238 formal responses, with the overwhelming majority being in favour of all proposals; 87 per cent of respondents favoured the idea of the 'register' (HC Debs, 25 October 1996, WA 965). In political terms the opposition party of the day was in almost total agreement (Labour Party, 1996).

The registration proposals included the requirement that the offender should notify the police of any change of address within 21 days of the change; special arrangements would exist for those of 'no fixed abode'. The requirement to notify would continue, depending on the severity of the original sentence. Any custodial sentence of more than 30 months meant a life time's requirement to notify changes to the police. Lesser sentences would result in time periods equivalent to the provisions of the Rehabilitation of Offenders Act 1974, which allow convictions to be 'spent' in designated circumstances after a given length of time, and all these time periods would be halved for juvenile offenders.

Details registered with the police were to be stored on the Police National Computer (PNC) and it was signalled that other agencies engaged in child protection activities might have access to it. Although unnamed, the assumption was that this meant the probation service, social services departments and other agencies such as the National Society for the Prevention of Cruelty to Children (NSPCC).

The Consultation Document was silent on the role of the police in using the information they received and on how they might disseminate it. It said nothing on the role of the police in actively enforcing the registration requirements and said only that defaulters should be fined up to £1,000 or imprisoned for a month.

The Bill

The Government published its Sex Offenders Bill on 18 December 1996. The Bill as published was divided into two parts. Part 1 was concerned with the registration arrangements and Part 2 with the commission of sexual offences outside the UK (sex tourism). For present purposes, we will focus on Part 1 (see Chapter 4 for further details on Part 2) which in turn constituted five clauses, specifying the offenders who will have to register and for how long they will be required to register; describing what information must be supplied and how; making failure to comply with the requirements an offence; outlining the position of young offenders (i.e. under 18 years); and empowering courts to issue certificates stating details of the court hearing.

How did the Bill compare to the Consultation Document? First we should note that, although putting forward options, the Consultation Document did contain what might be called the Government's 'preferred options'. These included, firstly, that we did actually have registration requirements, and that their duration should match that of the Rehabilitation of Offenders Act 1974. Failure to register was to be an absolute offence and the provisions should not be retrospective; the offence of failing to register would be a summary one. Registration was to be in the locality where the offender lived. The Government wanted access to the information on record to be given to those engaged in child protection activities.

The Bill reflected all of these 'preferred options', although again had nothing directly to say on the subject of allowing access to registered information. It is true to say that the Government continually held the line on all its preferred options, although some were held more easily than others.

Outside of parliamentary circles, there was a general consensus in the press on the need for the Bill. Having created the 'monsters' and the 'sex fiends', the press could not really 'disinvent' their creations and a register seemed a good way of tracking them. Only Matthew Parris in *The Times* was willing to criticise the Bill, which he dismissed as meaningless: 'there is no reason for this Bill. No reason at all. It is simply a piece of electioneering' (Parris, 1997); a general election was just four months away.

On some matters the Bill revealed some interesting departures from the Consultation Document. The Document, for example, had never mentioned offenders who had received a police caution as being in need of going on the register; the Bill now included such offenders and made them liable to register.

As we saw in the last chapter, part of the rationale for a caution was that the offence was 'atypical' and unlikely to be repeated. The rationale for registration was, if anything, the opposite; it was a typical offence and the offender was likely to do it again. As Liberty put it:

> Cautions are supposed to act as a salutary warning . . . if cautions are being used for sexual offences deemed so serious that they merit notification, they should not be.
>
> (Liberty, 1997a, para. 1.5)

The Bill also departed from the Consultation Document on the question of qualifying offences. The Document's original 32 offences in England and Wales were reduced in the Bill to just 14. Omissions include bigamy, abduction, soliciting by a man, giving drugs to facilitate intercourse, incest by a woman, causing prostitution of a woman and others. Indecent exposure, which is a category of offence for which the Home Office keeps records, appeared neither in the Consultation Document nor the Bill, even though some professionals believe it often to be a precursor to more serious sexual offending (see e.g. Worrall, 1997, p. 121; HMIP, 1998a, para. 5.58).

A comparison of the qualifying offences in the Consultation Document and the Bill is further confused by the fact that the former is directed only at England and Wales, whilst the Bill is intent on registration requirements for the whole of the UK. This meant further lists of qualifying offences for Scotland and Northern Ireland had to be added to the Bill because of the different laws in those two countries. In Scotland, the very age of criminal responsibility is two years below that in England, making registration a possibility for a Scottish youth (aged eight and upwards) whereas in England, a youth of the same age, doing the same things, cannot even have committed an offence (the age of criminal responsibility being ten).

The Bill made no mention of the four-week 'holiday period' that the Consultation Document thought was a reasonable period during which registration elsewhere is not required. It also made no reference to people of no fixed abode.

The parliamentary debate

The Parliamentary Committee discussions on the Bill – Standing Committee D – made no reference to the qualifying offences left out from the Consultation Document. No reference was made to the decision to include cautions as well as convictions as criteria for registering (although that issue was raised earlier, outside the Committee, on the main floor of the House (HC Debs, 27 January 1997, col. 60)). The debate did not consider the ways in which the police would ensure verification and compliance with requirements to register and whether or not they would be active in searching out defaulters and, if so, what extra resources they would need. It is, however, worth noting that right at the outset of discussions, the Government announced an increase in the penalties that would apply for failing to register – the original £1,000 rising to £5,000 and one month in prison rising to six months in prison – and that this decision was made 'after receiving representations from the police . . . to stop sex offenders from flouting the registration requirements' (Home Office, 1997 b; HC Debs, 27 January 1997, cols. 30–31).

In summary, the main criticisms aimed at the Bill as it passed through the House of Commons were the facts that: (i) it was not retrospective; (ii) it was unclear on how the police should use the information registered with them, and whether or not this might include public disclosure; and (iii) in concentrating only on convicted sex offenders it was missing out thousands of other potentially dangerous people. A number of minor amendments were made on the basis of discussions, but these three areas deserve closer attention.

(i) The Bill was not retrospective

Critics suggested this was a major loophole. Although the requirement to register would fall on anyone currently in contact with the criminal justice system (i.e. in custody or under supervision), those who had served their sentences and completed any supervision were not liable to registration. Peter Thurnham, for the Liberal Democrats, argued that up to 50,000 convicted offenders would thereby escape registration and 'it will be decades, therefore, before the register is of use to anyone'

(HC Debs, 27 January 1997, col. 31). And 'for now it only nibbles at the problems – it is a mouse of a Bill given the large numbers of previously convicted offenders' (HC Debs, Standing Committee D, 4 February 1997, col. 7); later estimates suggested that there were some 100,000 convicted sex offenders in the community (Marshall, 1997).

Thurnham's attempts to get the Bill amended were unsuccessful. Timothy Kirkhope, for the Government, argued that it would be impossible to make the Bill retrospective as 'in most cases we have no idea where those people are now living' and tracking them down would be an intolerable burden on the police and in any case, 'publicly unacceptable' (HC Debs, Standing Committee D, 4 February 1997, col. 9).

(ii) The Bill was unclear on how the police should use the information registered with them, and whether or not this might include public disclosure

What concerned the critics was the idea that registration might become simply a passive listing of names and addresses, and the Bill gave no indication of a more active registration process.

Kirkhope had made clear that registration was not a form of punishment, but was an administrative function that offered protection to the public. What worried critics was the lack of any necessary link from the police-held register to those activities that protected the public. No guidance was being given to the police in the Bill and there seemed no interconnection with a number of other child protection practitioners and databases (e.g. the Department of Health Consultancy Service – see Chapter 8) that had existed for a number of years.

Whilst the Government was happy with existing inter-agency arrangements to protect children and the public, efforts were made in Standing Committee D to make the Government more proactive, and to take a lead in saying how these systems should be integrated in more 'proactive packages'. For the opposition, Alun Michael argued for amendments to put the Secretary of State under a duty to provide either a Code of Practice or other guidance to the police and other agencies as to how information might be properly shared and acted on. At the very least, other public lists could automatically be updated on the basis of new registration information, but, perhaps more importantly, the police might be empowered to pass information they held on to other agencies. These proposals were resisted, with confidence being expressed in the existing arrangements.

It was at this juncture that debate moved on to the ideas of the public having access to the 'register' – what the Americans called 'community notification'. They had been raised earlier by the Conservative MP, David Mellor:

We shall have to confront the problem . . . that is already quite commonplace in America. The problem is that, if the police have a right to know, why do the public not have a right to know?

(HC Debs, 27 January 1997, col. 42)

Within the committee the discussion was more circumspect:

The general issue concerns the pressure for community notification or Megan's Law or whatever title is given.

(HC Debs, Standing Committee D,
4 February 1997, col. 56)

In effect, the Committee wished to discuss community notification only to be able to say it had considered it and felt it inappropriate for the UK. Instead, it was felt that more considered disclosure was in order, and that this could possibly include disclosure to one or two particular members of the community, but not to everyone. In the main, information of this nature would remain for use by professionals and practitioners only. Alun Michael concluded that 'we may learn some lessons from the United States [but] . . . our culture, law, police service and other services are different' (HC Debs, Standing Committee D, 4 February 1997, col. 58).

The debate was simultaneously carried on outside Parliament, and at one point Home Secretary Michael Howard looked willing to concede on community notification ('Howard set to name sex offenders' *Guardian*, 12 February 1997). The police, however, remained opposed to the idea and the Association of Chief Police Officers (ACPO) through its spokesperson, Tony Butler, Chief Constable of Gloucestershire, let it be known that notification on a wide scale would be 'fraught with dangers' and 'could drive offenders underground'. *The Times* believed:

Last night's statement from ACPO is likely to thwart the mounting pressure on Michael Howard to allow neighbourhoods to be told when convicted child sex offenders move in. Mr. Howard, who said earlier this week that he was giving serious consideration to the idea, is unlikely to want to press ahead in the face of opposition from senior police officers.

('Police Chiefs oppose plan to advertise paedophiles'
The Times, 15 February 1997)

Back within the confines of Parliament, attempts to amend the Sex Offenders Bill and introduce regulations and guidance on the use of information were unsuccessful. The status quo would remain, and existing channels of communication and areas of discretion were felt sufficient for the time being.

(iii) In concentrating only on convicted sex offenders the Bill was missing out thousands of other potentially dangerous people

Standing Committee D heard that convicted sex offenders could be as small a proportion of the total as five or ten per cent; truly this was the tip of the proverbial iceberg.

Arguments were made that other information systems could have suspects within them and that links to the 'register' would only enhance the general child protection package. In turn, it was held that some suitably validated suspects ought to be required to register. This could include, for example, those subject to injunctions in the civil courts, or those whose own children had been made subject to care orders in the same courts (HC Debs, Standing Committee D, 4 February 1997, cols. 16–17). The campaign group ACHE (Action on Child Exploitation) was reported to be behind these proposed amendments ('Communities take action on abusers' *Community Care*, 16–22 January 1997).

Reference was also made to the position of local authority child protection workers who had access to registers of children at risk and who often had access to their own compilation of offenders *and suspects* in a given locality. On occasion, this local authority information on offenders and suspects had been given out to particularly vulnerable members of the public, and the courts had ruled that this was the right and proper thing to do if it protected children (see below). It seemed anomalous to some parliamentarians that local authorities appeared under a duty to give out this information, yet received no guidance on storing it. What records were kept were of their own volition.

The amendments were again lost, with the Government arguing that not only could a 'suspect' not be forced to register, but 'civil courts have totally different standards of proof and can apply different sanctions'; for the moment, 'the proper forum for determining whether there will be a conviction and thereby a registration must remain the criminal courts' (HC Debs, Standing Committee D, 4 February 1997, cols. 17–18).

At the end of the three House of Commons Readings and the Committee stage, Part 1 of the Bill had received a number of amendments, but had remained untouched by the three main arguments referred to.

The Sex Offenders Act received its Royal Assent on 21 March 1997, and imposed the requirement on designated sex offenders to notify the police of their name and address and any changes to these details should they take place. The required details are much less than asked for by most American states.

The Sex Offenders Act 1997

The Sex Offenders Act, Section 1 applies to all those convicted or cautioned of an offence outlined in Schedule 1 to the Act. It also applies to those with mental health problems where there has been no finding of guilt, but a Hospital Order has been made under the 1983 Mental Health Act for reasons of insanity or being unfit to plead, and where an offence as listed in Schedule 1 would otherwise have been committed. The time period for which the Act applies is outlined in Table 7.1 (mirroring the Rehabilitation of Offenders Act 1974) and time periods commence from the day of conviction or caution, with subsequent time spent in custody or hospital being discounted.

Sex Offenders Act 'registration' periods

Sentence	Notification period
Life imprisonment	Indefinite
Admitted to hospital subject to a restriction order	Indefinite
30 months or more imprisonment	Indefinite
Imprisonment for less than 30 months but more that 6 months	10 years
6 months or less imprisonment	7 years
Admitted to a hospital not subject to a restriction order	7 years
A non-custodial sentence (including guardianship under the Mental Health Act 1983)	
or	
a Caution	5 years

Table 7.1

A restriction order attached to a hospital order usually implies the offence has been particularly serious, and means the restricted patient cannot be discharged from hospital by doctors without the consent of the Home Secretary; any discharge can also have conditions attached to it (Mental Health Act 1983, s. 41–42; see also Home Office/DHSS, 1987).

Schedule 1 to the Act lists the offences to which the 'register' will apply and divides into three parts for (1) the law in England and Wales, (2) the law in Scotland, and (3) the law in Northern Ireland.

Section 2 of the Act sets out the details which must be given to the police within 14 days of conviction or change of address. As we have seen, these are simply the person's name, or any other used names, and address. Date of birth and address at the time of conviction or caution may be required for purposes of identification. The details may be given in person, by a visit to a police station, or in writing. The police must also be notified if the offender stays at any other address for longer than two weeks in a 12-month period (s. 2(2)). Any failure to comply is punishable by a fine up to £5,000 and/or a period of imprisonment of up to six months.

For sex offenders below the age of 18, all registration periods were to be halved (s. 4). The NSPCC was amongst those that thought young offenders should not be on it at all and that alternative arrangements should have been devised (NSPCC, 1997); the Sexual Offences Act 1993 had abolished the presumption that boys under the age of 14 were incapable of sexual intercourse, and enabled charges to be brought against them for the first time for rape and various forms of unlawful sexual intercourse. All sentencing courts were also to be empowered to issue certificates for any age of offender as a form of evidence that they knew they had to comply with notification requirements (s. 5).

Implementing the Sex Offenders Act 1997

The Home Office published guidance on the new law for the police in England, Wales and Northern Ireland (Home Office, 1997c) and the Scottish Office did the same for Scotland (Scottish Office, 1997a; see also NIO, 1997). The Home Office Police Research Group circulated information on how registers worked in the US (Hebenton and Thomas, 1997). Further guidance was sent to local authority social services and social work departments and to hospital managers (NHS Executive, 1997; Scottish Office, 1997b). The stated intention was that this initial guidance was to be considered as 'interim' in status whilst further work continued on drawing in other agencies, such as housing departments and schools (see also Department of Health, 1998a, para. 3.9).

The interim guidance of 1997 (Home Office, 1997c) limited itself to taking practitioners through the Act and its implications and adding on an Appendix A entitled 'Managing Information Acquired under the Provisions of the Sex Offenders Act 1997'. The guidance had little to say on resource implications for the police, or exactly how they were supposed to ensure compliance and verification that addresses were being accurately notified. The guidance also skirted around another snag to implementation that had arisen: the new systems required the police to be given advance warning that a new name had been added to the register of those required to notify. Whilst the courts and prisons were happy routinely to advise the police each time a new name was added, the medical profession and health care professionals had been more reluctant. They interpreted the Act as putting duties and responsibilities on no-one other than the offender and, therefore, it followed that the offender should consent to them notifying the police, and that they would only override a withholding of consent if they judged it to be in the public interest. They disliked the idea of 'automatic' routine notifications. The NHS Executive could only say that it 'anticipated that the need to protect the public means that the balance will generally come down in favour of notification' (NHS Executive, 1997, Part A, para. 8).

The follow-up to the interim guidance appeared in draft form in the summer of 1999 and was described as drawing 'upon the good practices established since the 1997 Act came into force' (Home Office PSTU, 1999). This guidance reaffirmed the idea that information exchange between agencies was to be integrated into risk assessment and management systems, and was not to be seen as an end in itself. It also emphasised the principle that information sharing should 'be rooted in the powers and duties of any agency' (*ibid*, para. 13) and not be exchanged just because another agency requested it; in other language this might be termed the 'need to know principle'. The police and other agencies were encouraged to draw up inter-agency protocols outlining how information would be shared (*ibid*, paras. 17–18).

The register itself was, from the outset, to be held on the Police National Computer (PNC), which is available to all forces in the UK through 5,000 terminals from its operational headquarters in Hendon, North London. The PNC is accountable through its directorate to the Police Information Technology Organization (PITO) (see also Chapter 4).

The PNC holds various databases, or 'applications', for the police, including missing or wanted persons, registered car ownership, stolen vehicles and an index to fingerprints held; it handles between 150,000 and 200,000 inquiries a day. In 1995, work began on converting the national collection of criminal records from card index and microfiche to the PNC through Project PHOENIX (Police Home Office Extended Names Index). The PHOENIX application now has the subtitle 'The Criminal Justice Record Service', to reflect the growing use of criminal records throughout the criminal justice system, and beyond, for such activities as pre-employment screening (see Chapter 8). It was a relatively simple matter to designate sex offenders on the PHOENIX systems and state whether they were 'registered' or 'unregistered' and, in effect, create the sex offender 'register'.

Individual police forces can create their own local versions of the register and, through such innovative software as QUEST (Questioning Using Extended Search Techniques), can even pinpoint sex offenders around smaller geographic areas or areas near the scene of a crime; QUEST was launched in July 1998 ('QUEST for suspects' *PITO News*, February 1997, p. 12).

The sex offender register had come on-line on 1 September 1997, and despite some early concerns that offenders were not complying and were 'going to ground', and despite various pessimistic headlines from the press, by the end of the year, 88 per cent of offenders had notified the police of their whereabouts as requested; this amounted to 3,365 out of a possible 4,524 ('Hundreds of violent sex offenders go to ground' *Sunday Telegraph*, 28 December 1997). The youngest reported registrant in England has been a 10-year-old boy from Cheshire ('Boy of 10 to be registered as sex offender for assault' *Guardian*, 24 August 1999) and in Scotland, an 11-year-old Edinburgh boy ('Boy put on adult list' *Community Care*, 4–10 March 1999). By February 1999, 8,161 individuals were recorded on the PNC as having notified the police in England and Wales of their details (HC Debs, 12 May 1999, col. 159 WA).

On the first anniversary of the register, the professional social work journal *Community Care* conducted a survey of 200 social workers on their views of the register's usefulness. Most thought it had had a limited effect and had diverted public attention to the 'stranger danger', away from the much greater threat to children from their own immediate or extended families. Half of the social workers were in favour of 'community notification', and a majority also thought that a register of suspects and those found 'guilty' in civil actions should be kept, as well as those convicted before September 1997 (Valios, 1998); a more systematic evaluation is still being completed (HC Debs, 28 June 1999, col. 85 WA).

Community notification

'Community notification' is the American terminology for the public disclosure of sex offender register information. As we have noted, such disclosures were debated during the parliamentary discussions on the Bill, and then the Home Office guidance was able to shed some more light on the public's right to know whether sex offenders were living amongst them.

Even before the register was implemented, the police had been giving information to the public about known sex offenders. Information on child sex offenders had been disclosed to schools in Hampshire ('Schools sent lists of local paedophiles' *Daily Telegraph*, 18 October 1996) and schools in Wales had duly passed such information on to parents when they had received it ('Teachers name paedophile in letter to parents' *Independent*, 30 November 1996). The London Borough of Lewisham had also disclosed information it had on paedophiles to the general public living in the Forest Hill area of south London ('In the name of the children' *Independent*, 28 March 1997). When the North Wales Police disclosed information on two sex offenders to a local community in the summer of 1997, the two people concerned sought a judicial review of the police decision.

The community notification debate was fuelled by reports of 'Megan's Law' coming across the Atlantic from the US. In 1994, a Federal law (The Jacob Wetterling Crimes against Children and Sexually Violent Offender Registration Act) had required all States of the US to enact laws creating a sex offender register; many had already had them in place for a number of years, but now all were mandated to do so. In 1996, Megan's Law amended the Jacob Wetterling Act to require all States to allow public access to, or dissemination of, the registration information. The Law was named after Megan Kanka, a seven-year-old girl from New Jersey who had been sexually assaulted and killed by a convicted sex offender living in the same street as his victim and her family.

In the summer of 1997, as the UK public debate on community notification continued, Megan's mother, Maureen Kanka, visited the UK to add her weight to the calls for the sex offender register to be public. Tabloid headlines became ever more strident (e.g. '"I'll name the sex beasts" – Straw's pledge to parents as perverts head for freedom' *Daily Mirror*, 9 June 1997) and more controversy came with news of a book from Australia, based on press reports of court hearings, naming all that country's known sex offenders (Coddington, 1997); an earlier version had covered New Zealand and now one was being promised for the UK ('This woman has named 600 child abusers in Australia. Now she plans a British list' *Independent*, 19 February 1997).

In July, the High Court judicial review ruled that the North Wales Police had acted properly in alerting people of the conviction record of their neighbours (*R v. Chief Constable of North Wales Police, ex p. AB* (1997) Times, 14 July). At the time, the police had actually used press cuttings of the offender's court appearance that had been kept on file to try to avoid accusations of improper disclosure; using press cuttings meant the information was already in the public domain.

The High Court stated that, as a general principle, and in terms of good public administration, the police should keep criminal record histories confidential, but if there was specific reason to disclose, then they could do so. The specific reason would normally be a risk to the public, and that risk should be carefully assessed before any such disclosure. The High Court cited the Home Office guidance to the police regarding criminal record disclosures for pre-employment screening purposes (see Chapter 8) and an earlier case in Derbyshire, when the police had been found to have acted properly in circulating a photograph of a convicted shoplifter to certain shopkeepers to enable them to take preventive action (*Hellewell v. Chief Constable of Derbyshire* [1995] 1 WLR 804).

The two people involved later unsuccessfully appealed against the decision. The Court of Appeal discussed the sensitive balance involved in disclosure, the problems of accommodating such offenders and the possibility of others being driven 'underground'. They also thought the police should discuss disclosures with offenders in advance of taking any action, but that ultimately the police had to adopt 'a proactive rather than a reactive policy for dealing with offenders who had committed offences against children in the past' (*R v. Chief Constable of North Wales Police, ex p. Thorpe* (1998) Times, 23 March).

An earlier judicial review, not referred to in the ruling but which arguably had some relevance, was that made in favour of Devon County Council when that local authority's Social Services Department was found to have been acting properly in disclosing information to the public about a man only *suspected* of having committed sex offences against children (*R v. Devon CC, ex p. L* [1991] 2 FLR; see Hayes, 1992 for a critique of this ruling).

Although the North Wales case did not relate specifically to sex offender 'register' information – the Act was as yet unimplemented – the 1997 Home Office guidance was able to draw on the judgment – and indeed the *Devon* judgment – to give its interim guidance to the police on public disclosure from the register, whilst at the same time affirming its belief that authoritative statements on the law were for the courts and not the Home Office. The police were to make a risk assessment, involving other agencies as appropriate, make the information available to identified people and be prepared to give advice on how that information should be used (Home Office, 1997c, Appendix A; see also Power, 1999).

Not everyone was happy with this arrangement, and head teachers were one group who were confused by the idea of being given information by the police which they might then be unable to pass on to parents. Tony Butler, ACPO's spokesperson on sex offending, did not see it so starkly. Teachers might acquire information as part of a risk management strategy with other agencies and to that extent they could be faced with moral dilemmas – unfortunately, that was simply 'the reality of this area' ('Heads attack guidelines on naming paedophiles' *Daily Telegraph*, 12 August 1997); the National Association of Head Teachers and ACPO later agreed a Protocol on how information disclosed to schools should be handled, with the police being given the 'guiding' role (NAHT/ACPO, 1998).

As we have seen, the Home Office eventually produced a follow-up draft guidance on information disclosure and sex offenders to its interim 1997 version. This document covered inter-agency exchanges of information for risk analysis purposes, but also gave advice on disclosures to third parties including members of the public. Such disclosures were expected to be exceptional and only as part of an individual sex offender's risk management plan (Home Office PSTU, 1999, paras. 21–27).

Just how big the problems of disclosure were to be was revealed within a few weeks by the case of the 43-year-old discharged sex offender,

Robert Oliver. Oliver was assessed as dangerous and as posing a continuing risk, and so his neighbours were duly notified. Oliver moved on to a series of addresses in Swindon, Manchester, Liverpool, Dublin, London and, finally, Brighton. Each time the community was notified of his whereabouts, he effectively became an 'outlaw'. Each time, he had to keep moving for his own safety and eventually sought protective custody with the East Sussex police before moving on to 'secure accommodation' in a Midlands hospital. One mother in Brighton summed up the position: 'This man must go. I don't care where he goes to, as long as he goes away from here' ('Police keep watch on freed paedophile' *Independent*, 15 October 1997; see also Bowman *et al.*, 1998 for a detailed account of the professional response to Oliver during his stay in East Sussex).

The same thing happened in April 1998, when Sydney Cooke, a 71-year-old co-offender with Oliver, was released. He too started his return to the community living in a London police station and agreeing to voluntary supervision and voluntary electronic monitoring. Cooke soon moved to the West Country and, when word got out that he was in the Bristol area, a crowd of several hundred besieged the police station in the Knowle West area of the city. A peaceful protest deteriorated when bottles and stones were thrown and the police in riot gear had to be deployed. Similar spontaneous protests against Cooke had taken place in Bridgewater, Yeovil and Minehead in Somerset ('Riot police called in as paedophile protest turns violent' *PA News*, 24 April 1998).

The local services charged with managing these difficult situations – not to mention paying for them – turned to national Government for support and direction. The Government responded by announcing a new national steering group consisting of representatives from the police, the Home Office and the probation service that would, in future:

> . . . identify high profile, difficult to place, sex offenders while they are still in prison and assess their release plans . . . oversee their handling [after they have been released, and] . . . consider any funding necessary to meet likely additional accommodation costs.

> (HL Debs, 5 May 1998, col. 479)

By August 1998, the steering group was reported to be looking at the possibility of a new national facility dedicated to housing released men who have sexually abused children, catering for up to 50 serious offenders ('National Centre proposed to house 50 freed paedophiles' *Independent*, 13 August 1998).

In the absence of any immediate prospect of such a unit, a village in Oxfordshire made its own arrangements when it heard that a former resident sex offender, Rhys Hughes, intended to come home when released from prison. The residents of Sonning Common planned to establish a 24-hour help-line and a network of 'child safety houses' with window stickers advising children it was a safe place to go if need be. One 31-year-old mother, who lived in the village, warned 'He will be persecuted. People will drive him out and rightly so. I don't think he has got any right to be here' ('Return of the Beast' *Oxford Times*, 28 August 1998). The moral dilemmas were not going to go away. Later reports said Hughes would also go into secure accommodation for his own protection.

Nottingham was eventually chosen as the site for the promised 'national centre'. In May 1999, Home Secretary Jack Straw announced plans for a unit within the grounds of Nottingham Prison to house newly released sex offenders. The residents would be free citizens, but subject to supervision when they left the unit and safe from vigilante attacks when inside it. Local people immediately protested against the siting of the new facility, pointing out the nature of the residential area and the number of schools nearby ('Prison blockade attempts to stop paedophile unit' *Guardian*, 16 June 1999), but within a few weeks the protest had died down and the first resident moved in ('Paedophile unit gets first resident' *Guardian*, 20 July 1999).

Risk assessment

An unforeseen consequence of the Sex Offenders Act and the ruling that police could disclose information to the public on particularly dangerous sex offenders, was the requirement now to set up mechanisms to help police decide when they actually had a dangerous offender on their hands. Risk assessments had to be made on all new entrants on the register if the police were to fulfil their newly acquired duty to inform the public. Risk assessment required information exchange and, as we have seen, draft guidance on how this should take place was produced in August 1999 (Home Office PSTU, 1999).

Some police forces already had public protection panels where they met with other agencies, such as the probation service, to make multi-agency risk assessments of all kinds of dangerous offenders. Others were moving into the risk assessment business for the first time and wide variations were being noted:

> The most obvious example of lack of consistency was the way in which risk assessments were being undertaken. The speed with which the Act was introduced had led many forces to adopt their own risk assessment models drawing on the experience and expertise of specialists outside the police service.
>
> (HMIC, 1999, para. 5.10)

The Association of Chief Police Officers has moved in response to these criticisms and developed a standardised risk-assessment model, based on the good practice of various forces and the model used by the Home Office's Prison Department. By June 1999, it was reported that the model had been sent to all forces and training needs were being determined ('Risk model approved to identify sex re-offenders' *Policing Today* 5(2), June 1999, p. 9).

In Northern Ireland, a multi-agency working group on sex offenders, involving the RUC, the probation service and social services, started meeting to produce their own procedures for the assessment and management of risk; a first draft appeared in June 1998, and was still being worked on at the time of writing.

Apart from informing decisions on public disclosure, the risk assessment might also be expected to lead to appropriate action from the police by way of surveillance or other 'protective' action. In fact, reports from the Metropolitan police suggest that sometimes there is no such action forthcoming from the police simply due to lack of resources ('Checks on paedophiles collapse' *Evening Standard*, 12 October 1998).

Summary

The UK sex offender 'register' came about after a fairly short period of debate during 1996-97, which resulted in the Sex Offenders Act 1997. The 'register' is held by the police and offenders are required to notify them of any change of address within two weeks of that change. This can be seen as yet another exercise in data accumulation by the police on sex offenders (see also Chapter 4) with the innovation, this time, that the data subject himself has a responsibility for keeping the quality of the information at a high level.

Implementation of the Sex Offenders Act has, arguably, given the police a good deal of extra work they were not anticipating. The legal duty falls on the offender to notify the police of any changes, but additional work to ensure verification and compliance was not altogether seen. Yet a further unforeseen consequence was the need to inform local communities when a particularly high-risk offender was known to be living in their midst; the police had to engage in multi-agency operations with other practitioners (e.g. the probation service) in order to assess that risk before making a decision on community notification. Having disclosed 'personal information' on known offenders, the police then had to deal with the – often hostile – public outcry against having this offender in their locality.

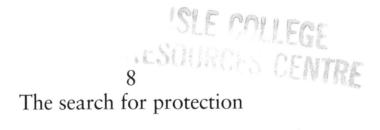

8
The search for protection

The wish to make our lives safer and our communities safer places in which to live is something that everyone would vote for, just as they would vote for a sunny day. The ideas of 'public protection', including 'child protection', and 'community safety' are very much vogue phrases at the beginning of the new century.

All the work of the criminal justice system described in Chapters 4 to 6 could be said to contribute to public protection by identifying, incapacitating and circumscribing the activities of offenders. In this chapter, we consider measures put in place outside the criminal justice system which seek to protect communities and individuals from becoming victims of sexual offending.

Much of the work on crime prevention and community safety has been premised on the idea that criminals calculate when to act by weighing up the opportunities and the likelihood of being caught. Whilst such a 'calculation' model might work for sex offenders, the fear was present that this kind of offending was 'different' and could happen any time and anywhere.

The approach taken here draws on the ideas of the 'continuum' of sexual assault and the divide that has been drawn between the private and the public space. We examine, therefore, first the measures available to protect people in their own home, including the local child protection arrangements to ensure the safety of children within their families, secondly, the protective arrangements that exist in the workplace and in terms of pre-employment screening for work involving children, and, finally, what provisions there are for making the wider community a safer place.

Protection in the home
Children and young people

The protection of children and young people from physical, sexual, emotional and psychological abuse within their own homes has always posed problems for the state. In general terms, we believe that families and households should be free to bring up their children the way they want to without 'official' interference. If it becomes apparent that they are struggling to meet identified levels of 'reasonable care', we can offer them 'family support', such as substitute day care for children or other support in cash or kind, on the basis that the children are still best cared for by their family. If the official concerns rise sufficiently, the state may intervene to protect the child by removing it from the household and providing it with alternative care in the way of a foster home or children's home. Whilst these different positions on intervention are easily set down and an awareness of children's rights brought into play, the actual implementation of child protection arrangements is invariably a complex arrangement.

The death of seven-year-old Maria Colwell at the hands of her step-father, and the resulting public inquiry in 1974 to investigate why this had been allowed to happen, led in turn to the formalisation of child protection arrangements as we know them today. In England and Wales, Area Child Protection Committees (originally called Area Review Committees) were established, with a membership of senior officers from all the local agencies in a local authority area likely to have contact with children and thereby child protection matters. Written policies and procedures were to be produced to guide all the practitioners of those local agencies in what to do in individual cases, and child protection conferences (originally called case conferences) were to be convened when there was a need to discuss a particular child or family (DHSS, 1974, 1976). These arrangements are still in place today, albeit with various additions and refurbishments (Home Office *et al.*, 1991).

In Scotland, the Area Child Protection Committees were called simply Child Protection Committees, but in Northern Ireland they took the same name as in England and Wales; Northern Ireland has a second tier committee called a Child Protection Panel.

In simple legal terms, the police investigate the criminal aspects of abuse and social workers take on the civil aspects of child care, with a duty to investigate and invoke procedures of child protection. Social workers act under the relevant laws for England and Wales (Children Act 1989), Scotland (Children (Scotland) Act 1995) and Northern Ireland (Children (Northern Ireland) Order 1995).

An innovative feature of the 1974 arrangements was the introduction of the local child protection register (originally named the 'at risk' or 'child abuse' register), containing the names of all children in the area where there were child protection issues. The decision to add a name to the register was to be made by a child protection conference; any local agency with concerns for a child could then check the register to see if they were already 'known' and who the 'key' or 'focal' agency was. The register was to be maintained by the social services department or the local branch of the NSPCC. In essence, the register is a mechanism to help identify the child where there are child protection concerns.

Child protection registers have been criticised for being bureaucratic, costly and ineffective (Morris *et al.*, 1980, pp. 116–17) and for being potentially oppressive and even 'dangerous' (*R v. Norfolk CC, ex p. M* [1989] 2 All ER 359). Nonetheless, they have stood the test of time and remain key features of local child protection arrangements.

In keeping with the times, the original guidance on registers said nothing about sexual abuse as a category of abuse needing registration. The sexual abuse of children in the 1970s was still well hidden away, and social workers, along with everyone else, were culturally blind to its existence. Further guidance on registers issued by the DHSS in 1980 made a point of saying that sexual abuse was a category that did *not* need registering (DHSS, 1980, para. 2).

This position changed slowly during the first half of the 1980s, as child sexual abuse was 'discovered' by those professionals who had previously overlooked it. Until that time, the sexual abuse of children would need to have been clear cut and obvious for action to have been taken. Then, as it came onto the professional agenda, practitioners could start to recognise symptoms, listen more carefully to children and seek out sexual abuse. Early surveys also suggested that Area Review Committees were unprepared for child sex abuse and had few procedures in place to guide practitioners (Mrazek *et al.*, 1983; see also Porter, 1984).

In Leeds, two paediatricians drew attention to a medical test they thought revealed evidence – or at least suspicions – of a child having been sexually abused. This was the so-called Anal Dilation Test, whereby the anal canal remained open on buttock separation rather than closing (Hobbs and Wynne, 1986). The same two paediatricians also noted the increasing awareness of child sexual abuse, which they attributed to 'doctors and others' willingness to confront an old problem and intervene' (Hobbs and Wynne, 1987).

In 1986 the BBC had broadcast its television programme 'Childwatch', presented by Esther Rantzen, to launch the organisation 'Childline'. Childline was a national freephone help-line for children to phone if they felt they were in trouble or danger. Appropriate referrals were passed on to the relevant social services departments (see Macleod, 1996). Parton has described the Childwatch programme, which had an estimated audience of 16.5 million, as:

> . . . a significant intervention into the issue of child abuse, particularly in relation to sexual abuse . . . its timing in late 1986 served both to raise public awareness but also disturb many previously untouched sensitivities.
>
> (Parton, 1991, p. 93)

This slowly wakening awareness of child sexual abuse was to be given a massive push the following year with the breaking of what came to be known as the 'Cleveland affair'. In June 1987, local newspapers in the Middlesbrough area started reporting huge numbers of children being admitted to local hospitals diagnosed by doctors as having been sexually abused. By the end of the month, the story had gone national and questions were being asked in the House of Commons ('Hand over your children, Council orders parents of 200 youngsters' *Daily Mail*, 23 June 1987).

The paediatricians in Cleveland, using the Anal Dilatation Test described in Leeds, had found enormous numbers of children displaying the symptoms of sexual abuse. The local social workers had accepted the diagnosis, but the police had not. A major inquiry was mounted to try and unravel what had gone on, and child sexual abuse would never be hidden away again.

The Cleveland Report sensitised all child care practitioners to the possibility of sexual abuse. All agencies were asked to rethink their approach to the problem, work more closely with parents and make better efforts at meaningful inter-agency work. The report reasserted the primacy of the child with its famous dictum:

> . . . there is a danger that in looking to the welfare of the children believed to be the victims of sexual abuse the children themselves may be overlooked. The child is a person and not an object of concern.
>
> (Cleveland Report, 1988, p. 245)

A flurry of Whitehall circulars were sent to the police, schools and everyone working with children. The key phrase was that we were all 'working together' for the child (DHSS, 1988; Home Office, 1988; DHSS (NI), 1989; Scottish Office, 1989a). Sexual abuse was a category of abuse that needed to be registered.

Work on the new Children Bill being put before Parliament was held up so that the Cleveland Report recommendations could be included where appropriate, and the new Children Act finally became law in 1989. Implementation came two years later, when the 1988 guidance was reconstituted, yet again, to include sexual abuse defined as the 'actual or likely sexual exploitation of a child or adolescent' and with new guidance on abuse within children's homes and organised abuse (Home Office *et al.*, 1991).

The new guidance also made reference to abuse of children by groups using 'bizarre or ritualised behaviour, sometimes associated with particular "belief" systems' (*ibid*, para. 5.26.2). Everyone else referred to this as 'ritual' or 'satanic' abuse.

The essence of ritual or satanic abuse was that the child was sexually abused as part of some ceremony hinting at 'witchcraft', which was supposed to frighten the child into silence when it was over. The arguments over whether or not this sort of abuse actually did exist or was imagined continued for some years, most infamously in the Orkney Islands, where a number of children were removed from home on the basis of such allegations (Clyde Report, 1992). The Government commissioned independent research to look at the phenomenon, but the research concluded that there was little evidence for it (La Fontaine, 1994; see also La Fontaine, 1998); the most recent edition of 'Working Together' omits any reference at all to this kind of abuse (Department of Health, 1999).

In other parts of the UK, changes in the law led to changes in the published guidance on child protection arrangements. In Northern Ireland, the Children (Northern Ireland) Order 1995 was followed by a new 'Protocol for Joint Investigation' (1996), produced by all the agencies that would make those investigations and in Scotland, the Children (Scotland) Act 1995 was accompanied by a series of books of regulations and guidance.

Today, the routine investigation of child sexual abuse goes on within social services departments as a normal part of their work. Most of this goes on unheralded and makes no headlines; an account of this work using research based on 40 case studies can be found in Corby (1998).

Women and adults

The position of women victims of violence and sexual assault in the home has traditionally been held to be different to that of children. Interventions to assist were held back by beliefs that adults, unlike children, had a choice in where they lived and the capacity to seek help when they needed it. On top of that, the 'privacy' of the home was held up as a 'cordon sanitaire' to keep official intervention at bay.

The women's movement of the early 1970s challenged this orthodoxy with its intellectual analysis of the subordinate position of women, their economic dependency and inability to leave a household as easily as the apologists would suggest. This analysis was backed up by listening to the experiences of women who had been subject to violence and sexual assault in the home. Some of these women now sought help from the newly formed 'safe houses' or 'refuges' for women wanting to leave violent husbands or partners.

Throughout this period, refuges were opened across the country. Run by women for women, they were co-ordinated nationally through the Women's Aid organisation. Today there are more than 300 Women's Aid groups throughout the UK, giving shelter to more than 70,000 women and children each year. Some refuges specialise in taking black and ethnic minority women. Priority is given to the acceptance of a woman's story without disbelief or questioning (Hague and Malos, 1998).

Rape Crisis Centres are another victims' group, taking a feminist analysis and run by women for women. The centres offer counselling services, telephone help lines and general support. They have a campaigning and educational side to dispel some of the myths of rape, such as the idea that it is only committed by strangers in public places. The campaigning also challenges the very use of the word 'victim':

> . . . there is not a separate category of women called victims –
> just as there [is] no category of men who are not 'rapists' –
> victim takes away our power and contributes to the idea that
> men can 'prey' on women.
>
> (London Rape Crisis Centre, 1984)

The preferred terminology was 'survivor'. The campaigning work of the Rape Crisis Centres was not always appreciated, especially in its early days. A survey of police surgeons found 36 per cent of the respondents thought they were a 'poor idea' and one doctor thought:

> The predominant role of a Rape Crisis Centre should be
> supportive. Unfortunately they are frequently used as feminist
> political tools using rape and rape victims in the general cause
> of women's lib rather than vice versa.
>
> (Geis *et al.*, 1978)

This antagonism to a contentious and challenging approach has been held to be responsible for Rape Crisis Centres not getting mainstream Government support, unlike the more 'respectable' Victim Support organisation (Williams, 1999, p. 94). Nonetheless, Rape Crisis has also stood the test of time and is now co-ordinated through a central Rape Crisis Federation based in Nottingham.

In the early 1970s, the campaigning work and 'raising of consciousness' carried out by the women's movement was drawn into the deliberations of the House of Commons Select Committee on Violence in the Family, and recommendations on new laws were examined.

Civil legislation followed, in the form of the Domestic Violence and Matrimonial Proceedings Act 1976 and relevant parts of the Domestic Proceedings and Magistrates' Courts Act 1978. Women could now apply for injunctions against a man molesting or attacking them even if he continued to live with them in the same house. Men ignoring the injunctions were in contempt of court, but sometimes powers of arrest were also added to them. The Housing (Homeless Persons) Act 1977 allowed women leaving violent men to be designated as homeless and in 'priority need' of alternative emergency accommodation (these same provisions are now in the Housing Act 1996, Part VII).

The laws were a great step forward, although implementation was not always as useful as it might have been (see e.g. Atkins and Hoggett, 1984). In 1988 (Scotland) and 1992 (England and Wales), the common law recognised for the first time that rape could take place within marriage and a number of women became causes célèbres when they had killed violent men after years of domestic violence. Arguments started to be made that these women could not use the defence of 'provocation' as easily as men could because of the wording of the law (see e.g. HC Debs, 23 January 1992, cols. 477–78).

After a Law Commission (1992) report on the subject and another Select Committee examination, the Family Law Act 1996, Part IV overhauled the civil law on domestic violence for England and Wales. The new Act made it easier to obtain 'occupation orders' and 'non-molestation orders' to protect the 'health, safety and well-being' of applicants, and made it easier to have a power of arrest attached to breach of these orders (Department of Health, 1997a).

The Family Law Act also contained provisions to protect children by amending the Children Act 1989. In future, the courts would have a discretionary power to add an 'exclusion requirement' to any emergency protection orders or interim care orders they were making on children. The 'exclusion requirement' meant the suspected adult abuser could be ordered to leave a household, or stay away from a household or even to stay outside of a defined area in which a house is situated (Children Act 1989, ss. 38A and 44A, as amended by Family Law Act 1996, s. 52 and Sch. 6). Until now the existing Children Act powers (in Sch. 2, para. 5) had been discretionary only for the assailant. These new public, rather than private, powers replicated powers provided for in Scotland with the 'exclusion orders' available under the Children (Scotland) Act 1995, section 76.

Although the Family Law Act improved the lot of those in relationships, the media had discovered at this time a new phenomenon that affected those not in relationships. The 'stalker' had become a new 'hate figure' who needed to be dealt with. In essence, this was the label attached to people – usually men, but not always – who seemed to be compulsively obsessed by a particular person who in turn became the target of letters, phone calls, personal calls and all manner of other interventions, despite it being made quite clear that these were all unwelcome. Of themselves, these acts were not necessarily hostile or violent, although their cumulative effect was harmful; new laws were going to be needed.

The Government responded with a consultation paper (Home Office/Lord Chancellor's Department, 1996) and followed this up with the Protection From Harassment Act 1997. The Act provided for both civil and criminal remedies, and came into force on 16 June 1997. The civil remedy introduced new restraining injunctions and two new criminal offences of causing harassment and the more serious charge of causing fear of violence.

Legal measures apart, the Government does appear to be directing more attention to violence against women, with activities such as the

Home Office's 'Break the Chain' campaign and the consultation papers produced in all parts of the UK by the respective Government offices (Scottish Office, 1998a; NIO, 1999; Cabinet Office/Home Office, 1999).

Protection in the workplace

Sexual offending can take place in any workplace, but here we will focus on offending against children in workplaces such as schools, sports clubs and children's homes. In taking this focus, this is not to ignore other workplaces or to avoid what has also been recognised as sexual harassment that can take place anywhere.

Sexual harassment in the workplace has not yet been defined as sexual offending by criminal statutes, although other laws may be used to combat it. It does fall within that concept of the 'continuum' of sexual violence experienced by women, and in its worst forms it may, of course, become a criminal offence recognised by law.

Sexual harassment has been described by the TUC as:

> ... conduct which is *imposed* on another person because of his/her sex. It is *unwanted, unreciprocated* and regarded as *offensive* by the recipient ... it can involve physical contact ranging from unnecessary touching through to rape. It can be verbal – suggestive remarks or 'jokes', sexual propositions, unwanted comments on dress and appearance or verbal abuse of a sexual nature ... leering, displaying pornographic pictures or pin ups, and making suggestive gestures.
>
> (TUC, 1990, emphasis in original)

Despite the neutral gender language in this definition, the TUC is clear that 'sexual harassment is overwhelmingly a problem experienced by women' (*ibid*), and elsewhere the women's group WASH (Women Against Sexual Harassment) has been formed to campaign for better protection for women in the workplace.

Some women who have experienced sexual harassment have used the Sex Discrimination Act 1975 to make an employer liable, whether or not they knew about the harassment. Others have used the employment protection laws to claim 'unfair dismissal' or 'constructive dismissal', with the latter implying a resignation took place only after sexual harassment made working conditions intolerable.

Women – and men – employed in a variety of settings have experienced general violence in the workplace when that work has brought them into contact with members of the public. In a survey carried out by the Trades Union Congress, nurses in the NHS were found to be the most vulnerable sector and, overall, younger women workers were the most likely to be attacked or threatened with attack (Gallagher, 1999).

The sexual exploitation of children in the workplace has been a source of concern for a number of years, especially when that workplace has been providing a form of 'care' or 'education' for children. Here, we consider just some of the prime sites for child abuse in institutional settings and the response that has been made; these workplace sites include schools, boarding schools, children's homes, sports clubs and the church. One popular theory has been that these workplaces act as a 'honey pot', attracting would-be offenders to them because it gives them access to children.

Schools

The worst excesses of violence and oppressive teaching has a special place in British literature, from *Tom Brown's School Days* to the Dickensian creations of Wackford Squeers and Mr Gradgrind. The school is seen as a potential site for the authority of the teacher to be used against the vulnerability of the pupil, and for that imbalance to lead on to possible sexual exploitation. Today, teachers are periodically found guilty of sexual offences against children (see e.g. 'School head jailed for sex assaults' *Independent*, 22 October 1991; 'Teacher jailed for decade of sexual abuse' *Daily Telegraph*, 23 June 1998).

Teachers were one group of employees, however, who thought it had become too easy for children to make allegations of sexual abuse, and that teachers were vulnerable to malicious accusations against which they were unable to defend themselves; any child or young person wanting to 'have a go' at a teacher had only to report inappropriate behaviour, which led to suspension and investigation. The problem was discussed in the House of Commons (HC Debs, 16 January 1992, cols. 1207–16) and Nigel de Gruchy, the General Secretary of the National Association of Schoolmasters Union of Women Teachers (NASUWT), said:

> Nobody wants special treatment for teachers or anyone else.
> But the pendulum has swung too far in the other direction.
> Our figures show that far too many teachers have suffered
> and are suffering from gross breaches of natural justice, often
> perpetrated by mischievous and cunning children.
>
> (NASUWT, 1994)

Mr de Gruchy was speaking at the launch of new guidelines designed by teachers' organisations to clarify the situation for teachers; he regretted that the police and social workers had not been able to sign their names to the guidelines (*ibid*; ATL *et al.*, 1994).

NASUWT claimed it had to deal with 450 investigations against teachers between January 1991 and July 1994, of which 34 resulted in prosecutions and 23 in convictions (NASUWT, 1994, Appendix A). By

April 1991, the figure of 450 had risen to 974, with an overall total of 792 cases finding no grounds for prosecution ('False abuse charges "ruin careers of 350 teachers each year"' *Daily Telegraph*, 10 April 1999).

The complexity of this area was further illustrated in the summer of 1998, when it was discovered that the Health Education Authority was drawing up guidelines to protect children from strong sunlight, which might cause skin cancer.

On behalf of teachers, the Local Government Association jumped in to say the guidelines should not ask teachers to apply sun tan creams to pupils for fear of being accused of child abuse:

> School teachers are very vulnerable to accusations of physical and/or sexual abuse. Their reluctance is well-founded . . . we would counsel strongly against any suggestion that teachers, with or without parental consent, should apply sunscreen products to children in their care.
>
> (LGA, 1998)

Yet more confusion was thrown on the subject when the reported comments of the Chief Inspector of Schools seemed to imply that sex between teachers and pupils was not so harmful and could even be 'educative' ('"Sex between teachers and pupils can be educative" – Schools Chief' *Independent*, 6 February 1999). These comments came just as the Commons was debating the Sexual Offences (Amendment) Bill, which sought to ban any relationships between adults in positions of authority and the children they cared for as an 'abuse of trust' (see below).

The British private boarding school has long held a special place in the popular imagination as a location for the sexual abuse of children. Abuse by teaching staff and other pupils has allegedly been 'covered up', dealt with internally and otherwise 'denied', or else seen as part and parcel of normal life in boarding schools (see e.g. 'Sex abuse "at 75% of boarding schools"' *Independent*, 9 December 1989). The journalist Paul Foot has recalled the 'sadism' of his former housemaster, Anthony Chevenix-Trench, at Shrewsbury School in the 1950s, where 'Trench was assaulting boys in his charge for one reason only: his own sexual gratification' (Foot, 1996).

Foot recalls how Trench moved on to be headmaster at Eton, where his practices continued until he was finally removed from office:

> Throughout the long process of dismissal there was hardly a public whisper about the conduct that had occasioned it. He applied [successfully] for the headmastership of Fettes.
>
> (Foot, 1996)

In the summer of 1990, another headmaster, a mathematics teacher and an English teacher were all imprisoned for sexually assaulting pupils at Crookham Court School in Berkshire ('A shocking abuse of trust' *Independent on Sunday*, 15 July 1990). According to some observers, it was these convictions and the investigation proceeding them that had led to the inclusion of section 87 in the Children Act 1989 ('An Inspector calls' *Guardian*, 31 May 1994).

Section 87 gave local authorities the duty to inspect the residential care provisions of private boarding schools. Starting in 1991, regular inspections are now made to ensure the welfare of the children in any school with more than 50 boarders; the educational side of the school remained the responsibility of HM Inspectorate of Schools. As if to emphasise the importance of this work, an experimental telephone help-line for boarding school children reported receiving over 10,000 calls ('Boarding school abuse help-line gets 10,000 calls' *Observer*, 29 September 1991). The Department of Health published guidance on how the new inspections should work (Department of Health, 1991a).

Sports clubs and voluntary organisations

Sports clubs have also been identified as places where the sexual exploitation of children may take place. The ambition of young sportsmen and women to achieve at the highest levels, together with the authority of the sports coach, has led to situations of 'grooming' and 'entrapment'. The closeness of the young athlete's bond with the adult figure has led some to describe any sexual abuse taking place as 'virtual incest' (Brackenridge, 1997).

A great deal of work in this area has been carried out by Professor Celia Brackenridge at the Leisure and Sport Research Centre at Cheltenham and Gloucester College of Higher Education. Professor Brackenridge has outlined the way in which an initial analysis of sex discrimination in organised sport has led to an understanding of sexual abuse.

The opening of the subject, however, has not been easy and sporting authorities have been, at best, slow to respond (but see e.g. NCF/NSPCC, 1995) and at worst have denied there has been a problem:

> [It] has been indeed a struggle to get the subject out of the ghetto: it is ironic, for example, that during a period when moral panics about 'stranger danger' and sexual abuse have escalated in society at large, many sport and leisure organisations have failed to acknowledge or confront sexual exploitation.
>
> (Brackenridge, 1998)

Despite revelations at the highest levels, including the 17-year prison sentence passed on a former Olympics swimming coach for convictions of rape and indecent assaults ('Swimming chiefs face legal action' *Daily*

Telegraph, 29 September 1995), sports organisations have been criticised for playing down the problem. Arguments summoned against sexual abuse taking place include the idea that overall more people benefit from sport; the problem is exaggerated or 'couldn't happen here'; people who allege it are 'trouble-makers'; and, even if it does take place, it's not the responsibility of the sports authorities (Brackenridge, 1998).

The Football Association is one authority that has included a statement of commitment to child protection in its policies for the development of young players (FA, 1997, Appendix G), and Bristol Rovers was the first professional club to launch its 'Child Safe' programme in early 1999 ('FA hunts out the football sex abusers' *Independent*, 15 February 1999).

The voluntary sector as a whole has had an ambivalent relationship with child protection matters. Voluntary organisations which employ staff to work directly with children are rigorous in their selection and screening of staff. Organisations that literally rely on unpaid volunteers fear such rigour might put people off volunteering, as does the idea of imposing fees for Criminal Conviction Certificates (see below).

In Northern Ireland, it is worth noting that the voluntary sector has been particularly proactive in addressing the problems posed by sex offenders directly. Following criticism when a convicted sex offender managed to get work in the voluntary sector which gave him access to children (DHSS (NI), 1993), the Voluntary Sector Working Group on Sex Offenders was formed. The group has been active since its formation, holding conferences and specialist working parties looking at accommodation, employment, confidentiality and other issues (VSWGSO, 1997a and b).

The church

One particular 'workplace' where child abuse was not anticipated was the church. Unfortunately, a series of scandals has shown that even here children have not been safe.

In the Republic of Ireland, the revelation that 'celibate' priests were abusing children or fathering children was reported to have undermined the very authority of the church:

> ... large numbers of Catholics in Ireland, many disillusioned by scandals within the church, have abandoned regular practice of their faith ... an MRBI poll showed ... more than 90% of Catholics believe controversies involving convicted paedophile priest Fr. Brendan Smyth who has since died, and Bishop Eamon Casey, have damaged the authority of the church.
> ('Scandals undermine Irish Church authority – survey'
> Reuters, 4 February 1998)

134

Bishop Casey had moved to South America following allegations that he had fathered a child (see also ICBA, 1996 and O'Mahony 1996, esp. Chapter 6).

In the UK, a Catholic priest was sentenced to five years imprisonment by Preston Crown Court in September 1997 and another priest received an eight-year sentence at Cardiff Crown Court in December 1998; both had been convicted of sexual offences against children. A Church of England priest from Essex was imprisoned by a Bucharest court in July 1998 for having sex with under-age boys whilst in Romania, and the school chaplain from the private Tonbridge School in Kent was arrested and charged in Germany for importing pornographic videos in May 1998.

What bothered some observers was the apparent ability of the churches to cover up the activities of their employees by moving them to different geographic locations to put off complaints and disrupt investigations. Whether these allegations were true or not remains debatable. The Church of England has produced its own guidance on child protection within church organisations, with particular reference to appointing workers with children (CCPAS, 1998).

Children's homes

Residential care for children unable to live with their families takes many forms but, in essence, they are all children's homes. Most children's homes are run by local authorities through their social services departments, social work departments or Health and Social Services Boards; some children's homes are independent or in the voluntary sector. Children's homes have been accused of providing a haven for the abuse of children.

Reports of sexual crimes against children in residential care came to light from time to time in the 1970s, but were mostly dealt with on an individual basis. It was not seen as the major problem it was to become (see Ferris, 1977 for an interesting account of local authority attitudes to the employment of homosexual people in social services departments at this time).

The slow realisation during the 1980s that children's homes could be prime sites for sexual offending has been described by the former Chief Inspector of Social Services at that time:

> The subject of sex abuse of children in institutions did not really become an issue until the early 1980s . . . and there were tremendous pressures, I think, on everybody in the system at that time, to deny that those of us working in the system and accepted by the community as being devoted to the interests of children were in fact exploiting them and abusing them.
>
> (House of Commons, 1998, para. 799)

In Belfast, there were continuing stories emerging about the Kincora children's home and the long-term abuse of its residents. The Dublin-based *Irish Independent* had first published stories in January 1980 about Kincora being the centre of a homosexual vice-ring, but the true extent of the activities there and the alleged 'cover-ups' continued to mystify for many years (see e.g. Rafferty, 1986).

A 1984 parliamentary review of all forms of care for children, including residential care, made no mention of sexual abuse as a problem area. A passing reference was made to the 'trouble [sic] at the Kincora Boys Hostel' and the need for better complaints systems, and the imbalance between care staff as figures of authority and vulnerable children was noted:

> The risk of abuse of power by social workers and other adults concerned with children in care is . . . sufficiently serious for there to be a need for some means by which a child can contact, without fear of reprisal, their local authority parent.
>
> (House of Commons, 1984, para. 364;
> see also paras. 360–65)

The pre-employment screening of staff going to work in children's homes in England and Wales started in 1986 (see below), but cases of abusing staff continued to crop up, most prominently in the case of Frank Beck. Beck was sentenced to life imprisonment for a series of offences against children in his care in Leicestershire ('Head of Children's Homes jailed for life, five times' *Independent*, 30 November 1991). We return to the impact of the Beck affair later in this chapter.

In the meantime, the Children Act 1989, with its greater emphasis on listening to children, had been passed and its accompanying guidance outlined what should be done if staff in a children's home suspected that one of their number was abusing children (Department of Health 1991b, paras. 1.34–1.37 and 1.179–1.192).

What everyone agreed was that the child sex offender was effectively 'invisible' once he had gained work with children in residential care. Many were also very good at that work:

> . . . paedophiles tend to work very secretively, planning to gain the confidence of children and those responsible for their care over a long period. They groom and seduce the children into sexual activities gradually by means of involvement in other activities which themselves may be acceptable and even commendable and they win the confidence of colleagues by taking on extra duties and responsibilities.
>
> (SFCRC, 1997, p. 88)

The Waterhouse Report, appearing in February 2000 after three and a half years of deliberation, was an exhaustive account of child physical and sexual abuse in the former local authority areas of Gwynedd and Clwyd in North Wales; the full report was over 900 pages long, and tracked events back to 1974 in all forms of residential child care and fostering provided by the councils concerned, the private sector and the health services. The report found evidence of 'widespread sexual abuse of boys . . . in children's residential establishments in Clwyd' (Waterhouse Report, 2000, para. 53–10) and singled out two institutions for particular attention: the local authority community home Bryn Estyn near Wrexham, and the private homes run by the Bryn Alyn Community, also in the Wrexham area. The report made no less than 72 recommendations on recruitment, selection, screening, management, inspection and other matters, including the specific role of the Welsh Office.

Many of the sexual offenders who had been active in North Wales had been apprehended and convicted by the time of the Waterhouse Report, but of equal concern to the inquiry was the length of time it had taken for the offending to be brought to light. At Bryn Estyn, the report found two senior members of staff engaged in sexual abuse of many of the young residents without detection. The Deputy Principal, Peter Howarth, who was eventually convicted and subsequently died in prison, abused children in his flat, which was part of the residential complex:

> Invitations to these sessions were by a 'flat list' compiled by Howarth or made up on his instructions and boys who went to the flat were required to wear pyjamas without underpants. Attendance was part of the agreed programme of activities available to boys in the evening. The sessions would begin at about 8.30pm and end at 11.00pm to 11.30pm.
> (Waterhouse Report, 2000, para. 8.05)

The report said it was satisfied that all senior and junior members of staff knew about the 'flat list' but chose not to do anything (*ibid*, paras. 8.10 – 8.12), and criticised what it called the 'cult of silence' that reigned (*ibid*, paras. 11.01 and 29.22; overall see paras. 29.01–29.33). Many of the report's recommendations were to try to open up the closed world of the residential care system that allowed such offending.

The key to 'identification' was to recognise potential offenders at the point of entry to work with children and make sure they did not get past that first point of entry. Screening mechanisms were needed to allow only suitable people into employment with children.

The pre-employment screening of child care workers

Applicants for any employment undergo a recruitment and selection procedure, but if that employment is for work with children they also undergo an additional screening process. Since the 1980s, applicants for work as teachers, social workers, probation officers, youth workers, children's homes workers, or any other public employment giving them 'substantial access to children' have been subject to pre-employment screening by means of a 'police check'; in effect a check made against any possible criminal record they may have.

As far back as the 1950s, arrangements had been made to allow police to notify the education authorities if they had arrested a teacher committing any offences that might put children at risk (Home Office, 1954), but the new arrangements entered into in the 1980s were to ensure that people unsuitable for work with children never got that work in the first place. The model for this pre-employment screening already existed, in terms of vetting would-be childminders and people wishing to foster or adopt children, but the new scale of screening was wider than anything seen before.

First into the field was Northern Ireland. The impetus for action came from the long-running allegations of sexual abuse emerging from the Kincora children's home in Belfast. Various forms of inquiry tried to ascertain exactly what had gone on at Kincora, and one report suggested the introduction of effective pre-employment screening (Sheridan Report, 1982).

The Northern Ireland Department of Health and Social Services instituted its Pre-Employment Consultancy Service (PECS) in October 1983. Designated employers could now request background information from PECS on all short-listed candidates for a child care job. That information included all *relevant* offences – obtained by PECS from the Royal Ulster Constabulary and with the relevance decided on by PECS officials – and other information from the Department of Health and Social Security's Consultancy Service in London (see below). The system at this time did not include the vetting of teachers.

When England and Wales introduced its system of pre-employment screening in 1986 (see below), Northern Ireland reviewed its own PECS arrangements. Changes were made to ensure that checks only took place on a successful candidate and not whole shortlists, and that the full record was disclosed rather than a selected version (NI Working Party, 1988). PECS was also supplemented by a separate system for vetting teachers; records were disclosed by the RUC directly to employing authorities (DENI, 1990).

By 1990, the PECS arrangements screened applicants for the Northern Ireland Health and Social Services Boards and Trusts, the National Board for Nursing, Midwifery and Health Visiting, the probation service, the 26 District Councils and 57 voluntary organisations. In all, some 400 checks were being made each month (DHSS (NI), 1995, para. 2.11). In 1996, the DHSS issued revised guidelines on how the system should work (DHSS (NI), 1996b) and separate guidance to the voluntary sector on how they should be protecting children (DHSS (NI), 1996c).

Criminal record checks on child care workers in England and Wales started in 1986. The impetus for these checks is attributed to the murder of four-year-old Marie Payne by Colin Evans in 1984. It emerged that Evans had a record of previous offences against children, but that had not stopped him obtaining voluntary work in the course of which he was able to associate with young children. Evans had not met Marie through his work, but concern was aroused (see 'List of errors that ended in child's death' *Guardian*, 18 December 1984) and the Home Secretary announced the forming of a working party with a brief to:

> . . . devise a system under which information about the unsuitability by reason of criminal background of people seeking positions where they will have substantial opportunities for access to children can be communicated to those bodies which are responsible for employing such people, whether in a paid or voluntary capacity.
>
> (HC Debs, 27 March 1985, cols. 244–45 WA)

The working party's report (Home Office/DHSS, 1985) formed the basis for pre-employment screening in England and Wales. Screening was to be a non-statutory arrangement, laid down in Government circulars outlining how local authorities as employers would have Senior Nominated Officers who would liase with their local police forces and establish a channel of communication for requests going one way and criminal record information going the other; requests were supported by the written consent of the applicant concerned. The full criminal record was disclosed and the employing authority would make its appointment decision based on this information. The police were entitled to disclose 'other background information' in addition to past convictions if that other information gave 'cause for serious concern'. Adjustments were made to build 'exemptions' into the Rehabilitation of Offenders Act 1974 and the Rehabilitation of Offenders (NI) Order 1978 so that past convictions could never be considered 'spent' when applying for work with children (Home Office, 1986b; see also Home Office, 1986c).

Minor adjustments were made to this system in 1988 and again in 1993, with the latter circular being the basis for checks throughout the 1990s (Home Office, 1993a). As child sexual abuse rose, so to did the numbers subject to vetting; in 1985, it had been anticipated that some 100,000 people would be checked each year but in 1993, the actual number was 665,000 per year (Home Office, 1993b, para. 23).

In 1989, three pilot schemes were started to try and extend pre-employment screening beyond its local authority and public sector standing to the voluntary sector. The pilot schemes were of only middling success (Unell, 1992) but did result in a system modelled on the Northern Ireland PECS arrangements, whereby national voluntary organisations went through the Voluntary Organisations Consultancy Service (VOCS), who obtained police records and Consultancy Service records (see below) for them (Home Office, 1994b; see also Home Office, 1994c).

Scotland followed the 1985 Home Office/DHSS working party guidelines to start its checking system in 1989 (Scottish Office, 1989b); some vetting already existed in residential establishments and schools (SWSG, 1985). Instead of liaising with their local police forces, Scottish authorities contact the Scottish Criminal Record Officer (SCRO) in Glasgow, where their requests are handled by the SCRO's User Support Bureau.

Apart from the 'police checks', employing authorities had two other sources of information they could access to screen would-be employees. The Consultancy Service was an index held by the Department of Health and made up of names sent into them by employers where, for example:

- a member of staff had been prosecuted for an offence against a child;
- a member of staff had been dismissed or resigned after a child's welfare had been put at risk;
- a member of staff had been disciplined and re-deployed away from work with children;
- any other circumstances where a child had been put at risk.

Until now, it has been up to employers to decide when to submit information to the index, unless it is an employee in a children's home, when it becomes a legal duty to submit (Children's Homes Regulations, 1991, S.I. No. 1506, reg. 19(2)(b)); this position will change when the Protection of Children Act 1999 is implemented and it becomes a duty to submit on all staff (see below). There are a reported 7,000 names on the Index and some 53,000 checks made annually, but the latter figure will rise considerably when the new Act requires organisations to always check it (HC Debs, 28 October 1996, WA 779; Home Office, 1993a, Annex C).

'List 99' is the second source of information open to employers to consult. It is much like the Consultancy Service, but applies to teachers and is held by the Department for Education and Employment. The Secretary of State has had powers to 'direct' that certain people are 'unsuitable' and should have their names added to the list (Education (Teachers) Regulations 1993, S.I. No. 543), although this power applied only to England and Wales; the list itself covers the whole of the UK. In 1995, these Regulations were amended to allow for the 'automatic barring' of people from teaching if they commit a designated offence against a child (see DFEE, 1995).

From time to time, both the effectiveness and the ethics of these pre-employment screening arrangements, based on old criminal records and the two lists held at Government level, have been questioned. This questioning, however, has done little to stop the inexorable growth in their use from 1986 to the present day.

From the initial brief given to the 1985 Home Office/DHSS Working Party to 'devise a system', pre-employment screening has been largely a bureaucratic exercise of information (criminal records) exchange and decision making. The civil liberties questions of privacy and rehabilitation rights have been raised (see e.g. NCCL, 1988) and the inclusion of posts outside the 'access to children' criteria, the taking into account of non-relevant offences and the relatively powerless position of the job applicant in terms of effective redress have been examined (Hebenton and Thomas, 1993, esp. Chapter 6). The journal *Social Work Today* said these questions 'ought to be generating a fierce debate' but feared they were not ('Disclosing Criminal Convictions' *Social Work Today*, Editorial, 11 February 1988) and Essex Police declared its dissatisfaction with local authorities 'abusing' the Home Office circulars (cited in AMA, 1995, p. 19). Organisations representing the interests of ex-offenders produced guidance of 'damage limitation' to help ex-offenders into work (Apex Trust, 1990; NACRO 1996b).

Researchers produced evidence to show the variation in decision-making based on criminal record disclosure, including the continuing possibility of sex offenders getting through (Smith, 1998, 1999), and even a Government-appointed Task Force reported that it was unhappy with the 'varying interpretations' and 'geographical inconsistencies' of checking arrangements (Better Regulation Task Force, 1999, para. 4.3.4). None of it made any difference. The conventional wisdom prevailed that criminal record checks were essential and should be an integral part of selection procedures, that information technology would improve things and the only real question was how we could possibly have managed without them before the 1980s.

Meanwhile, periodic reports of individuals sexually abusing children in their care still made the headlines. The most notorious was the case of Frank Beck, who had abused children for over 13 years in the Leicestershire area (D'Arcy and Gosling, 1998). The Beck affair led directly to two reports on improving residential care for children (Department of Health, 1991c; Warner Report, 1992) and the establishment of a central Support Force for Children's Residential Care; the Support Force produced further guidance on recruitment and selection of residential care staff (SFCRC, 1997). The Warner Report focused on the recruitment and selection of staff for children's homes and the need to ensure that police checks were part of an integrated and effective system of selection; those responsible for selection started referring to new staff having been 'Warner interviewed' or 'Warnered'.

Despite all this activity, concerns continued to be raised and not just within children's homes. In Belfast, a sex offender had gained access to children through voluntary organisations (DHSS (NI), 1993) and in Newcastle, a man committed sexual offences in a nursery school against a number of children (Hunt Report, 1994). In Scotland, the inquiry report into the Dunblane Primary School shootings went on to look at how Thomas Hamilton, the man responsible, had been able to find work in youth clubs that he himself had set up. Hamilton was not a convicted sex offender, but his behaviour toward children had been the subject of persistent complaints and concerns (Cullen Report, 1996, Chapter 11).

In the entrepreneurial spirit of the times, a private company called 'Faircheck' was established in London to see if the independent sector could lead the way in good practice in pre-employment screening. Launched on 9 May 1995, Faircheck offered a package of background checks, personality tests and interviews, primarily to local authorities and others looking for workers with children, elderly people or any other vulnerable group. The cost of the package was reported to be £950 per check, which seems to have been too high for some authorities and in less than a year the company went out of business ('Faircheck private vetting agency folds' *Community Care*, 15–21 February 1996).

The Home Office's 1996 Consultation Document on the 'Sentencing and Supervision of Sex Offenders' recognised a continuing need for measures to prevent sex offenders gaining work with children, and duly proposed making it a criminal offence for a convicted sex offender to apply for work with children, or even to accept the offer of such work (Home Office, 1996a, paras. 64–77). This proposal was refined in yet another consultation paper, which tried to define more accurately concepts that included 'seeking work' and 'accepting an offer of work' involving contact with children (Home Office/Scottish Office, 1997); civil liberty groups pointed out the inherent problems, such as someone obtaining work with no access to children but later being redeployed by an employer (Liberty, 1997b).

At the same time as these proposals were made, a further White Paper was published suggesting an overhaul of all criminal record checks for employment screening, whether or not children were involved.

'On the Record' proposed a new Criminal Records Agency to take this work away from the police and to arrange for conviction disclosures on three levels:

1   an 'enhanced' criminal record check for child care workers, including non-conviction information;
2   a 'full' check for those with some contact with children; and
3   a Criminal Conviction Certificate for any employment and which individual applicants would apply for and pay for.

(see Home Office, 1996d)

A similar consultation paper was published for Scotland, making similar proposals (Scottish Office, 1996). Both consultation papers provided model codes of practice which they thought should be agreed to by employers having access to records, with the withdrawal of access being the sanction to ensure compliance.

The Police Act 1997, Part V received its Royal Assent on 21 March 1997 and gave the statutory underpinning for these new 'three-tier' arrangements. The Act made no reference to the creation of a Criminal Record Agency, but the new Government coming in that year, after taking a careful look at the law, confirmed that it would go ahead and renamed the Agency as the Criminal Records Bureau. The Bureau was to be based on Merseyside and was expected to start operations in July 2001 (Home Office, 1999f); Scotland was to have the same system but based on the Scottish Criminal Record Office in Glasgow rather than the Bureau (Scottish Office, 1998b). Voluntary sector organisations immediately started campaigning against the cost element which had been introduced and which they foresaw as putting many volunteers off (see e.g. HC Debs, 5 July 1999, cols. 432–35 WA).

The conviction and sentencing of Roger Saint at Chester Crown Court in May 1997 for charges of indecent assault of children in his care prompted further action from the Government; the Saint case was later reviewed by the Waterhouse Report, 2000 (paras. 25.01–25.28). The children in question had been placed in Saint's care as a foster and adoptive parent, despite the fact that he had previous convictions against children which were known to the local authorities who made the placements. The Children (Protection from Offenders) (Miscellaneous Amendments) Regulations 1997, S.I. No. 2308 came into force on 17 October 1997 to amend various other Regulations in England and Wales, with a view to making some prohibitions on fostering and adoption approvals automatic and to put the requirement for police checks on a statutory footing, and including an amendment of the Children's Homes Regulations 1991, S.I. No. 1506, regulation 5 to make checks mandatory before any appointment (Department of Health, 1997b).

After the 1996 conviction of a number of residential care workers in North Wales for sexual and other crimes against children in their care, the Government had commissioned Sir William Utting to conduct a review of the adequacy of safeguards against the abuse of children living away from home in England and Wales, and Roger Kent to carry out a similar review in Scotland. They also established a judicial tribunal of inquiry, to be chaired by Sir Ronald Waterhouse, to examine the events that led to the North Wales convictions; the Waterhouse inquiry was eventually published in February 2000 but, as the report itself says, many of the Utting and Kent recommendations were by then already in place (Waterhouse Report, 2000, para. 56.01); on the question of police checks, there was no substantial criticism, although the system had not always worked as effectively as it should and not least in the case of the foster parent Roger Saint (ibid, paras. 25.10–25.13).

The Utting Report entitled 'People like Us' made wide-ranging recommendations for tougher safeguards to protect children living away from home, including the need for a complete rehabilitation of residential care, and action both to keep potential abusers out and to ensure that 'sexually and physically abusive terrorists' did not prosper in children's homes due to neglectful management. The warning was that:

> Abusers may be good at their jobs, winning respect, affection or fear from their colleagues and admiration from the parents whose children they corrupt. They are adept at avoiding detection and disciplinary or criminal charges . . . they are very dangerous people.
>
> (Utting Report, 1997, p. 5)

The report pointed out that recommendations of the 1992 Warner Report and the more recent Burgner Report were still unimplemented. The Burgner Report had called for the extension of police checks to small unregistered children's homes; the Government duly closed this loophole for would-be abusers (Home Office, 1997d).

In Scotland, the Kent Report made some 61 recommendations to improve the safety of children, including the idea of a child care register in the continuing absence of any national registration schemes for social care workers, comparable to nursing or medical registration. On the specific work of the Scottish Criminal Record Office, it recommended that a note be kept of all the people subjected to a police check on entering child care work, so that if any future offences were committed by them, the connection could be instantly made and employers informed (Kent Report, 1997).

The Government made a full response to the Utting Report (Department of Health, 1998b), but also referred direct questions about preventing sex offenders getting work with children to an interdepartmental working group that had already been formed. The group was to draw upon the Utting Report and also the 1997 consultation exercise 'Sex Offenders – a ban on working with children'. Specifically, its terms of reference were:

- the definition of a position of trust;
- the scope of occupations to be covered;
- the definition of those who need to be protected;
- the kind of behaviour prohibited;
- the possible mechanisms for prohibiting such behaviour, including a possible criminal offence.

(HC Debs, 17 July 1998, cols. 348–49 WA)

The working group produced an interim report on 25 November 1998, which recommended a new criminal offence of 'abuse of trust'; it would be an offence for an adult – aged over 18 – to have sexual intercourse or engage in other sexual activity with a person below the age of 18 where they are in a 'position of trust' in relation to the younger person. The recommendation was taken up almost immediately, and without waiting for the working group's final report. The Sexual Offences (Amendment)

Bill was published on 16 December 1998, its clauses 2 to 4 creating a new offence of 'abuse of trust' aimed at those under 18 in schools, children's homes, hospitals and penal establishments.

The progress of the Sexual Offences (Amendment) Bill through Parliament was held up by the House of Lords, who refused to accept other clauses in the Bill, which sought to equalise the age of consent between heterosexual and homosexual activities. The Bill was being re-presented into the 1999–2000 session when the Lords' objections could be overturned (HC Debs, 23 July 1999, col. 732 WA).

The working group published its main report on 25 January 1999 outlining the principles of any scheme designed to protect children:

1 the overriding need was to protect children from those who might abuse them;
2 the right of an individual to seek work should not to be jeopardised any more than was necessary to ensure that; and
3 the scheme must be fair and compliant with the European Convention on Human Rights; anyone who might be deemed as unsuitable for work with children or unable in practice to obtain such work should have received the benefit of a proper process before reaching this position and know where he stood.
(Home Office, 1999g, para. 3.4)

Recommendations included the need to have a fully integrated information system that drew on criminal records, List 99 and the Consultancy Service through a form of 'one-stop-shop' arrangement; that focal point was to be the Criminal Records Bureau, emanating from the Police Act 1997, once it was up and running.

In fact, the Protection of Children Bill, published in advance of the working group paper on 13 January 1999, had already drafted the law on how such a one-stop-shop might be created. This private Members Bill, promoted by Labour MP Debra Shipley, put List 99 and the Consultancy Service on to a statutory footing for the first time, and introduced a tribunal to hear appeals from anyone who thought their names should not go on the various lists; the Bill also amended the Police Act 1997, section 112 to facilitate the Criminal Records Bureau handling personal information other than criminal records. The Bill became law in the summer of 1999.

Having produced its report in January, the working group continued its deliberations and reported again in July 1999, when it put forward further key recommendations:

1 to identify and ban unsuitable people from working with children;
2 to create a new criminal offence which the 'unsuitable person' would commit if they worked with children;
3 to provide a new definition of 'working with children'.
(Home Office, 1999h)

It also affirmed the need for the one-stop-shop system, and for:

> Similar schemes to be put in place for Scotland and Northern Ireland with access to all information on those banned in each country to be available in all three and with reciprocal bans in place.
>
> (Home Office, 1999h)

Implementing these further recommendations was going to require new primary legislation. In the meantime, without any recourse to legislation, an agreement was entered into between the Home Office, the probation service and the employment service to ensure that information about sex offenders and other potentially dangerous offenders was passed to the employment service, so that these offenders were not directed towards work with children or work that would give them opportunities to re-offend, whether against children or adults (Home Office, 1999i).

Protection in the community

The search for 'protection' has been made in the home, the workplace and now the wider community itself. The rising crime rate had made 'law and order' a political issue throughout the 1980s, with the perceived failure of treatment approaches and the rise of the 'victim' movement putting protection of the public on the political agenda. When the Government had produced its White Paper on a new legislative framework for sentencing, it was significantly entitled 'Crime, Justice and *Protecting the Public*' (Home Office, 1990a, emphasis added).

Outside the criminal justice system, the search for protection in the community was taking place in other directions. Crime prevention policies had been around in one form or another since the 1960s, but now moved from a 'situational' concern, with more secure housing and better street lighting, to social and communal strategies which, by the time of the 1998 Crime and Disorder Act, meant 'partnership' between agencies and the Labour Government's self-styled 'joined-up policies' (Crawford, 1998).

In this section, we consider some of the protective measures taken that are specific to sex offending. These include the idea of making public space safer, action to clean up 'red-light' areas, the accommodation needs of known sex offenders and the problem of the 'unregistered' sex offender at large in the community.

The 'freedom of the city'

Urban environments have become synonymous with being 'unsafe' environments. The 'public' space of cities and towns has become space to be travelled through as quickly as possible, whether as a pedestrian, on 'public' transport or by private transport. Certain areas became 'known' as being particularly 'dangerous' and we are expected to use 'common sense' to avoid them. Worpole and Greenhalgh have summarised the position:

> few modern city dwellers truly feel that they have the 'freedom of the city', the freedom to walk, roam and wander where they want.
>
> (Worpole and Greenhalgh, 1996, p. 7)

It was not always like this. In the seventeenth century, public space was a space to linger in and be seen in. Dressing up and promenading was, for certain classes, the order of the day. 'Public' houses and coffee houses supported this use of public space, as did the building of squares and other public areas for meeting. The fall of 'public' man and woman to today's privatised lifestyles has been recorded by Sennett (1974).

The 'city of strangers' has brought with it its own mythologies of impersonality, coldness and alienation. In the 1970s, women's groups often demonstrated to 'reclaim the night', but today we fall back more often on the silent gaze of closed-circuit television looking down on public space, or retreat and regroup into 'safe' shopping malls on the outskirts of towns, policed by their own private security guards.

For Worpole and Greenhalgh, it is the depopulation of public space that causes much of the problem. The car park attendant replaced by the ticket machine, the underground ticket office by another machine, the caretaker gone from the public toilet or the park-keeper from the park. As the culture of the car downgrades public transport, the bus conductor disappears in favour of one man/woman operated buses. The answer is not CCTV, but a re-populating of public space to encourage back the pedestrians, the joggers and the dog walkers (Worpole and Greenhalgh, 1996).

The Department of the Environment, Transport and the Regions has commissioned research to highlight what makes being a pedestrian so difficult these days. Features that make us feel unsafe included: people, such as drunks, who just hung around; poor street lighting; isolated areas; subways and alleyways; and fear of people who displayed erratic behaviour:

> When I'm waiting at the station, I look up and down the platform and see the ones that are talking to themselves and avoid them . . . try and sit right away from them . . . there are so many people in London who are ill . . . I'm aware of them when I'm walking . . . what's frightening is that there is no way of knowing if they are going to be violent or whatever.
>
> (DETR, 1999, p. 33)

Much has been said about trying to encourage people out of their cars and on to public transport, not least because of the volume of traffic now on our streets. The poor quality of much public transport, in terms of overcrowding or unreliability, has been cited as a reason people prefer to sit in traffic jams listening to their car radios. In general, public transport is perceived as relatively 'safe' once you are on it, but the walk to it and the waiting for it to arrive are seen as problem times when people feel less safe. The presence of drunks, vagrants or other undesirable people is frequently commented on as a contributing factor to the fear of crime (Department of Transport, 1997).

The London Underground has been identified as posing unique problems, including the very fact of being 'underground' which caused a feeling of 'timelessness' for some travellers:

> Whether it was day or night, the environmental conditions remained constant and were said to foster feelings of anxiety, including for personal safety.
>
> (Department of Transport, 1997)

One form of public transport considered somewhat safer has always been that of the licensed taxi. Even here, however, that safety has been qualified because some taxi drivers could still pose a threat, not least to women travelling alone at night or when used for unescorted children. Once out on the streets, the regulation of taxi drivers is difficult, but attention has been directed at how they obtain their licence to drive in the first place.

In 1991, a campaign was started to introduce a form of vetting by way of a criminal record check on all applicants for a licence to drive a taxi. Local authorities, it was agreed, could link up with their local police, in much the same way as for child care checks, in order to weed out the unsuitable drivers.

The Association of District Councils outlined the sort of problems that existed without a criminal conviction check. A dossier was compiled of incidents from over 40 of their members revealing the sort of person who was getting a licence:

- a taxi driver in Exeter imprisoned for unlawful sexual intercourse with a 15-year-old girl he regularly drove to school; he had previous convictions for indecency;
- a man in Hereford imprisoned for rape getting a licence almost immediately on release;
- taxi drivers in Portsmouth having their licences revoked when offences of rape and unlawful sexual intercourse came to light.

> (ADC, 1991)

Without checks on criminal records, the authorities were dependent on people recognising taxi drivers and remembering what had happened.

When cases did come to light, the police sometimes prosecuted using the Theft Act 1968 to charge people with obtaining a job and pecuniary advantage by deception (see e.g. 'Sex case man in court over CV lie' *Daily Mail*, 16 August 1989).

Members of Parliament took up the cause, and amendments were made to the Road Traffic Bill. In future, all applicants would be subject to a police check against their criminal records (Road Traffic Act 1991, s. 47; Department of Transport/Home Office, 1992). The city was deemed to be that much safer and freer as a result.

The 'red-light area'

In the past, sex offending has often been synonymous with prostitution and what has come to be called the 'sex industry'. The arguments that this is a 'crime without a victim' are being challenged, as is the idea that women and men ('rent-boys') choose voluntarily to enter this 'industry'. The facts of economic insecurity and gender-specific poverty that drive people into prostitution are becoming clearer and the concept of a continuum of abuse, from economic and social through to sexual abuse of the person selling their services, becomes more credible.

Prostitution is not of itself illegal in England and Wales, but the selling of sexual services in a street or public place is (Street Offences Act, 1959, s. 1). Special 'prostitutes cautions' are given to women by the police (Home Office, 1959) and from time to time there is talk of regulating the premises used by the women and the possible introduction of sanctions against those placing prostitutes' advertising cards in telephone boxes. Despite all of this, prostitutes continue to 'work' on the streets and in turn create problems for those areas in which they choose to work.

'Red-light' areas, where prostitutes regularly walk the streets, have posed particular problems for other women walking in the same area when they are mistaken for prostitutes by men who accost them. Men who cruised these areas in their cars looking for women were termed 'kerb-crawlers'.

A woman in the Canning Street district of Liverpool described the problem:

> It's a constant nuisance here. Young children and elderly women as well, we're all accosted by kerb-crawlers at times. There are also a fair number of frightening people always hanging around.
>
> (quoted in 'Police curb the kerb-crawlers'
> *Observer*, 6 November 1983)

Another woman in the Streatham area of London said:

> I have been physically assaulted five times in the last few years. The last time a man pulled up beside me in the car and asked

me how much I charged, I turned away and tried to ignore
him. He stopped the car and grabbed me and pushed my face
into a wall. He then got back into his car and drove off.
(quoted in Matthews, 1993, p. 1)

For local residents, the 'public' activity of street prostitution could be
seen as an intrusion into their 'private' area, and sometimes into their gardens
or up to the front door. In some communities, residents organised themselves
to take direct action to get rid of the intruders (see e.g. Henshaw, 1986).

Before 1985, the police appeared to be powerless to take any action.
The police in Nottinghamshire and South Yorkshire had tried prosecuting
the men under the Justices of the Peace Act 1361 with some success
('Police curb the kerb-crawlers' *Observer*, 6 November 1983), but in
1985, the police were given more direct powers in the Sexual Offences
Act of that year.

The 1985 Act made it an offence for a man to solicit a woman for the
purposes of prostitution, either from a motor vehicle in a street or public
place or by a man having just left such a vehicle. The soliciting had to
be 'persistent' or in such a manner as to cause annoyance to the woman or
to other persons in the neighbourhood (Sexual Offences Act 1985, s. 1).

Enforcement of the Act has been problematic for the police, who
believe 'convictions are difficult to achieve' (Matthews, 1993, p. 18).
Some forces have tried alternative 'high-visibility' operations to use
embarrassment to force kerb-crawlers out of an area. Avon and Somerset
Police were amongst those forces who sent warning letters to the home
addresses of motorists, having tracked them through their car registration
numbers, and were reportedly considering sending similar letters to
employers if they could be identified ('Police may warn employers after
study finds typical kerb-crawlers' *Independent*, 13 November 1989).
Comprehensive multi-agency operations involving community
consultation and traffic control have been more successful (Matthews,
1993), but, more recently, the Home Office has hinted at introducing
greater powers to arrest kerb-crawlers (Bratby, 1999).

The red-light district of Lumb Lane in Bradford had been tolerated
for many years by its local community; Peter Sutcliffe, the Yorkshire
Ripper, had lived only a mile or so away. In early 1995, however, the
area was to receive national prominence through the television drama,
'Band of Gold'. The unwelcome image of the area portrayed was later
said to be one of the triggers for vigilante action from the local Muslim
community to 'clean up' the area.

Anti-prostitution patrols took to the streets over Easter 1995. Groups
of young Asian men 'persuaded' the women to move elsewhere; for their
part, the women undoubtedly felt 'harassed' off the streets.

A later Commission of Inquiry, looking into public disorder in the streets
that were unconnected to the vigilante patrols, was able to reflect that:

There is no doubt that Lumb Lane and its nearby streets no longer have a red light trade, and the campaign has been seen locally as successful. Direct and, at least technically, illegal, action was seen to work.

(Bradford Commission, 1996, p. 107)

West Yorkshire was also the site of a different approach to kerb-crawlers. An agreement was reached between the West Yorkshire Police and Leeds Metropolitan University to give men apprehended as kerb-crawlers a choice of either appearing in court and risking a fine, or attending classes at the University's Research Centre on Violence, Abuse and Gender Relations. The men would have to pay a tuition fee for the classes, aimed at stopping them from re-offending, but would avoid a court hearing and a conviction. The classes were nicknamed the 'John School' – US slang for a prostitute's client – and participants received lectures from police officers, health officials, former prostitutes and academics on matters relating to law, health and the lifestyle of prostitutes ('Kerb-crawlers face lessons in shame' *Observer*, 30 November 1997).

The housing of sex offenders

The accommodation of sex offenders has always been a fraught subject. Much of the spontaneous community action witnessed in the late 1990s was focused on particular localities and a desire to get these offenders out of that locality. The 'not in my backyard' or 'NIMBY' mentality, that had in the past applied to new roads, power stations and planning decisions, was now brought to bear on sex offenders. The former head of education at Wandsworth Prison in London went on record to say we needed a special 'paedophile town' built on an island or peninsula away from centres of population ('Ex-jailer calls for paedophile town' *Daily Telegraph*, 11 April 1997).

The Housing Act 1996, section 161 had introduced the concept of 'qualifying persons', who were entitled to housing from local authorities and section 161(4) had gone on to say that local authorities could decide 'what classes of person are, or are not, qualifying persons'. An interim Code of Guidance on the Act confirmed the right of authorities to exercise their 'discretion about who is a qualifying person' and that this could include such groups as 'people with a history of anti-social behaviour' (D of E/D of H, 1996, paras. 4.25 and 4.27). The whole area of anti-social tenants was one that was exercising local authorities generally, and the adding on of sex offenders to those who were noisy, inconsiderate or drug dealing seemed quite appropriate.

In Birmingham, there was confusion when a housing official took it upon himself to tell local residents that a man with a record of sex offences had moved into their area. The official was the subject of disciplinary proceedings, whilst the tenants got up a petition in support of him. A spokesman for the council bemoaned the fact that 'there is no register to which we can refer to find out whether prospective tenants have a record of sex crimes' ('Paedophiles face being banned from renting council homes' *The Times*, 9 January 1997). Meanwhile, Middlesbrough Council was reported to be considering a 'blanket ban' on council homes for any child sex offenders (*ibid*).

Support for such bans came indirectly from another court ruling on homelessness legislation (at that time the Housing Act 1985, Part III). The High Court supported the London Borough of Hounslow's decision to refuse housing to a convicted sex offender who had lost his accommodation whilst in prison. This was not a question of blanket bans and policies, because each applicant claiming homelessness had to be dealt with on an individual basis; in the general climate, however, the ruling appeared to give a 'green light' to further action to exclude sex offenders from access to housing (*R v. Hounslow LBC, ex p. R* (1997) Times, 25 February).

In April 1997, the Labour-controlled Rhondda Cynon Taff Council was reportedly the first council to introduce a blanket policy banning sex offenders from local authority housing. The chair of the housing committee said:

> We had to do something positive about this dreadful problem because all our accommodation is on estates where young families live and the safety of our children is paramount. We are aware of the infringement of civil liberties question but we feel that safeguarding our children comes before any other consideration.
>
> (quoted in 'Council home ban for paedophiles' *Daily Telegraph*, 2 April 1997)

The Northern Ireland Housing Executive tried to be more positive, and focused on its role as a landlord trying to give people accommodation. The Executive published a consultation paper in October 1997 laying out what its position was and inviting comments. They accepted the 'community safety' argument, but did not see it as their role to turn people away and thought the best option was to house child sex offenders amongst adult-only residents wherever possible (NIHE, 1997).

To help clarify the situation, the Chartered Institute of Housing in England drew up its own guidance on the housing of sex offenders, which it distributed to local authorities and other providers of housing, such as Housing Associations. The advice was to avoid blanket bans, work closely with the police and probation service and be positive about engaging with others in the rehabilitation and reintegration of sex offenders (CIH, 1998).

The 'unregistered' sex offender

Another continuing concern related to the sex offender register not being retrospective. As we have seen, one estimate from the Home Office put the number of convicted sex offenders in the community at over 100,000 (Marshall, 1997). The vast majority of these would not be on the register simply because their offences had been committed too early for inclusion; they were not 'in the system' – in custody or under supervision – at the time of implementation on 1 September 1997. The problem had been raised during parliamentary discussion on the Sex Offenders Bill, but now the Act was in place it was seen as something requiring resolution.

The Home Office responded with its consultation paper on the 'Community Protection Order' (Home Office, 1997e). These orders were designed to rein in all those convicted sex offenders in the community who were not required to keep their details up to date on the register. The sex offender would not automatically be required to start registering, but if a so-called 'trigger event' was spotted by the police, such as a person acting suspiciously near a playground or school, and the police knew they had previous convictions for sex offences against children, an application could be made to a court for a Community Protection Order. The order would not only initiate a requirement on the person concerned to register, but also could lay down areas of the community which they could not enter because of the risk they posed to children.

The Community Protection Order was renamed as the Sex Offender Order when it appeared in the Crime and Disorder Act 1998, sections 2–4 (covering England and Wales) and sections 20–22 (covering Scotland) (see Home Office, 1998d); the Criminal Justice (NI) Order 1998, articles 6–7 extended the Sex Offender Order to Northern Ireland.

The Greater Manchester Police were reportedly the first force to apply for a Sex Offender Order. The courts made an order on a 35-year-old man, requiring him to keep out of much of the southern part of Manchester between the hours of 10 p.m. and 7 a.m. for a period of eight years. The man had previously served a custodial sentence for rape after breaking into student bed-sits, and the trigger behaviour involved being seen by police peering through bed-sit windows at night before running away ('Bed-sit rapist becomes subject of first legal exclusion order' *Independent*, 24 December 1998). By October 1999, the Home Office was aware of 14 orders having been made, but no information existed on how many had been applied for (HC Debs, 25 October 1999, col. 691 WA).

Summary

The search for community safety or community protection moved inexorably up the political agenda as the turn of the century grew closer.

In this chapter, the search has been outlined in terms of safety for women and children within their own households, for possible victims of sexual offending in various work places and, finally, the wider community protection on the streets and in matters of the accommodation and public activities of known sex offenders who are not currently on the sex offender register.

Particular attention has been paid to the pre-employment screening of child care workers to ensure that unsuitable people do not get work giving them access to children. These arrangements epitomise the current use of 'personal information' held by the police (i.e. criminal records), whereby that information is disseminated to those in the best position to make a risk assessment on a particular individual – in this case local authorities. The ethical and civil liberty implications have also been considered in terms of the various different decisions made by local authorities and the lack of due process for the ex-offenders concerned.

9
Conclusions

As we complete this survey of sexual offending and the social responses being made to it, a number of recurring themes keep emerging: the relative nature of sexual offending and how we define it; the need to hold 'personal information' in various databases in order to identify the otherwise 'invisible' sex offender; and the need to use that personal information to carry out risk assessment and thereby achieve better 'risk management' on those who pose a threat to us.

Here, we consider the debate on child prostitution as an example of how we rethink traditional approaches to sexual offending; we look in more detail at the phenomena of risk and dangerousness, and the need for ever more personal information to identify the sex offender and assess the risk they pose.

Child prostitution

Child prostitution has been with us since Victorian times at least. In recent years, a campaign has gathered momentum to force a rethink on our approaches to young people below the age of consent who resort to prostitution. In essence, the argument has been that the selling of sexual services by these young people and any associated criminal behaviour by them should be reconstituted as a form of child abuse and even be de-criminalised.

As far back as 1959, the Home Office had advised the police when cautioning prostitutes to ensure:

> That no opportunity should be neglected of putting a girl or young woman who is in danger of drifting into prostitution into touch with a social welfare agency which may be able to persuade her to take up regular employment or to go home to her parents.
>
> (Home Office, 1959, para. 5)

During the 1980s, a loosely co-ordinated campaign was started to improve the lot of child prostitutes. Non-governmental organisations have taken a lead in this campaign. The Children's Society 'Safe in the City' project in Manchester found schoolgirls, engaged in prostitution, who they felt needed protection rather than punishment (Chamberlain, 1993; Lee and O'Brien, 1995). Barnardos set up its 'Streets and Lanes' project in Bradford in 1994 to work directly with these young girls on a multi-agency basis; they too argued for protection over punishment (Barnardos, 1998). The argument was that any criminality going on here should be ascribed to the male purchasers of sexual services, who should be recategorised as child abusers. Lynne Ravenscroft, a magistrate, put the subject on the agenda of the Magistrates' Association to add weight to the campaign (Ravenscroft, 1997).

What was coming to light was the dreadful social circumstances of the young girls and boys (rent-boys) that was turning them to prostitution: runaways from home; children leaving local authority care; children using drugs.

The campaign started to see results. The police launched two pilot schemes in Nottingham and Wolverhampton in mid-1997, to try to take a different approach and to take the 'victims' not 'criminals' line. In February 1998, the Government accepted the ease with which young people could become 'trapped in an unhealthy and illegal lifestyle' which led to prostitution, and saw the case for moving the focus of attention to the abusing adult:

> Children who become involved in prostitution should be seen primarily as children in need of welfare services and in many instances protection under the Children Act.
> (Department of Health, 1998a, para. 5.40)

In the meantime, cases of child prostitution continued to come to light. A number of men in their 50s were arrested in Middlesbrough and Darlington to be questioned about organising prostitution rings ('Town rocked by child prostitution' Northern Echo, 15 April 1998) and in Scotland, reports were made of a growing 'market' for young boys in the Calton Hill area of Edinburgh and around the two main railway stations – Queen Street and Central – in Glasgow ('Fears for under age rent boys' Scotsman, 1 February 1999).

At the end of 1998, the Government introduced a set of draft guidelines on how the police and other agencies in England and Wales could change the focus of their work with child prostitutes. The guidelines held back from actually discriminalising under-age prostitute activities, because it was thought that this would 'send out the wrong message', but it did favour a more child-centred approach, with multi-agency co-operation to develop expertise, consider individual cases and devise overall strategies. The offering of individual 'exit strategies' for those caught up in prostitution was considered the best way forward (Home Office/ Department of Health, 1998; see also Swann, 1999).

Child prostitution throws a spotlight on many of the questions raised in this book. The age of consent could be said to invalidate the 'consent' of everyone under 16 and yet we hold them criminally responsible for their behaviour because the age of criminal responsibility is ten (eight in Scotland). We choose to see the person buying the sexual service as the criminal, and see him as a possible child abuser, yet we refuse to decriminalise the activities of the young person because it would send the 'wrong message' to the men ('pimps') who organise and control these young people. Are we really holding back from dealing with the male abuser as well, because of his 'normality' on the 'continuum' of male attitudes and behaviour?

Risk and dangerousness revisited

We first encountered risk and dangerousness in Chapter 1 and have bumped into both concepts at frequent intervals thereafter. The assessment and management of the risk posed by sexual offenders has become an all consuming task for the police, prisons, probation service, social services departments and those health care professionals who come across these offenders.

In its wider context, 'risk' has taken on a greater significance in all areas of life, and we are now told we live in the 'risk society'. The risk being described is invariably a negative one in terms of crime or where there is some kind of deficit and something may happen to us; risk does have a positive side where taking a risk can lead on to greater things, but in terms of crime reduction that is not the side we are looking at.

As the world grows more complex, and some would say more fragmented, so the areas of unfamiliarity in life increase. In so doing, they increase the perceived risks of life which it is then incumbent upon us to try and reduce. Insofar as sexual offenders pose a risk, we need to identify them and have information about them to calculate the risk or degree of danger they pose in order to then manage that risk. In turn, we are making 'calculations' of an almost actuarial nature to determine who is or is not a risk. Some practitioners literally use the calculus of 'tick-boxes' to record the information on a sex offender which then becomes part of their risk assessment.

The wider social theories of risk and risk society are beyond the brief of this book (see e.g. Beck, 1992; Young, 1999), and the degree to which risk work now predominates in the 'social care' field has been noted by writers such as Parton (1996).

The role of law enforcement in the risk society has, in turn, started to reshape our very understanding of what policing means. Ericson and Haggerty describe the move from traditional policing to a policing that is more about information production and dissemination. The police have become just part of a network of agencies that move information around to the most appropriate location for risk assessment or risk management to take place (Ericson and Haggerty, 1997).

This new form of policing challenges the police to develop new skills of information management and to use the new tools of information technology. At its most simple, it is the police disclosure of criminal records held by them to local authorities in order that the pre-employment screening of child care workers can take place. Fifteen years ago, there were no such disclosures and criminal records were used mainly by the police themselves and the courts; today, over 600,000 applications for disclosures of this kind are made to the police every year.

In the case of sex offenders, other examples arise as information rebounds between the police, the courts, the prisons, local authorities, the probation service and others as we try to get the right information to the right person at the right time for them to do their job; in many instances that 'job' is part of a risk analysis.

Peter Neyroud, the Assistant Chief Constable of the West Mercia Police, believes it is leading to fundamental changes:

> The nature of the new skills and the requirement to work across agency boundaries raises the question as to whether the current 'pillared' structure of independent agencies – each with its own operational independence – is the best way of protecting the public. It certainly challenges the old professional model and creates an argument for a new cross-agency discipline of risk management.
>
> (Neyroud, 1999)

Whether or not risk assessment – the prediction of the future behaviour of others – can ever be an exact science remains debatable. For some critics, it will only ever be a haphazard 'guessing game' that will inevitably draw in and label people who would never go on to be a risk to anyone. Advocates of risk assessment believe otherwise and have faith in their abilities to refine their techniques and make ever better predictions, but some people will inevitably be wrongly assessed and punished or constrained for crimes they would never have committed in the future, and we have to ask if this does not conflict with our notion of justice.

Risk analysis also needs information, and it especially needs personal information about identifiable people.

The central role of personal information

As risk assessment and management moves to centre stage in law enforcement and crime reduction, it drags with it the role of personal information to inform those risk analysis tasks. Personal information, information technology and the information 'superhighways' are all familiar terms in the information society. But what actually is 'personal information'?

Personal information relates to a particular individual and includes all that information we might expect to be considered private or personal, such as information about health, sexual matters or family. It would include all that information about which the community at large has no particular interest, because it holds no significance for the community. According to the academic Raymond Wacks, we might define it as follows:

> 'Personal information' consists of those facts, communications, or opinions which relate to the individual and which it would be reasonable to expect him (or her) to regard as intimate or sensitive and therefore want to withhold or at least to restrict their collection, use, or circulation.
>
> (Wacks, 1989, p. 26)

The individual sex offender would probably subscribe to this definition. His intentions are personal to him, his activities often in private and his victims – especially children – are asked or threatened to keep 'the secret'. Within feminist analysis, wider cultural forces (male) may support this 'containing' of information, narrowing of the definition of a sexual offence and refusal to take the victims' views seriously.

The role of the law enforcement and other public protection agencies has been to move this personal information on the sex offender from the private to the public domain. In this instance, public domain is only the various agencies who have a 'need to know' in order to identify, track and intervene in the sex offenders' activities as appropriate. As the sex offender seeks to restrict the 'collection, use or circulation' of personal information about him, so these agencies are trying to do the exact opposite by collecting, using and circulating that same information.

To this end, we have seen the creation of the sex offender 'register', the promotion of 'intelligence-led' policing, the build up of the NCIS Paedophile Section database and the more active use of the national collection of criminal records and their routine dissemination to other agencies to help them make their risk assessments. Elsewhere, we have seen the upgrading of the Department of Health Consultancy Service Index, the 'List 99' and the Forensic Science Services National DNA Database. All these initiatives put personal information at the centre of activities to combat the sex offender.

This personal information is not being collated for its own sake, but is increasingly being actively used and also exchanged between agencies charged with law enforcement or public protection. As we have seen, this inter-agency work seeks to get the right information to the right agency at the right time to enable them to do their job.

At one time, police-held criminal record repositories were for the police alone, to help them do their work and for the police to produce them in court (as antecedents) to help sentencers make appropriate decisions.

Today, police-held criminal records are available to numerous other agencies throughout the criminal justice system and beyond. As we saw in Chapter 7, the national criminal record collection was renamed as PHOENIX and computerised in 1995, when, significantly, it took on the subtitle 'The Criminal Justice Record Service' to reflect the changing priorities.

Personal information becomes the 'currency' that all agencies value, and personal information thereby facilitates the overall interactions that make up inter-agency work. To use another metaphor, personal information is the oil that keeps the cogs of the inter-agency machine working. Traditional frictions and 'turf-wars' are reduced as personal information is put into circulation to make manifest the old cross-discipline cliché that 'at the end of the day we are all working to the same end'.

The circulation of personal information has been furthered by changes in the law (see e.g. Crime and Disorder Act 1998, s. 115, implemented 30 September 1998) and by information technology which gives real time information exchange rather than the old index cards, microfiche and telephone.

Traditional ideas of 'confidentiality' and 'privacy' are breaking down as 'serious crime' demands the production and exchange of personal information. Data Protection Acts offer some safeguards, but exceptions exist for investigating crimes and protecting children (see e.g. Thomas, 1995). Worrall has expressed pessimism about any future positive work with sex offenders:

> the debate on working with sex offenders in the community has been virtually foreclosed . . . official government discourse now rejects the language of rehabilitation in favour of the language of surveillance and control through information.
>
> (Worrall, 1997, p. 125)

Much of this information exchange is to allow agencies to intervene appropriately; to make an arrest, remove a child from a harmful situation, make a sentencing decision, make an employment selection decision or a housing decision. All of these interventions are made on the basis of the information in question being used for risk assessment and risk management.

The rights of the sex offender

In general terms, the aim of penal policy is to identify and punish those who break the criminal law. Punishment, in turn, involves a degree of censure, containment and attempts to circumscribe and reduce the activities of the offender. At one end of the line is the custodial sentence and at the other the community sentence, which still tries to delimit and reduce the offenders' activities. Since the early 1970s, there has been a retreat from sentences designed to reform or rehabilitate the offender in favour of sentences commensurate with the seriousness of the crime and which deliver 'just deserts'. This retreat has been accompanied by a questioning of the value of treatment – 'what works?' – the rediscovery and renaissance of dangerousness and the rise of the 'victim movement', which prefers to see some direct redress for the victim rather than help for the offender. The 'law and order' political lobby has been able to mobilise these features to argue for longer sentences, electronic tagging, more active databases, extended supervision and indeterminate sentences. The sex offender has been a prime candidate for all of these measures.

More recently, these moves to commensurate punishments have been complemented by new forms of 'regulation' to ensure sufficient degrees of public protection and safeguards are in place to reduce the risk posed by offenders. As with punishment, regulation seeks to contain and circumscribe the activities of offenders. Registers tell us where they are and DNA databases confirm their identity. 'Paedophile towns' may not yet exist, but electronic tagging, Sex Offender Orders and pre-employment screening all help to reduce the risk they pose by circumscribing their activities.

The detection and prosecution of sex offenders and the measures of protection from them have, nonetheless, to accept that the offenders concerned are still entitled to the 'due process' of law and other rights enjoyed by all citizens. However awful the crimes, and however much we give priority to the rights of the victims or potential victims – especially children – the residual rights of the sex offender remain.

Freedom of movement, for example, is usually considered a fundamental right, even if not always spelt out in statutory form. Sex offenders may find their freedom of movement curtailed in the UK by conditions attached to supervisory arrangements, electronic tagging or Sex Offender Orders that require them to stay away from certain localities.

Privacy is held to be another basic right and is enshrined in article 8 of the European Convention on Human Rights (Council of Europe, 1950, now incorporated into the Human Rights Act 1998). From privacy has emerged the additional right to 'information privacy' and 'data protection' when that information – personal information – is held on computer (Council of Europe, 1980) and most industrialised countries now have data protection legislation. In turn, this legislation becomes qualified when it comes to the 'suppression of criminal offences' (*ibid*, art. 9(2)), and separate recommendations may be made on law enforcement-held information (see e.g. Council of Europe, 1988). A balance must be struck between the need to 'know' and the sex offender's individual right to privacy.

The right to rehabilitation or to be accepted back into society after a period of punishment – custodial or non-custodial – is another 'right' that is not clearly defined. The old adage that once you have 'paid your debt to society' you are a free man or woman again has been stated more fully:

> Rehabilitation implies the action of re-establishing a degraded person in a former standing with respect to rank and legal rights, and to attempt to ensure that those rights are maintained over time.
>
> (McWilliams and Pease, 1990)

The sex offender thought to be 'once a paedophile always a paedophile' and hounded out of his home by vigilante crowds and newspaper reporting, may find this statement has a somewhat hollow ring to it.

What McWilliams and Pease are saying is that the ending of a period of punishment, whether or not the offender is 'reformed', should still be marked by that offender's 'rehabilitation' to society in terms of the restoration of all their civic and legal rights and duties. In this sense, rehabilitation serves as a means of limiting the extent of the punishment to that time period decreed by the court; without it the punishment continues.

The offender, having to submit to a pre-employment criminal record check years after the end of his or her sentence, might argue that their punishment continues. The sex offender subject to regular home visits by probation officers or social workers or required to 'register' for life might feel the same way. The argument that these community interventions are still less of an imposition than a custodial sentence, or that certain activities are for purposes of 'regulation' rather than 'punishment', might not lessen the degree of grievance they believe they are experiencing (see also von Hirsch, 1990).

An international problem

The phenomenon of sex offending is an international one. The United Nations describes the sexual exploitation of children as a 'global phenomenon', to be found in both developing and developed countries and becoming increasingly complex due to its transnational scope (UN, 1996). The International Labour Organization (ILO) has described prostitution in South East Asia as growing so rapidly in recent decades that the sex industry has assumed the dimensions of a commercial sector, contributing substantially to employment and national income in the region (ILO, 1998).

In Europe, the Council of Europe has asked its member states to review their legislation and practice to better protect children (Council of Europe, 1991) and the European Union has made the same demand of its members following the massive public demonstrations in the streets of Brussels against child kidnap and murder in Belgium (EU Joint Action,

97/1 54 JHA). The European Parliament has passed its own resolution (12 December 1997) calling for better integration of agencies' efforts to protect children (Official Journal C.20, 20 January 1997); for a further exposition of European initiatives see Thomas *et al.* (1999) and Hebenton and Thomas (1999).

Closer to home, we can see an almost domino effect in social responses to sex offenders. When the UK sex offender register came into being in September 1997, stories began emerging of offenders in Northern Ireland moving over the border to the Republic of Ireland to avoid having to register ('Paedophiles go South to avoid sex register' *The Sunday Times*, 7 December 1997). These newspaper allegations were officially refuted (see Houses of the Oireachtas – Official Report, 9 December 1997), but it started a debate in the Republic on the need for a sex offender register of its own. A discussion paper put the arguments for and against (Department of Justice, Equality and Law Reform 1998, Chapter 10) and eventually a newly drafted Sex Offenders Bill appeared (10 January 2000), containing provisions for not only a register but also for a sex offender order (comparable to the UK's), more post-release supervision and a ban on sex offenders seeking work with children.

As Ireland plans its sex offender register, the European Parliament calls for a Europe-wide register (Official Journal C.20, 20 January 1997), and some politicians have even suggested a world-wide register ('Mitchell argues for world-wide register of paedophiles' *Irish Times*, 26 April 1996). Such wide-ranging registers would seem to be completely impractical at this point in time, not least because of the different definitions of a sex offence in different countries, but the idea certainly demonstrates the centrality of personal information databases in the regulation of sex offenders, and the seriousness accorded the problem by politicians.

Bibliography

Ackroyd, S., Harper, R., Hughes, J., Shapiro, D. and Soothill, K. (1992) *New Technology and Practical Police Work*. Milton Keynes: Open University Press.

ACOP (Association of Chief Officers of Probation) (1996) *Community Based Interventions with Sex Offenders Organised by the Probation Service – a Survey of Current Practice*. London.

ACOP (Association of Chief Officers of Probation)/Victim Support (1996) 'The Release of Prisoners: informing, consulting and supporting victims – joint statement', July, London.

ACPO (Association of Chief Police Officers) (1995) *Code of Practice for Data Protection*. London.

Adams, C. and Horrocks, C. (1999) 'The Location of Child Protection in relation to the Current Emphasis on Core Policing', in The Violence Against Children Study Group *Children, Child Abuse and Child Protection*. Chichester: Wiley.

ADC (Association of District Councils) (1991) 'Hackney Carriage and Private Hire Vehicle Licence Applicants: Non-Disclosure of Criminal Convictions', April, London.

Alder, Z. (1987) *Rape on Trial*. London: Routledge and Kegan Paul.

Adler, Z. (1991) 'Picking up the Pieces', *Police Review*, 31 May, 1114–1115.

AMA (Association of Metropolitan Authorities) (1995) Social Services Circular 95/1995. London.

Anna, T. (1988) 'Feminist Responses to Sexual Abuse: The Work of the Birmingham Rape Crisis Centre', in M. MaGuire and J. Pointing *Victims of Crime – a new deal*. Milton Keynes: Open University Press.

Apex Trust (1990) *Realising the Potential: the recruitment of people with a criminal record*. London.

Atkins, S. and Hoggett, B. (1984) *Women and the Law*. Oxford: Blackwell.

ATL (Association of Teachers and Lecturers), National Association of Head Teachers, NASUWT, National Union of Teachers, Professional Association of Teachers, Secondary Heads Association and the Council of Local Education Authorities (1994) *Teachers Facing Allegations of Physical/Sexual Abuse: Guidelines on Practice and procedure*. 13 June. London.

Bagshaw, M. (1997) 'Inside Track', *Policing Today*, 3 (4), 20–22.

Bailey, V. (ed.) (1981) *Policing and Punishment in Nineteenth-Century Britain*. London: Croom Helm.

165

Bailey, V. and Blackburn, S. (1979) 'The Punishment of Incest Act: a case study of law creation', *Criminal Law Review*, 708–718.

Bancroft, J. (1974) *Deviant Sexual Behaviour: Modification and Assessment*. Oxford: Clarendon Press.

Barker, M. and Morgan, R. (1993) *Sex Offenders: a framework for the evaluation of community based treatment*. March. London: Home Office.

Barnardos (1998) *Whose Daughter Next? Children Abused Through Prostitution*. London: Barnardos.

Bartley, P. (2000) *Prostitution: Prevention and Reform in England, 1860–1914*. London: Routledge.

Bartrip, P.W.J. (1981) 'Public Opinion and Law Enforcement: the ticket of leave scares in mid-Victorian Britain', in V. Bailey (ed.) *Policing and Punishment in Nineteenth-Century Britain*. London: Croom Helm.

Beattie, J.M. (1986) *Crime and the Courts in England 1660 –1800*. Oxford: Clarendon Press.

Beck, U. (1992) *Risk Society*. London: Sage.

Beckett, R. (1994) 'Cognitive-Behavioural Treatment of Sex Offenders', in T. Morrison, M. Erooga and R.C. Beckett (eds) *Sexual Offending Against Children: Assessment and Treatment of Male Abusers*. London: Routledge.

Beckett, R., Beech, A., Fisher, D. and Fordham, A.S. (1994) *Community-Based Treatment for Sex Offenders: an Evaluation of Seven Treatment Programmes*. August. London: Home Office.

Beech, A., Fisher, D., Beckett, R. and Scott-Fordham, A. (1998) *An Evaluation of the Prison Sex Offender Treatment Programme*. Research Findings No.79. Research, Development and Statistics Directorate. London: HMSO.

Benyon, J., Turnbull, L., Wilks, A., Woodward, R. and Beck, A. (1993) 'Police Cooperation in Europe: An Investigation', Centre for the Study of Public Order, University of Leicester.

Better Regulation Task Force (1999) *Fit Person Criteria*. May. Londnon: Cabinet Office.

Bibby, P.C. (ed.) (1996) *Organised Abuse: the Current Debate*. Basingstoke: Arena.

Booth, W. (1890) *In Darkest England and the Way Out*. Pamphlet.

Bosanquet, H. (1914) *Social Work in London 1869–1912*. London: John Murray.

Bottoms, A.E. (1977) 'Reflections on the Renaissance of Dangerousness', *Howard Journal of Penology and Crime Prevention*, 16 (2), 70–96.

Bowman, A., Buller, P., Lewis, M. and Smith, G. (1998) 'Practical Difficulties Encountered by Police, Probation and Social Services; the key issues for inter-agency working within the Sex Offenders Act 1997', in S. Hayman (ed.) *Child Sexual Abuse: Providing for Victims Coping with Offenders*. London: Institute for the Study and Treatment of Delinquency.

Brackenridge, C. (1997) '"He Owned me Basically . . .", Womens Experiences of Sexual Abuse in Sport', *International Review for the Sociology of Sport*, 32 (2), 115–130.

Brackenridge, C. (1998) 'Casting a Shadow: the Dynamics and Discourses of Sexual Abuse in Sport', Paper presented at the Leisure Studies Association International Conference, *The Big Ghetto: Gender, Sexuality and Leisure*, Leeds Metropolitan University, July.

Bradford Commission (1996) *The Report of an Inquiry into the Wider Implications of Public Disorders in Bradford which occurred on 9, 10 and 11 June 1995.* London: The Stationery Office.

Bratby, L. (1999) 'Home Office Pledges Introduction of Power to Arrest Kerb-Crawlers', *Police Review*, 9 July.

Bristow, E.J. (1977) *Vice and Vigilance.* Dublin: Gill and Macmillan.

Brongersma, E. (1988) 'A Defence of Sexual Liberty for All Age Groups', *Howard Journal of Criminal Justice*, 27 (1), 32–43.

Brown, D. (1997) *PACE Ten Years On: A Review of the Research.* Research Study 155. Research and Statistics Directorate. London: Home Office.

Brown, W. (1993) 'DNA Fingerprinting Back in the Dock', *New Scientist*, 6 March.

Brownlee, I. (1998) *Community Punishment: A Critical Introduction.* London: Longman.

Burn, G. (1985) *Somebody's Husband, Somebody's Son.* London: Pan Books.

Cabinet Office/Home Office (1999) 'Living Without Fear: An Integrated Approach to Tackling Violence Against Women, June', The Womens Unit, London.

Cameron, D. and Frazer, E. (1987) *The Lust to Kill.* Cambridge: Polity Press.

CCPAS (Churches Child Protection Advisory Service) (1998) *Protecting Children and Appointing Children's Workers: Guidance to Churches.* 9th edition. Swanley, Kent: CCPAS.

Chamberlain, L. (1993) 'Valuable Young', *Community Care*, 19 August, 7.

Chambers, G. and Millar, A. (1983) 'Investigating Sexual Assault', Scottish Office Central Research Unit Study. Edinburgh: HMSO.

CIH (Chartered Institute of Housing) (1998) 'Rehousing Sex Offenders – A Summary of the Legal and Operational Issues', February, Coventry.

Clark, P. and Erooga, M. (1994) 'Groupwork With Men Who Sexually Abuse Children', in T. Morrison, M. Erooga and R.C. Beckett (eds) *Sexual Offending Against Children: Assessment and Treatment of Male Abusers.* London: Routledge.

Clark, H. and Johnston, D. (1994) *Fear the Stranger.* Edinbugh and London: Mainstream Publishing.

Cleveland Report (1988) *Report of the Inquiry into Child Abuse in Cleveland 1987.* (cm 412). London: HMSO.

Clyde Report (1992) *The Report of the Inquiry of the Removal of Children from Orkney in February 1991.* Edinburgh: HMSO.

Cobbe, F.P. (1992) 'Wife Torture in England', in J. Radford and D. Russell (eds) *Femicide: The Politics of Woman Killing.* Milton Keynes: Open University Press.

Coddington, D. (1997) *The Australian Paedophile and Sex Offender Index.* Sydney: The Mount View Trust.

Coggan, G. and Walker, M. (1982) *Frightened for my Life: An Account of Deaths in British Prisons.* London: Fontana.

Cohen, S. (1972) *Folk Devils and Moral Panics.* London: MacGibbon and Kee Ltd.

Coker, J.B. and Martin, J.P. (1985) *Licensed to Live.* Oxford: Blackwell.

Collins, P. (1999) 'Operation Osprey', *Cross Border Control*, No. 11, 44–48.

Corby, B. (1998) *Managing Child Sexual Abuse Cases.* London: Jessica Kingsley Publishers.

Council of Europe (1950) European Convention on Human Rights, Strasbourg.

Council of Europe (1980) Convention for the Protection of Individuals with Regard to Automatic Processing of Personal Data, Strasbourg.

Council of Europe (1988) *The Use of Personal Data in the Police Sector.* Recommendation R (87) 15, Strasbourg.

Council of Europe (1991) Sexual Exploitation, Pornography and Prostitution of, and Trafficking in, Children and Young Adults. Recommendation R(91)11, Strasbourg.

Council of the European Union (1997) *Council Resolution on the Exchange of DNA Analysis Results.* Ref. 97/C 193/02, Brussels.

Cox, B., Shirley, J. and Short, M. (1977) *The Fall of Scotland Yard.* Harmondsworth: Penguin Books.

CPS (Crown Prosecution Service) (n.d.) *Code for Crown Prosecutors.* London.

CPS (Crown Prosecution Service) (1994) *Code for Crown Prosecutors.* June, London.

CPS (Crown Prosecution Service) (1996) *An Explanatory Memorandum for use in Connection with The Code for Crown Prosecutors.* June, London.

CPSI (Crown Prosecution Service Inspectorate) (1998) *Cases Involving Child Witnesses.* Thematic Report 1/98, January, London.

Crane, P. (1983) *Gays and the Law.* London: Pluto Press.

Crawford, A. (1998) *Crime Prevention and Community Safety.* London: Longman.

Criminal Law Revision Committee (1984) *Sexual Offences.* 15th Report. (Cmnd 9213). London: HMSO.

Critchley, T.A. (1967) *A History of Police in England and Wales.* London: Constable.

Cullen Report (1996) *The Public Inquiry into the Shootings at Dunblane Primary School on 13 March 1996.* (Cm 3386). London: The Stationery Office.

D of E (Department of the Environment)/D of H (Department of Health) (1996) 'Code of Guidance on Parts VI and VII of the Housing Act 1996 – Allocation of Housing Accommodation – Homelessness', 20 December, London.

Daley, H. (1986) *This Small Cloud: A Personal Memoir.* London: Weidenfeld and Nicolson.

D'Arcy, M. and Gosling, P. (1998) *Abuse of Trust: Frank Beck and the Leicestershire Children's Homes Scandal.* London: Bowerdean.

Davies, G., Williams, C., Mitchell, R. and Milson, J. (1995) *Video Taping Children's Evidence: An Evaluation.* London: Home Office.

DENI (Department of Education Northern Ireland) (1990) *Disclosure of Criminal Background of Persons with Access to Children.* Circular 28/1990. Belfast.

Departmental Committee (1925) *Sexual Offences Against Young Persons.* (Cmd 2561). London: HMSO.

Departmental Committee (1926) *Sexual Offences Against Children and Young Persons in Scotland.* (Cmd 2592). London: HMSO.

DETR (Department of the Environment, Transport and the Regions) (1999) 'Personal Security Issues in Pedestrian Journeys', *DETR*, May, London.

Department of Health (1991a) 'The Children Act 1989: Guidance and Regulations', Volume 5, *Independent Schools.* London: HMSO.

Department of Health (1991b) 'The Children Act 1989 – Guidance and Regulations', Volume 4, *Residential Care*. London: HMSO.

Department of Health (1991c) *Children in the Public Care – a review of residential child care*. London: HMSO.

Department of Health (1994a) 'Introduction of Supervision Registers for Mentally Ill People from 1 April 1994', *HSG*, (94) 5, London.

Department of Health (1994b) 'The Child, The Court and The Video', *SSI*. London.

Department of Health (1995) *Annual Reports of Area Child Protection Committees 1993/4*. London.

Department of Health (1997a) *Family Law Act 1996: Part IV Family Homes and Domestic Violence*. Circular LAC (97) 15. London.

Department of Health (1997b) *Guidance to the Children (Protection from Offenders) (Miscellaneous Amendments) Regulations SI 1997/2308*. Circular LAC(97)17. London.

Department of Health (1998a) 'Working Together to Safeguard Children: New Government Proposals for Inter-Agency Co-operation', Consultation Paper, February, London.

Department of Health (1998b) *The Government's Response to the Children's Safeguards Review*. (Cm 4105). London: The Stationery Office.

Department of Health (1999) *Working Together to Safeguard Children*. London: The Stationery Office.

Department of Justice, Equality and Law Reform (1998) *The Law on Sexual Offences – a discussion paper*. May, Dublin.

DFEE (Department for Education and Employment) (1995) *Misconduct of Teachers and Workers with Children and Young Persons*. Circular 11/1995. London.

DHSS (Department of Health and Social Security) (1974) *Non-accidental injury to children: Area Review Committees*. Circular LASSL (74) 13. London.

DHSS (Department of Health and Social Security) (1975) *Report of the Committee Inquiry into the Provision and Coordination of Services to the Family of John George Auckland*. London: HMSO.

DHSS (Department of Health and Social Security) (1976) *Non-accidental injury to children: the police and case conferences*. Circular LASSL (76) 26. London.

DHSS (Department of Health and Social Security) (1978) *Release of prisoners convicted of offences against children in the home*. Circular LAC (78) 22. London.

DHSS (Department of Health and Social Security) (1980) *Child Abuse: Central Register Systems*. Circular LASSL (8) 4. London.

DHSS (Department of Health and Social Security) (1988) *Working Together: a guide to arrangements for inter-agency cooperation for the protection of children from abuse*. London: HMSO.

DHSS (Department of Health and Social Services) (NI) (Northern Ireland) (1978 Release of prisoners convicted of offences against chi

DHSS (Department of Health and Social Services) (NI) (Northern Ireland) (1989) *Cooperating to Protect Children*. Belfast: DHSS.

DHSS (Department of Health and Social Services) (NI) (Northern Ireland) (1993) *An Abuse of Trust: the report of the SSI investigation into the case of Martin Huston*. Belfast: DHSS.

DHSS (Department of Health and Social Services) (NI) (Northern Ireland) (1995) *Review of the DHSS Pre-employment Consultancy Service (PECS).* May. Belfast: DHSS.

DHSS (Department of Health and Social Services) (NI) (Northern Ireland) (1996a) *Interagency guidance on the movement of the persons charged , held or cautioned in connection with certain offences against children or young people under the age of 17.* Circular HSS (CC) 3/1996, as revised. Belfast: DHSS.

DHSS (Department of Health and Social Services) (NI) (Northern Ireland) (1996b) *Making the right choice: a guide to using the Pre-employment Consultancy Service (PECS).* Belfast: DHSS.

DHSS (Department of Health and Social Services) (NI) (Northern Ireland) (1996c) *Our Duty to Care.* Belfast: DHSS.

Department of Transport (1997) *Perceptions of Safety from Crime on Public Transport.* June. London.

Department of Transport/Home Office (1992) *Disclosure of Criminal Record: Applicants for Hackney Carriage and Private Hire Vehicle Drivers' Licences.* Circular 2/1992. London.

Donnelly, L. (1999) 'Dangerous Precedent', *Health Service Journal*, 25 February.

Dovaston, D. and Burton, C. (1996) 'Vital New Ingredient', *Policing Today*, April, 44–48.

Drew, B. (1997) 'On Paedophile Patrol in the Philippines', *Nexus*, No.4, July, 16–17 (internal NCIS bulletin).

East, W.N. and Hubert, W.H. (1939) *Report on the Psychological Treatment of Crime.* HMSO: London.

Eldridge, J., Kitzinger, J. and William, K. (1997) *The Mass Media and Power in Modern Britain.* Oxford: Oxford University Press.

Emsley, C. (1991) *The English Police: a political and social history.* Cambridge: Harvester Wheatsheaf.

Ericson, R.V. and Haggerty, K.D. (1997) *Policing the Risk Society.* Oxford: Clarendon Press.

Europol Convention (1995) *Convention based on Article K3 of the Treaty on European Union, on the Establishment of a European Police Office.* Brussels.

FA (Football Association) (1997) *A Charter for Quality: Football Education for Young Players.* October. London.

Fennell, P. (1988) 'Sexual Suppressants and the Mental Health Act', *Criminal Law Review*, 660–676.

Fennell, P. (1996) *Treatment without Consent.* London: Routledge.

Ferguson, H. (1990) 'Rethinking Child Protection Practices: a case for history', in The Violence Against Children Study Group *Taking Child Abuse Seriously.* London: Unwin Hyman.

Ferris, D. (1977) *Homosexuality and the Social Services.* London: National Council for Civil Liberties.

Finkelhor, D. (1986) *A Source Book on Child Sexual Abuse.* London: Sage.

Foot, P. (1996) 'Sir, the Sadist', *Guardian*, 4 September.

Franklin, B. (1997) *Newszak and News Media.* London: Arnold.

Gallagher, B. (1998) *Grappling with Smoke: Investigating and Managing Organised Child Sexual Abuse – A Good Practice Guide*. London: NSPCC.

Gallagher, J. (1999) *Violent Times: TUC Report on Violence at Work*. London: Trades Union Congress.

Geis, R., Wright, R. and Geis, G. (1978) 'Police Surgeons and Rape – A Questionnaire Survey', *The Police Surgeon*, 14, 7–14.

Gibbons, S. (1997) 'Catching the Killers', *International Police Review*, July/August, 32–33.

Glidewell Report (1998) *The Review of the Crown Prosecution Service – A Report*. (Cm 3960). London: The Stationery Office.

Grace, S., Lloyd, C. and Smith, L.J.F. (1992) 'Rape: From Recording to Conviction', Home Office Research and Planning Unit Paper No. 71, London.

Greenlees, L.T. (1991) 'Washington State's Sexually Violent Predators Act: Model or Mistake?', *American Criminal Law Review*, 29 (35), 107–132.

Gregory, J. and Lees, S. (1999) *Policing Sexual Assault*. London: Routledge.

Grover, C. and Soothill, K. (1995) 'Miscarriages of Justice: Sex Crime Appeals in the News', *The Police Journal*, April, 120–128.

Grubin, D. (1998) 'Sex Offending Against Children: Understanding the Risk', Police Research Series Paper 99. *Policing and Reducing Crime*. London: Home Office.

Guy, E. (1992) *The Prison Services Strategy in (PRT)*. London: Prison Reform Trust.

Hague, G. and Malos, E. (1998) *Domestic Violence: Action for Change*. Cheltenham: New Clarion Press.

Harris, J. and Grace, S. (1999) *A Question of Evidence: Investigating and Prosecuting Rape in the 1990's*. Home Office Research Study 196, London.

Hawton, K. (1983) 'Behavioural Approaches to the Management of Sexual Deviations', *British Journal of Psychiatry*, 143, 248–255.

Hayes, M. (1992) '*R v Devon County Council ex p. L*: Bad Practice, Bad Law and a Breach of Human Rights?', *Family Law*, 22 June, 245–257.

Hayman, S, (ed.) (1998) *Child Sexual Abuse: Providing for Victims Coping with Offenders*. London: Institute for the Study and Treatment of Delinquency.

Hebenton, B. and Thomas, T. (1993) *Criminal Records: State, Citizen and the Politics of Protection*. Aldershot: Avebury.

Hebenton, B. and Thomas, T. (1997) *Keeping Track? Observations on Sex Offender Registers in the US*. Crime Detection and Prevention Series Paper 83, Police Research Group. London: Home Office.

Hebenton, B. and Thomas, T. (1999) 'Capacity Building Against Transnational Crime: European Measures to Combat Sexual Offenders', *European Journal of Crime, Criminal Law and Criminal Justice*, 7 (2), 150–163.

Heilbron Committee (1975) *Report on the Advisory Group on the Law on Rape*. (Cmnd 6352). London: HMSO.

Heim, N. and Hursch, C.J. (1979) 'Castration for Sex Offenders: Treatment or Punishment? A Review and Critique of Recent European Literature', *Archives of Sexual Behaviour*, 8 (3), 281–304.

Henham, R. (1996) 'Recidivist Sentencing in the United States: the Implications for UK Sentencing Policy', Paper Presented at the Socio-Legal Studies Association Annual Conference, University of Southampton, April 1996.

171

Henham, R. (1998) 'Sentencing Sex Offenders: Some Implications of Recent Criminal Justice Policy', *Howard Journal of Criminal Justice*, 37 (1), 70–81.

Henshaw, D. (1986) 'Vigilante Groups Move in to fill the Law and Order Vacuum', *The Listener*, 23 Jan, 2–4.

Heywood, J.S. (1959) *Children in Care*. London: Routledge and Kegan Paul.

Hill, B. and Fletcher-Rogers, K. (1997) *Sexually Related Offences*. London: Sweet and Maxwell.

Hill, C. (1996) Liberty Against the Law. London; Penguin Books.

HM Prison Service (1989) *Suicide Prevention*. Circular 20/1989. London.

HM Prison Service (1991) 'Treatment Programmes for Sex Offenders in Custody: A Strategy', Directorate of Inmate Programmes, July, London.

HM Prison Service (1994) 'Release of prisoners convicted of offences against children or young persons under the age of 18', Guidance notes to: *Instruction to Governors 54/1994*. London.

HM Prison Service (1996) 'The Treatment of Imprisoned Sex Offenders – Programme Development', February, London.

HM Prison Service (1998) 'The Prison Service Sex Offender Treatment Programme', Offending Behaviour Programmes Unit, June, London.

HMIC (Her Majesty's Inspectorate of Constabulary)(1997) *Inspection Report*. London: The National Criminal Intelligence Service.

HMIC (Her Majesty's Inspectorate of Constabulary) (1999) *Child Protection*. HMIC Thematic Inspection Report. London: Home Office.

HMIP (Her Majesty's Inspectorate of Probation) (1995) *Dealing with Dangerous People: The Probation Service and Public Protection*. Report of a Thematic Inspection. London : Home Office.

HMIP (Her Majesty's Inspectorate of Probation) (1998a) *Exercising Constant Vigilance: the role of the Probation Service in Protecting the Public from Sex Offenders*. Report of a Thematic Inspection. London: Home Office.

HMIP (HM Inspectorate of Probation) (1998b) *Evidence Based Practice: a guide to effective practice*. London: Home Office.

Hobbs, C.J. and Wynne, J.M. (1986) 'Buggery in Childhood – a common syndrome of child abuse', *The Lancet*, 4 October, 792–796.

Hobbs, C.J. and Wynne, J.M. (1987) 'Child Sexual Abuse – an increasing rate of diagnosis', *The Lancet*, 10 October, 837–841.

Home Office (1954) *Convictions on Teachers*. Circular 151/1954, London.

Home Office (1959) *Street Offences Act 1959*. Circular 109/1959. London.

Home Office (1963) *Preventive Detention: report of the Advisory Council on the Treatment of Offenders*. London: HMSO.

Home Office (1964) *Children and Young Persons Act 1963: Parts I and II*. Circular 22/1964. London.

Home Office (1983) *Investigation of Offences of Rape*. Circular 25/1983. London.

Home Office (1986a) *Violence Against Women*. Circular 69/1986. London.

Home Office (1986b) *Protection of Children: disclosure of criminal background of those with access to children*. Circular 44/1986. London.

Home Office (1986c) *Police Reports on Convictions and Related Information*. Circular 45/1986. London.

Home Office (1987) 'The Use of Video Technology at Trials of Alleged Child Abusers', 8 May, London.

Home Office (1988) *The Investigation of Child Sexual Abuse*. Circular 52/1988. London.

Home Office (1990a) *Crime, Justice and Protecting the Public*. (Cm 965). London: HMSO.

Home Office (1990b) *Domestic Violence*. Circular 60/1990. London.

Home Office (1991) *Misuse of witness statements in sexual offences cases: a consultation paper*. London: HMSO.

Home Office (1993a) *Protection of Children: Disclosure of Criminal Background of those with access to children*. Circular 47/1993. London.

Home Office (1993b) *Disclosure of Criminal Records for Employment Vetting Purposes*. (Cm 2319). London: HMSO.

Home Office (1994a) *The Cautioning of Offenders*. Circular 18/1994. London.

Home Office (1994b) *Protection of Children: Disclosure of Criminal Background to Voluntary Sector Organisations*. Circular 42/1994 London.

Home Office (1994c) *Safe From Harm?: Code of Practice for Safeguarding the Welfare of Children in Voluntary Organisations in England and Wales*. London.

Home Office (1995a) 'DNA Database goes Live', 10 April, Press Release, London.

Home Office (1995b) *Probation Service Contact with Victims*. Probation Circular 61/1995. London.

Home Office (1996a) *Sentencing and Supervision of Sex Offenders – A Consultation Document*. (Cm 3304). London.

Home Office (1996b) 'Review of Extra-Territorial Jurisdiction – Steering Committee Report', Sentencing and Offences Unit, July, London.

Home Office (1996c) *Protecting the Public: The Governments Strategy on Crime in England and Wales*. (Cm 3190). London: HMSO.

Home Office (1996d) *On the Record: The Governments Proposals for Access to Criminal Records for Employment and Related Purposes in England and Wales*. (Cm 3308). London: HMSO.

Home Office (1997a) 'Electronic Monitoring – The Future of Community Punishment', 12 November, Press Release, London.

Home Office (1997b) 'Sex Offenders to Face Tougher Penalties – MacLean', 27 January, Press Release. London.

Home Office (1997c) *Sex Offenders Act 1997*. Circular 39/1997. London.

Home Office (1997d) *Police Checks on Staff Working in Registered Private Children's Homes and Small Unregisterable Children's Homes*. Circular 43/97. London.

Home Office (1997e) 'Community Protection Order: A Consultation Paper', November, London.

Home Office (1998a) 'Speaking Up For Justice', June 1998, London.

Home Office (1998b) 'Joyce Quinn Commends Rigorous Supervision of Sex Offenders in the Community', 28 April, Press Release, London.

Home Office (1998c) *Effective Practice Initiative: A National Implementation Plan for the Effective Supervision of Offenders*. Probation Circular 35/1998. London.

Home Office (1998d) *The Crime and Disorder Act – Sex Offenders Orders: Guidance*. London.

Home Office (1999a) 'Sex Offences Review: Terms of Reference Announced', 25 January, Press Release, London.

Home Office (1999b) 'Managing Dangerous People with Severe Personality Disorder: Consultation Document', 19 July, London.

Home Office (1999c) 'Paul Boateng announces new name for Probation Service', 1 December, Press Release, London.

Home Office (1999d) 'The Work of the Probation Services with Sex Offenders', Probation Unit, March, London.

Home Office (1999e) '32 Probation 'Pathfinder' Projects to Reduce Re-Offending', 14 July, Press Release, London.

Home Office (1999f) 'Criminal Records Bureau – outcome of timetable review', 16 December, Press Release, London.

Home Office (1999g) Report of the Interdepartmental Working Group on Preventing Unsuitable People from Working with Children and Abuse of Trust, 25 January, London.

Home Office (1999h) 'Tough Measures to Weed Out Child Abusers', 29 July, Press Release, London.

Home Office (1999i) *Disclosure to the Employment Service of Restrictions that should be placed on the employment of potentially dangerous offenders.* Probation Circular 48/1999. London.

Home Office (2000a) 'Recorded Crime Statistics England and Wales October 1998–September 1999', Statistical Bulletin Issue 1/00, 18 January.

Home Office (2000b) *National Standards for the Supervision of Offenders in the Community.* London.

Home Office (2000c) 'Pilot Project to assess dangerous personality disorder announced by Home Office', 10 February, Press Release, London.

Home Office PSTU (Police Science and Technology Unit) (1999) 'Draft guidance on the disclosure of information about sex offenders who may present a risk to children and vulnerable adults', 31 August, London.

Home Office/Department of Health (1992) *Memorandum of Good Practice.* London: HMSO.

Home Office/Department of Health (1998) 'Draft guidance on children involved in prostitution', 29 December, London.

Home Office/DHSS (Department of Health and Social Security) (1985) 'Disclosure of Criminal Convictions of those with access to Children: First Report', July, London.

Home Office/DHSS (Department of Health and Social Security) (1987) 'Mental Health Act 1983: Supervision and After-Care of Conditionally Discharged Restricted Patients – Notes for the Guidance of Social Supervisors', London.

Home Office/Lord Chancellor's Department (1996) 'Stalking – the Solutions', Consultation Paper, July, London.

Home Office/Scottish Office (1997) 'Sex Offenders: a ban on working with children', Consultation Paper, January, London.

Home Office, Department of Health, Welsh Office (1995) *National Standards for the Supervision of Offenders in the Community.* 2nd edition. London.

Home Office, Department of Health, DES and Welsh Office (1991) *Working Together: a guide to arrangements for inter-agency cooperation for the protection of children from abuse.* London: HMSO.

House of Commons (1984) 'Children in Care', Second Report from the Social Services Committee, Session 1983–1984, HC 360–351, London: HMSO.

House of Commons (1998) 'Children Looked After by Local Authorities', Health Committee 2nd Report, Session 1997–1998, HC 319 II. London: The Stationery Office.

Howard League (1985) *Unlawful Sex: Offences, Victims and Offenders in the Criminal Justice System of England and Wales*. London: Waterlow.

Hucklesby, A. (1994) 'The Use and Abuse of Conditional Bail', *Howard Journal of Criminal Justice*, 33 (3), 258–270.

Hughes, B., Parker, H. and Gallagher, B. (1996) 'Policing Child Sexual Abuse: the view from police practitioners', Police Research Group. London: Home Office.

(HRW) Human Rights Watch (1997) *To Serve Without Favour: Policing, Human Rights, and Accountability in Northern Ireland*. Helsinki: Human Rights Watch.

Hunt Report (1994) 'Report of the Independent Inquiry into Multiple Abuse in Nursery Classes in Newcastle-Upon-Tyne', City Council of Newcastle-Upon-Tyne.

ICBA (Irish Catholic Bishop's Advisory Committee)(1996) *Child Sexual Abuse: Framework for a Church Response*. Dublin: Veritas.

Ignatieff, M. (1978) *A Just Measure of Pain*. London: Penguin.

ILO (International Labour Organization) (1998) 'The Sex Sector: the economic and social bases of prostitution in South East Asia', Geneva.

Interpol (1997) 'Handbook on Good Practice for Specialist Officers dealing with Crimes Against Children', November, Lyon.

Interpol – General Secretariat (1995) 'Interpol and the struggle to combat offences against minors', (ICPO), *International Criminal Police Review*, 452–453.

Jackson, L.A. (2000) *Child Sexual Abuse in Victorian England*. London: Routledge.

Janus, E. (1996) 'Preventing Sexual Violence: Setting Principled Constitutional Boundaries on Sex Offender Commitments', *Indiana Law Journal*, 72 (65), 157–214.

Jenkins, P. (1994) *Using Murder: the social construction of serial homicide*. New York: Aldine de Gruyter.

Jones, D. (1982) *Crime, Protest, Community and Police in 19th Century Britain*. London: Routledge and Kegan Paul.

Jones, D.J.V. (1992) *Crime in Nineteenth Century Wales*. Cardiff: University of Wales Press.

Kane, J. (1998) *Sold for Sex*. Aldershot: Arena.

Kelly, L. (1988) *Surviving Sexual Violence*. Cambridge: Polity Press.

Kelly, L. (1996) 'Weasel Words: Paedophiles and the Cycle of Abuse', *Trouble and Strife*, 33, Summer, 44–49.

Kelly, L. and Radford, J. (1990–91) "Nothing Really Happened': the invalidation of womens's experiences of sexual violence', *Critical Social Policy*, 30, Winter, 39–53.

Kent Report (1997) 'Children's Safeguards Review', Social Work Services Inspectorate for Scotland, Edinbugh.

Kilbrandon Report (1964) *Children and Young Persons: Scotland.* (Cmnd 2306). Edinburgh: HMSO.

King, D. (1999) *In the Name of Liberalism.* Oxford: Oxford University Press.

Labour Party (1996) 'Protecting our Children', September, London.

La Fontaine, J.S. (1994) *The Extent and Nature of Organised and Ritual Abuse: Research Findings.* London: HMSO.

La Fontaine, J.S. (1998) *Speak of the Devil.* Cambridge: Cambridge University Press.

Laurence, A. (1994) *Women in England 1500–1760.* London: Wiedenfeld and Nicolson.

Law Commission (1992) 'Family Law, Domestic Violence and Occupation of the Family Home', No. 207. London: HMSO.

Law Commission (1995) 'Consent in the Criminal Law – a Consultancy Paper', No. 139. London: HMSO.

Lee, M. and O'Brien, R. (1995) *The Game's Up: Redefining Child Prostitution.* London: Childrens Society.

Lees, S. (1997) *Carnal Knowledge: Rape on Trial.* Harmondsworth: Penguin.

Levy, A. and Kahan, B. (1991) 'The Pindown Experience and the Protection of Children', Staffordshire County Council, Stoke-on-Trent.

LGA (Local Government Association) (1998) 'Don't Apply Sun Lotions to Children, LGA Warns', 13 August, Press Release, London.

Liberty (1996) 'Response to the Home Office Consultation Paper on Sentencing and Supervision of Sex Offenders', August, London.

Liberty (1997a) 'Briefing on the Sex Offenders Bill', January, London.

Liberty (1997b) 'Response to the Home Office Consultation Paper, Sex Offenders: A Ban on Working with Children', May, London.

Linebaugh, P. (1991) *The London Hanged: Crime and Civil Society in the Eighteenth Century.* London: Allen Lane, The Penguin Press.

London Rape Crisis Centre (1984) 'Sexual Violence: The Reality for Women', The Women's Press Handbook Series, London.

McGowen, R. (1995) 'The Well-Ordered Prison: England 1780–1865', in N. Morris and D.J. Rothman, (eds) *The Oxford History of the Prison: the Practice of Punishment in Western Society.* Oxford: Oxford University Press.

MacLean, N.M. (1979) 'Rape and False Allegations of Rape', *The Police Surgeon,* (15), April, 29–40.

MacLeod, M. (1996) 'Talking with Children About Child Abuse', Childline, London.

McLeod, N. (1991) 'English DNA Evidence Held Inadmissable', *Criminal Law Review,* 583–590.

McWilliams, M. and Spence, L. (1996) *Taking Domestic Violence Seriously: Issues for the Civil and Criminal Justice System.* Belfast: The Stationery Office.

McWilliams, W. and Pease, K. (1990) 'Probation Practice and an End to Punishment', *Howard Journal of Criminal Justice,* 29 (1), February, 14–24.

Maguire, M. and Norris, N. (1992) 'The Conduct and Supervision of Criminal Investigations Research Study No. 5', Royal Commission on Criminal Justice. London: HMSO.

MaGuire, M. and Pointing, J. (eds) (1988) Victims of Crim – a new deal. Milton Keynes: Open University.

Mair, G. and Mortimer, E. (1996) 'Curfew Orders with Electronic Monitoring', Home Office Research Study No. 163, London: HMSO.

Marshall, P. (1997) 'The Prevalence of Convictions for Sexual Offending', Research Finding No. 55, Research and Statistics Directorate. London: Home Office.

Matthews, R. (1993) 'Kerb-Crawling, Prostitution and Multi-Agency Policing', Police Research Group; Crime Prevention Unit Series, Paper 43. London: Home Office.

Mearns, A. (1883) 'The Bitter Cry of Outcast London', Pamphlet, London.

Meyers, D.W. (1970) *The Human Body and the Law*. Edinburgh: Edinburgh University Press.

Miller, W.R. and Heather, N. (eds) (1986) *Treating Addictive Behaviours: Processes of Change*. New York: Plenum Press.

Morris, A., Giller, H., Szwed, E. and Geach, H. (1980) *Justice for Children*. London: Macmillan.

Morris, N. and Rothman, D.J. (eds) (1995) *The Oxford History of the Prison: the Practice of Punishment in Western Society*. Oxford: Oxford University Press.

Morrison, T., Erooga, M. and Beckett, R.C. (eds) (1994) *Sexual Offending Against Children: Assessment and Treatment of Male Abusers*. London: Routledge.

Mrazek, P.J., Lynch, M.A. and Bentovim, A. (1983) 'Sexual Abuse of Children in the United Kingdom', *Child Abuse and Neglect*, 7 (2), 147–153.

NACRO (National Association for the Care and Resettlement of Offenders) (1996a) *Sentencing and Supervision of Sex Offenders – NACRO's Response to the Consultation Document*. London.

NACRO (National Association for the Care and Resettlement of Offenders) (1996b) *Disclosing Convictions*. London.

NAHT (National Association of Head Teachers)/ACPO (Association of Chief Police Officers) (1998) 'Protocol Regarding Sex Offenders Act 1997', July, Haywards Heath.

NASUWT (National Association of School Masters Union of Woman Teachers) (1994) 'Teachers and Child Protection', 5 July, Press Statement, London.

NCCL (National Council for Civil Liberties) (1988) 'NCCL urges reform of police checks system', 26 September, Press Release, London.

NCF (National Coaching Foundation)/NSPCC (National Society for the Prevention of Cruelty to Children) (1995) *Protecting Children: A Guide for Sports People*. London.

NCIS (National Criminal Intelligence Service) (1995) 'Child Sex Tourism Comes Under Scrutiny', 20 November, Press Release, London.

Neyroud, P. (1999) 'Danger Signals', *Policing Today*, June, 5 (2), 10–15.

NHS (National Health Service) Executive (1997) *Guidance to Hospital Managers and Local Authority Social Services Departments on the Sex Offenders Act 1997*. Circular HSG (97)37. London.

NIHE (Northern Ireland Housing Executive) (1997) 'The Sexual Abuse of Children: Housing Implications – the Executives Proposals', 23 October, Belfast.

(NIO) Northern Ireland Office (1997) 'The Sex Offenders Act 1997 – Introductory guide for Northern Ireland', August, Belfast.
(NIO) Northern Ireland Office (1999) 'Tackling Violence Against Women: a consultation paper', April, Belfast.
NI (Northern Ireland) Working Party (1988) 'Disclosure of Criminal Background of Persons Seeking Access to Children', Interdepartmental, March, Belfast.
NSPCC (National Society for the Prevention of Cruelty to Children) (1997) 'NSPCC concerned re inclusion of juvenile offenders on sex offenders register', 24 October, Press Release, London.
Nuttall, J. (1970) Bomb Culture. London: Paladin.

Oates, T. (1998) 'The Difficulties Encountered when Investigating Abuse that has taken Place in The Past', in S. Hayman (ed.) Child Sexual Abuse: Providing for Victims Coping with Offenders. London: Institute for the Study and Treatment of Delinquency.
O'Carroll, T. (1980) Paedophilia: the radical case. London: Peter Owen.
O'Mahony, P. (1996) Criminal Chaos: Seven Crises in Irish Criminal Justice. Dublin: Round Hall Sweet and Maxwell.

Parker, T. (1970) The Frying Pan: a prison and its prisoners. London: Hutchinson.
Parker, H. (ed.) (1979) Social Work and the Courts. London: Edward Arnold.
Parris, M. (1997) 'All-party witch-hunt', The Times, 24 January.
Parry, N., Rustin, M. and Satyamurti, C. (eds) (1979) Social Work, Welfare and the State. London: Edward Arnold.
Parsloe, P. (1979) 'After-custody: supervision in the community in England, Wales and Scotland', in H. Parker (ed.) Social Work and the Courts. London: Edward Arnold.
Parton, N. (1991) Governing the Family. London: Macmillan.
Parton, N. (1996) 'Social Work, risk and the blaming system', in N. Parton (ed.) Social Theory, Social Change and Social Work. London: Routledge.
Parton, N. (ed.) (1996) Social Theory, Social Change and Social Work. London: Routledge.
Pattullo, P. (1984) 'Judging Women', National Council for Civil Liberties, London.
Petrow, S. (1994) Policing Morals: the Metropolitan Police and the Home Office 1870–1914. Oxford: Clarendon Press.
Pigot Report (1989) Report of the Advisory Group on Video Evidence. London: Home Office.
Pinchbeck, I. and Hewitt, M. (1973) Children in English Society. Volume II. London: Routledge and Kegan Paul.
Plotnikoff, J. and Woolfson, R. (1998) 'Policing Domestic Violence: Effective Organisational Structures', Police Research Series Paper 100, Policing and Reducing Crime Unit. London: Home Office.
Policy Advisory Committee on Sexual Offences (1981) Report on the Age of Consent in Relation to Sexual Offences. (Cmnd 8216). London: HMSO.
Porter, R. (ed.) (1984) Child Sexual Abuse Within the Family. The Ciba Foundation. London: Tavistock Publications.

Porter, R. (1985) 'Rape – Does It Have a Historical Meaning?', in S. Tomaselli and R. Porter (eds) *Rape*. Oxford: Blackwell.

Potter, K. (1997) 'The Right to Know', *Police Review*, 21 February, 18–19.

Power, H. (1999) 'Sex Offenders, Privacy and the Police', *Criminal Law Review*, 3–16.

PRT (Prison Reform Trust) (1992) *Beyond Containment: The Penal Response to Sex Offending*. London.

PRT (Prison Reform Trust) (1995) 'A Suitable Case for Treatment?', Briefing Paper, August, London.

Prochaska, J. and Di Clemente, C. (1986) 'Towards a Comprehensive Model of Change', in W.R. Miller and N. Heather (eds) *Treating Addictive Behaviours: Processes of Change*. New York: Plenum Press.

Radford, J. and Russell, D. (eds) (1992) *Femicide: The Politics of Woman Killing*. Milton Keynes: Open University Press.

Radzinowicz, L. (1948) *A History of English Criminal Law*. Volume 2. London: Stevens and Sons.

Radzinowicz, L. (1956) *A History of English Criminal Law*. Volume 3. London: Stevens and Sons.

Radzinowicz, L. and Hood, R. (1990) *The Emergence of Penal Policy in Victorian and Edwardian England*. Oxford: Clarendon Press.

Rafferty, E. (1986) 'The Kincora Casualties', *Social Work Today*, 10 February.

Ranyard, R., Hebenton, B. and Pease, K. (1994) 'An Analysis of a Guideline Case as Applied to the Offence of Rape', *Howard Journal of Criminal Justice*, 33 (3), 203–217.

Ravenscroft, L. (1997) 'The Need to Decriminalise Child Prostitution', *Childright*, No. 141, November, 16.

RCCJ (Royal Commission on Criminal Justice) (1993) (Cm 2263). London: HMSO.

RCHWC (Royal Commission on the Housing of the Working Classes) (1885) (C (2nd series) 4402–1). London: HMSO.

Report of the Street Offence Committee (1928) (Cmd 3231). London: HMSO.

Ross, E. (1982) '"Fierce Questions and Taunts": Married Life in Working Class London 1870–1914', *Feminist Studies*, 8 (2).

Sampson, A. (1994) *Acts of Abuse: Sex Offenders and the Criminal Justice System*. London: Routledge.

Scottish Office (1979) *Release of Inmates Convicted of Offences Against Children in the Home*. Circular 14/1979 (Criminal). Edinburgh.

Scottish Office (1989a) 'Effective Intervention: Child Abuse – Guidance on Cooperation in Scotland', Edinburgh.

Scottish Office (1989b) *Protection of Children: Disclosure of Criminal Convictions of those with Access to Children: Local Authorities*. Circular SW9/1989. Edinburgh.

Scottish Office (1990) *Investigation of Complaints of Domestic Assault*. Circular 3/1990. Edinburgh.

Scottish Office (1994) *Child Protection: The Imprisonment and Preparation for Release of Offenders Convicted of Offences Against Children*. Circular SWSG 11/1994. Edinburgh.

Scottish Office (1996) 'On The Record in Scotland: Proposals for Improved Access to Criminal Records', June, Edinburgh.

Scottish Office (1997a) *Sex Offenders Act 1997 Guidance on Implementation.* Circular HD 12/1997 2154. Edinburgh.

Scottish Office (1997b) *Implementation of the Sex Offenders Act 1997 – Implications for Local Authorities.* Circular SWSG 11/1997. Edinburgh.

Scottish Office (1998a) 'Preventing Violence Against Women: a Scottish Office Action Plan', Edinburgh.

Scottish Office (1998b) 'Child Protection to be Strengthened with Introduction of Criminal Record Checks – McLeish', 14 December, Press Release, Edinburgh.

Scottish Office (1999) *The MacLean Consultation Paper.* Edinburgh.

Sennett, R. (1974) *The Fall of Public Man.* Cambridge: Cambridge University Press.

Seven, P. (1991) 'Treating Sex Offenders in Prison', *The Journal of Forensic Psychiatry*, 2 (1), May, 8–9.

SFCRC (Support Force for Children's Residential Care) (1997) Code of Practice for the Employment of Residential Child Care Workers, Department of Health, London.

Sheridan Report (1982) Homes and Hostels for Children and Young Persons in Northern Ireland. Belfast: DHSS.

Skidmore, P. (1995) 'Telling Tales: media power, ideology and the reporting of child sexual abuse in Britain', in D. Kidd-Hewitt and R. Osbourne *Crime and the Media: the post-modern spectacle.* London. Pluto.

Smith, J. (1998) 'How Consistent are Social Services Departments in Appointing Children and Family Social Workers?', *Childright*, 144, March, 9–10.

Smith, J. (1999) 'Prior criminality and employment of social workers with substantial access to children: a decision board analysis', *British Journal of Social Work*, 29, 49–68.

Sone, K. (1995) 'Lack of Conviction', *Community Care*, 8–14, June, 22–23.

Soothill, K. and Walby, C. (1991) *Sex Crime in the News.* London: Routledge.

Soothill, K., Francis, B. and Ackerley, E. (1998) 'Paedophilia and Paedophiles', *New Law Journal*, 12 June, 882–883.

Sparks, R., Bottoms, A. and Hay, W. (1996) *Prisons and the Problem of Order.* Oxford: Clarendon Press.

Swann, S. (1999) 'Children involved in prostitution: the Government's draft guidance', *Childright*, No. 157, March, 15–16.

SWSG (Social Work Services Group) (1985) 'Disclosure of Criminal Convictions of those with access to children', Consultation Paper, November, Edinburgh.

Temkin, J. (1993) 'Sexual History Evidence – the ravishment of Section 2', *Criminal Law Review*, 1, 3–20.

Temkin, J. (1999) 'Reporting rape in London: a qualitative study', *Howard Journal of Criminal Justice*, 38 (1), 17–41.

Thomas, T., Katz, I. and Wattam, C. (1999) *CUPICSO: the Collection and Use of Personal Information on Child Sex Offenders.* London: NSPCC.

Thomas, T. (1995) *Privacy and Social Services.* Basingstoke: Arena.

Tomaselli, S. and Porter, R. (eds) (1985) *Rape.* Oxford: Blackwell.

Tsang, L. (1998) 'Ensuring Justice for all Children', *The Lawyer*, 2 June.

TUC (Trades Union Congress) (1990) *Sexual Harassment at Work: TUC Guidelines.* London.

Unell, J. (1992) 'Criminal Record Checks within the Voluntary Sector: an evaluation of the pilot schemes', Volunteer Centre, UK.

UN (United Nations) (1948) *Universal Declaration of Human Rights*. New York.

UN (United Nations) (1996) 'Sexual Exploitation of Children: Study Series 8', Centre for Human Rights, Geneva.

Unsworth, C. (1979) 'The balance of medicine, law and social work in mental health legislation 1889–1959', in N. Parry, M. Rustin and C. Satyamurti (eds) *Social Work, Welfare and the State*. London: Edward Arnold.

Utting Report (1997) 'People Like Us – report of the review of the safeguards for children living away from home', Department of Health/Welsh Office.

Valios, N. (1998) 'Social Workers warn register is flawed', *Community Care*, 27 August–2 September.

Valios, N. (1999) 'Mental health groups angered by Straw's plans for indefinite detention', *Community Care*, 18–24 February.

Violence Against Children Study Group (1990) *Taking Child Abuse Seriously*. London: Unwin Hyman.

Violence Against Children Study Group (1999) *Children, Child Abuse and Child Protection*. Chichester: Wiley.

von Hirsch, A. (1990) 'The Ethics of Community-Based Sanctions', *Crime and Delinquency*, 36 (1), 162–173.

VSWGSO (Voluntary Sector Working Group on Sex Offenders) (1997a) 'Sex Offenders in the Community', NIACRO, Belfast.

VSWGSO (Voluntary Sector Working Group on Sex Offenders) (1997b) 'Sex Offenders in the Community – Conference Report', 19 February, NIACRO, Belfast.

Wacks, R. (1989) *Personal Information: Privacy and the Law*. Oxford: Clarendon Press.

Walkowitz, J.R. (1992) *City of Dreadful Delight*. London: Virago.

WAR/LAW (Women Against Rape/Legal Action for Women) (1995) *Dossier: The Crown Prosecution Service and the Crime of Rape*. London: Crossroads.

Warner Report (1992) *Choosing With Care: Report of the Committee of Enquiry into the Selection, Development and Management of Staff in Children's Homes*. London: HMSO.

Waterhouse, L., Dobash, R. and Carnie, J. (1994) *Child Sexual Abusers*. Edinburgh: HMSO.

Waterhouse Report (2000) 'Lost in Care – Report of the Tribunal of Inquiry into the abuse of children in care in the former county council areas of Gwynedd and Clwyd since 1974', (Summary) HC 201, London: The Stationery Office.

Webster, R. (1998) *The Great Children's Home Panic*. Oxford: Orwell Press.

Webster, R. (1999) 'How the police trawl the innocent', *New Statesman*, 19 July.

Whitfield, D. (1997) *Tackling the Tag: The Electronic Monitoring of Offenders*. Winchester: Waterside Press.

Williams, B. (1999) *Working with Victims of Crime*. London: Jessica Kingsley Publishers.

Wilson, E. (1983) *What is to be Done about Violence Against Women?* Harmondsworth: Penguin.

Wohl, A. (ed.) (1978) *The Victorian Family*. London: Croom Helm.

Wohl, A. (1978) 'Sex and the Single Room: Incest among the Victorian Working Classes', in A. Wohl (ed.) *The Victorian Family*. London: Croom Helm.

Wolfenden Report (1957) *Report of the Committee on Homosexual Offences and Prostitution*. (Cmnd 247). London: HMSO.

Worpole, K. and Greenhalgh, L. (1996) *The Freedom of the City*. London: Demos.

Worrall, A. (1997) *Punishment in the Community – the Future of Criminal Justice*. London: Longman.

Wyre, R. (1996) 'The Mind of the Paedophile', in P.C. Bibby (ed.) *Organised Abuse: the Current Debate*. Basingstoke: Arena.

Young, J. (1999) *The Exclusive Society*. London: Sage.

Index

All references are to page numbers

Children—*contd*
church, abuse by priest, 134-135
Cleveland enquiry, 126
Colwell, Maria, 124
crimes against,
committed abroad, 4, 67-68
development of awareness of,
43-44, 46, 125-126
history of, 35
dawn raids by police, 60
disqualification from caring for, 5
Dunblane, 142
evidence by, 73, 76-78
exclusion order, 129
foster parents,
prohibitions on, 51-52
gross indecency with, 3
history of offences against, 35
home, attacks on in the, 123-127, 129
NSPCC,
Justice for Children campaign, 78
regional investigation units, 62
local authority care, grounds for, 53
moral danger, 53
organised abuse of, 4
Prevention of Cruelty Acts, 43
priest, abuse by, 134-135
prostitution, 4, 155-157
protection,
development of, 51-52
home, in the, 123-127, 129
police, 60
reasonable cause to believe over 16, 9
Satanic abuse, 4, 126-127
school,
sexual abuse allegations, 131-134
sex offences against,
recognition of, 43-44, 46, 125-126
teachers, by, 132-134
sex tourists, 4, 67-68
Sexual Offences (Conspiracy and
Incitement) Act 1996, 68
sports clubs, 133-134
supervision orders, 86
teachers,
abuse by, 132-134
false allegations against, 131-133
unlawful sexual intercourse with, 9
video-recording of statement, 73, 77
voluntary sector, 133-134
witness, protection for, 76-78
workplace, sexual exploitation in,
131

Children's homes
awareness of abuse, 135-137
Bryn Estyn, 137
false allegations, danger of, 62
investigation of, 61
List 99, 140
NSPCC investigation of, 62
offences committed in, 2, 126
Operation Clyde, 61
Protection of Children Act 1999, 140
rehabilitation of offenders, 139
staff, pre-employment screening of,
137-146
duty to check, 140
Utting report, 143
Warner report, 141
Waterhouse Report, 61, 136-137, 143
Church
child abuse by priests, 134-135
Cities
protection in the, 146—149
red light areas, 149-151
Cognitive-behavioural approach
effectiveness of, 29
use of, 27-29
Colwell, maria, 124
Community
protection in the, 146
Computers
CATCHEM, 66
Data Protection Act, 64
HOLMES, 61
Internet,
pornography on, 2
sexual exploitation via, 4
PHOENIX, 116
police Code of Practice, 64
Police National Computer, 64
QUEST, 116
Consent
age of. *See* AGE OF CONSENT
children, by, 8
concept of, 7-8
defence, as a, 10
invalid, 7
lack of, 3-4
prohibited relationships, 9
prostitution, to, 10
rape, 74-75
sado-masochism, to, 10
Spanner case. 10
Continuum
sexual assault, of, 31